Six Greek T

Aeschylus **Persians, I**
Sophocles **Women of T**
Euripides **Trojan V**

Aeschylus, the earliest Greek playwright whose work has survived, was born in Athens around 525 BC, probably shortly after the founding of the festival of the Great Dionysia and the introduction of the form known as tragedy. Aeschylus was the first to refine the dramatic art, and the seven plays from the more than eighty that he wrote show a remarkable sophistication of stagecraft for so fledgling a form. His first victory with a set of four plays was not until 484 but he went on to win the first prize on another twelve occasions. *Persians* (472 BC), the earliest we have, is based, untypically, on recent history and the defeat of the Persians by the Athenians in the sea-battle at Salamis. Aeschylus himself had fought at Marathon against the Persians in 490, perhaps at Salamis too. Later plays, *Seven Against Thebes*, *Suppliants* and the three plays of *The Oresteia*, are set in the world of the epic cycles. *Prometheus Bound*, of uncertain date, is a powerful poetic drama from deepest myth, but like *Persians*, it examines the abuse of power and the progress of civilisation. Aeschylus died in Sicily in 456 BC.

Sophocles was born about 496 BC at Colonus, just outside Athens. He first won the prize for tragedy in 468 BC, defeating the veteran Aeschylus, and went on to win twenty-four victories in all. His long life virtually spanned the rise and fall of Athenian democracy and included public service as a financial trustee and as an elected general. He died in 406 BC soon after Euripides. He is said to have written some 123 plays in all, but, as with Aeschylus, only seven are extant, among them an *Electra*, *Ajax*, and the three plays that deal with Oedipus and his children. All of them demonstrate an increasing interest in the human condition and picture heroic figures, women and men, who undergo great physical and mental suffering before coming to appreciate, whatever the influence of the gods, their responsibility for their own lives. *Women of Trachis* shows Heracles, the strongest of men, brought to his death by his wife's misplaced attempts to rekindle his love. *Philoctetes* presents a fascinating moral debate and shows another hero facing up to physical torment, this time with a more hopeful conclusion.

Euripides was born near Athens between 485 and 480 BC and grew up during the years of Athenian recovery after the Persian Wars. His first group of plays was presented in 455 and he wrote about ninety-two in all. Younger than Sophocles, he died a few months before him in 406, but they were for many years dramatic rivals. Sophocles won the prizes, Euripides only four in his lifetime but the vote of posterity. Nineteen of Euripides' plays have come down, including our only satyr play, several which anticipate New Comedy and some of the most savage of tragedies. A constant striving for new approaches may have puzzled and aggravated his contemporaries but makes Euripides seem the most modern of the ancient playwrights. Representing human beings with all their faults and complexities he has even been described as the first psychologist. *Trojan Women*, set in the aftermath of the Greek defeat of the Trojans and seen through the eyes of the losers, is a powerful parable for contemporary history in Athens, as well as being a great anti-war play for all time. *Bacchae*, produced posthumously, dramatises the confrontation between Pentheus, King of Thebes, and the god Dionysus whose worship Pentheus has forbidden. Dionysus, god of the theatre, is the inevitable and only winner.

in the same series

SIX GREEK COMEDIES

Aristophanes
Birds, Frogs, Women in Power

Menander
The Woman from Samos

Euripides
Cyclops, Alkestis

FOUR ROMAN COMEDIES

Plautus
A Funny Thing Happened on the Way to the Wedding (Casina),
The Haunted House (Mostellaria)

Terence
The Eunuch, Brothers

Six Greek Tragedies

AESCHYLUS

Persians
Prometheus Bound
translated by Frederic Raphael and Kenneth McLeish

SOPHOCLES

Women of Trachis
translated by J. Michael Walton

Philoctetes
translated by Kenneth McLeish

EURIPIDES

Trojan Women
translated by Marianne McDonald

Bacchae
translated by J. Michael Walton

introduced by
Marianne McDonald and J. Michael Walton

METHUEN DRAMA

1 3 5 7 9 10 8 6 4 2

This collection first published in the United Kingdom in 2002 by
Methuen Publishing Ltd
215 Vauxhall Bridge Road, London SW1V 1EJ

These translations of *Persians* and *Prometheus Bound* first published in
1991 by Methuen Drama
Copyright © 1991 by Volatic Ltd and the Estate of Kenneth McLeish
This translation of *Women of Trachis* first published in 1990
by Methuen Drama
Copyright © 1990 by J. Michael Walton
This translation of *Philoctetes* published by Methuen Drama in 1990
Copyright © 1979, 1990 by the Estate of Kenneth McLeish
This translation of *Bacchae* first published in 1988
by Methuen London Ltd; revised version 1998
Copyright © 1988, 1998 by J. Michael Walton
This translation of *Trojan Women* first published in 2002
by Methuen Drama
Copyright © 2002 by Marianne McDonald

Introduction copyright © 2002 by Marianne McDonald
and J. Michael Walton

The rights of the translators to be identified as the translators of these
works have been asserted by them in accordance with the Copyright,
Designs and Patents Act, 1988

Methuen Publishing Limited Reg. No. 3543167

A CIP catalogue record for this book
is available from the British Library

ISBN 0 413 77256 X

Typeset by Wilmaset Ltd, Birkenhead, Wirral
Printed and bound in Great Britain by
Cox and Wyman Ltd, Reading, Berkshire

Caution

CONTENTS

Introduction vii

Aeschylus
PERSIANS 1

PROMETHEUS BOUND 37

Sophocles
WOMEN OF TRACHIS 73

PHILOCTETES 121

Euripides
TROJAN WOMEN 177

BACCHAE 223

A Note on the Translators 275

INTRODUCTION

Tragedy in Athens

In a period which lasted no more than sixty-six years,
between the first surviving Greek tragedy and the deaths of
Sophocles and Euripides, three Athenian playwrights produced a series of tragedies which lasted on page and stage for
the next two thousand four hundred years. To be accurate
that sixty-six years was both more and less than that.
Aeschylus' *Persians*, the first play in the present collection,
was produced in 472 BC. Aeschylus had been writing,
directing, choreographing and acting in his plays for nearly
thirty years already but none of his early output has survived.
Euripides' *Bacchae*, the last play in this volume, was first
performed posthumously in 405, the year after Euripides'
death; and Sophocles' final play, *Oedipus at Colonus*, was not
played until 401 when the playwright had been dead for over
five years. By a nice, if contrived, coincidence it was sixty-six
years between the opening of the first purpose-built play-
house in London by James Burbage, The Theatre, in April
1576, and the closing of all the London theatres by
Parliament in 1642. There can be little arguing with this
sixty-six years having been the most fertile and innovative in
the history of the English-speaking theatre.

Just as what has come to be known as the Jacobethan
drama covered a growing and developing range of types and
formats, from Marlowe to Shakespeare to Jonson to the
Court Masque to City Comedy, so the theatre of the Greeks
was fluid and wide-ranging. The labels, Tragedy, Satyr play
and Old Comedy covered all the plays that are known, from
the first ever performed in the sixth century BC, before
Aeschylus was born, through to the deaths within months of
one another of Euripides and Sophocles. Aristophanes, the
only writer of Old Comedy whose work has survived, was so
affected by Euripides' death that he wrote a play called *Frogs*
in which Dionysus, god of the theatre – indeed the same
Dionysus who also features as a character in *Bacchae* –
travels down to the underworld to bring back a playwright to
help save the city of Athens.

The writers of tragedy presented plays in groups of four. The first three were serious but the fourth was a comic coda called a satyr play. Featuring a chorus of satyrs, animalistic supporters of Dionysus with horses' tails and sporting a phallus, a satyr play dealt with a mythological story but in farcical terms, usually a kind of 'send-up' of some theme or situation handled seriously in the first three pieces. The need to conclude a group of tragic plays with a comic afterpiece is an important indication of what the scope and purpose of Greek theatre really was. Most Greek tragedy was on mythological themes. The exception is *Persians* (see below). In part this is the result of Greek tragedy developing as a performing art from the oral tradition of story-telling. The epic poems of Homer, *The Iliad* and *The Odyssey*, do not provide the immediate subject-matter of any surviving Greek tragedy except Euripides' *Rhesus*. The action of *Trojan Women* occurs between the two. These epics do provide a mythic framework in which the Trojan War and its aftermath are part of the background. Aeschylus is recorded in a later writer, Athenaeus, as claiming that all he wrote was 'slices from Homer's banquet'. Add to these surviving poems a number of lost sagas, which included the stories of such as Prometheus, Heracles, Philoctetes and Pentheus, and you have the world of myth, much of it handed down by word of mouth. Myth was malleable. There were no authorised versions, only outlines of character and situation whose details and variations formed the base material of drama.

So all of the surviving tragedies – *Persians* excepted – and a few others on historical themes known only by title, were from a past that had no historical authority to back it. Drama was invented before history. The Greeks had little sense of a fixed past. What they did have was a strong sense of stories from the past serving as parables for what could and should happen in the present. The theatre rapidly became a place for informed debate on issues of the present through the medium of the past. These issues might be moral, political, social or philosophical. They could be broad-based or direct. But they involved the spectators in a serious – Aristotle's later word was *spoudaios* – consideration of issues that were immediate. It is this that links not only the six plays here but all Greek tragedy.

Generalisations about Greek drama are frequently misleading. Most pervasive are that going to the theatre for the Athenians was like going to church; that the audience knew exactly what was going to happen; and that Greek tragedy was created out of some kind of formula invented by Aristotle (who was not born until twenty years after Sophocles and Euripides died). It is risky to make any sort of pronouncement about the frame of mind of any audience in any period but Athens was a *polis*, a city-state. Affairs of state were, by definition, 'political'. Theatre in Athens developed at the same time as a new democratic system of government that in itself was the cause of the Persian invasions of 490 and 480. That was when the Persians set up expeditions to try and restore the last king of Athens, who had been expelled in 510 BC. *Persians* includes an eyewitness account of the battle of Salamis of 480 where the Greek fleet won a decisive victory. Clearly that is a play of immediate political impact.

But so is *Prometheus Bound*, a story set in the deepest past, about a Titan who gave fire to mortals and defied Zeus. For this he was pinned to a rock in the Caucasus by Hephaestus, Might and Force, visited by a chorus of winged women, and by Io, transformed into a bull and tormented by a gadfly. How political was that in Athens? How political was it in Ireland when Tom Paulin used the same myth in his *Seize the Fire: A Version of Aeschylus' Prometheus Bound* (1989) as a story about power and about victims? 'Prometheus,' wrote Karl Marx, 'is the foremost saint and martyr in the philosopher's calendar.' An Athenian audience may not have known much about saints but they knew their martyrs well enough.

Seamus Heaney chose Sophocles as his starting point in his examination of the Irish question, *The Cure at Troy: after Philoctetes by Sophocles* (1990). Sophocles' original play deals with questions of honour and deceit, patriotism and expedience, selfishness and selflessness. Political issues? Certainly. Such issues affected the *polis* every day in its dealings with its own citizens, its allies and its enemies. Aeschylus, Sophocles and Euripides all wrote a *Philoctetes*. Only the Sophocles

survives but what we still do have is an intriguing essay from
400 years later by a rhetorician, Dio Chrystostom, comparing
the three versions. For the Greeks there were major issues
embodied here.

Sophocles' *Women of Trachis* is a play about love and
about power. Deianira, in an attempt to rekindle her
husband's love for her, succeeds only in destroying him.
Her love for him destroys him but his love for Iole was the
initial cause. 'Your husband may be the best man-at-arms in
the world,' says Lichas, 'but he met his match when he fell
for this girl' (ll. 488–9). The Heracles of this play is not the
strongest man in the world. He *was* the strongest man in the
world but, thanks to his wife's love, is dying slowly and
painfully by the time he makes his belated entrance.
Sophocles is still the primary playwright of heroism, but
he tackles heroism in all its phases and inevitably at points of
crisis, the hero trying to endure the unendurable.

The Euripides plays included here, *Trojan Women* and
Bacchae, are two of his finest, but in markedly contrasting
styles. *Trojan Women*, produced in 415, was inspired by an
actual atrocity committed against the island of Melos by the
Athenians the previous year. The Peloponnesian War against
Sparta lasted from 431 BC until 404 and was the background
to the majority of surviving tragedies and comedies. *Trojan
Women* has something in common with *Persians* in that it
chooses to concentrate not on the winners in war, but on the
losers. Whereas Aeschylus, who probably fought at the battle
of Salamis which the Persian messenger so graphically
describes, demonstrates the scope of the Athenian triumph
through the degradation of the losers, Euripides offers as
scathing a denunciation of war and, by implication, of his
fellow countrymen as in any play written since. No member
of that first audience could have been in any doubt about why
the play was written when it was: or where the playwright's
political sympathies lay.

Many people find *Bacchae* the most perplexing of all Greek
tragedies. Dionysus, god of the theatre, is one of its leading
characters but the other is his cousin, Pentheus, King of
Thebes. The play deals in an almost Pirandellian way with
the balance between real and unreal, between truth and

illusion. And yet, ultimately, it is a play about a family destroyed by one of its members who feels excluded. Domestic
politics mingle with questions of the exercise of authority but,
as in most Greek tragedies – and here is a generalisation that
has some truth to it – there are few winners.

Politics in Athens encompassed everything that it took to
be a citizen. All these plays, and the others too, tragedies and
comedies, looked at the vicissitudes of life, and subjected
them to rigorous and often uneasy scrutiny. The theatre in
Athens was exciting, entertaining, emotional and dangerous.
Comfortable it was not.

Play and festival

There were local festivals in Athens at which plays were
performed, known as Rural Dionysia, but the two civic
occasions were the Lenaea in mid-winter, and the Great
Dionysia in the spring. Only Athenians and resident aliens
could attend the Lenaea at which parochial comedy
dominated the occasion. The Great Dionysia was held at
the beginning of the sailing season and was open to foreign
guests. Other events, processions, award ceremonies, sacrifices, occupied the early part of the proceedings, to be
followed by a number of days devoted to the presentation of
three sets of tragedies (including their satyr play) and old
comedies of the sort that Aristophanes wrote. Groups of
tragedies were offered to a state official by the playwrights
the previous autumn and were selected on a competitive
basis. Three sets were 'granted a chorus' which meant that
the state would pay for three actors, a musician and some of
the general costs, including the leasing arrangements for an
architekton to manage the theatre space and its surrounds.
They would appoint a *choregos* to cover the rest, including
the training and maintenance of the chorus, costume and the
provision of masks. The *choregos* was a wealthy private
citizen who had been identified as someone to finance one of
a number of civic duties in any year.

Aeschylus originally acted and chose his fellow actors but,
as the fifth century progressed, acting became professional.

In the fourth and third centuries BC, a guild system was to develop, each guild acting as a go-between for professional troupes who would tour throughout the Greek-speaking world with a repertoire of revivals of the classics and some new work. In the fifth century prizes were eventually awarded for writers and actors in tragedy and in comedy. A ten-man jury was appointed, one selected by lot from each of the ten Attic tribes. All the jury cast their votes but only a random five were selected so that no one could be held responsible and, to some extent, decisions were left with the gods. Already, then, in the ancient world we have theatre managers, angels, casting directors and agents. There must have been a stage manager and dressers too. A front-of-house manager probably saw to it that important people, including the priests of Dionysus, sat in the best seats. Tickets were sold at a cost of two obols (a day's wage for a juryman and subsidised for those on low incomes), so somebody must have checked them. And somebody probably controlled the lucrative refreshment franchise too.

Performance

The place of performance was not always the theatre in the precinct of Dionysus that was used in the latter part of the fifth century. There is a story that Aeschylus first put on his plays in a makeshift theatre in the agora, the commercial and political heart of the old city. A collapse of seating with loss of life resulted in a move to the south-eastern slope of the Acropolis. When the victorious Athenians returned to their sacked city after Salamis, a restoration programme began. Soon after the death of Aeschylus in Sicily in 456 BC, Pericles, the leader of the democratic party, inaugurated a building programme which included major modifications to the Precinct of Dionysus as well as the building of a number of temples above it, including the Parthenon. It was this theatre space for which the surviving plays of Sophocles and Euripides were all written, and where revivals of Aeschylus' plays – permitted by special decree – were performed after his death.

The theatre consisted of three linked parts, all, of course, in the open air. The *theatron* was for the spectators, cut into the hillside and arranged around two thirds of the *orchestra*, or 'dancing-place'; the third side was confined by the stage-building or *skene*. There are several different ideas current about the shape of the performance space; who used which bits and when; and the extent to which there might have been scenery and scenic effects. The problems are difficult to solve because this was basically a temporary stage. It was made of wood and wood does not survive, particularly when later stone theatres are built over the top of it. References within the surviving texts and later vase-paintings seem to create more difficulties than they solve but some things are reasonably sure.

The audience was large, not, perhaps, the thirty thousand that Plato talks of, but possibly as many as seventeen thousand. That takes up a significant proportion of the three hundred thousand who lived in and around Attica, but the real potential audience was probably nearer fifty thousand, allowing for the slave population and those for whom the trek in to the city was impractical. This is still significantly higher than the thirteen per cent of London's population that attended the theatre in 1605.

The *skene* needed to have at least one main entrance, possibly two or three, with two additional entrances available up the side passages (*parodoi*) which divided the ends of the *theatron* from the playing space. The chorus would usually have entered by these *parodoi* and remained in the *orchestra*. In front of the *skene* was a wide but shallow 'stage' area, perhaps raised, if only by a few feet, with steps up from the floor. Actors could play wherever the action could be most effectively presented which would have included the *orchestra* on occasions. If the plays and vases prove anything, it is that there was a sense of physical relationships and stage action which was promoted and fortified by furnishings, properties, an awareness of stage space and a sense of stage picture. There is evidence in the plays of Aristophanes of a wheeled truck (*ekkuklema*), and a stage crane (*mechane*) which could be used, for instance, for the arrival of gods. There may have been means of indicating location, at least emblematically, by painted panel and even *periaktoi*, used in later times to swivel different settings on a prism-shaped device. Almost none of this is any help in deciding the original staging of *Prometheus Bound* which would probably have benefited from elaborate choreography and a lot of imagination. The six plays in this volume seem to ask for two earthquakes, a cave on a desert island, a tent, and a flying entrance, amongst other things.

Actors were male and masked. This is much less of a hindrance to subtle performance than is usually assumed as long as the actors were properly trained and working within a masked tradition. Greek actors were, and to think of the mask simply as a disguise is to misunderstand the whole nature of physical performance. There was clearly some doubling but the 'rule' of three actors may well have been breached on occasion. The word *choros* means dance, the *orchestra* was a dancing-place, but the chorus also punctuated passages of dialogue and interspersed choral odes in lyric metres between scenes. In some plays they could be closely involved with the action, as in *Persians* and *Bacchae*. In other plays they seem more remote. The performance overall made considerable use of musical accompaniment from a player of the *aulos*, a kind of oboe, but close detail of these vital performance elements is sadly lost.

Persians

The first performance of *Persians* took place at the Great Dionysia in 472 BC, only eight years after the second Persian expedition trying to reinstate Hippias, the former king of Athens. The first expedition, under King Darius, had been driven off after the celebrated Athenian victory at Marathon. This time Darius' son, Xerxes, had chosen to come overland through northern Greece. Greek resistance at Thermopylae was overcome by treachery and the Persians overran Athens. The whole population had to decamp to the island of Salamis. Threatened with extinction, the Athenians gambled everything on one last stratagem. The Persians were tricked into fighting in the narrow channel between the island and the mainland. Their larger ships proved less manoeuvrable than the Athenians' and the result was the disaster for the Persians related in graphic detail by the Messenger (ll. 249–514). Disaster for the Persians, maybe, but for the Athenians Salamis was a triumph. Aeschylus fought in the battle which was, in later times, such an important point in Athenian history that it was used as a date to link the three tragedians. Sophocles, it was said, sang in the victory ode, while Euripides – somewhat fortuitously if it is true – was born on Salamis on the very day that the two fleets met.

As the only surviving 'history' play, and the earliest surviving tragedy at that, *Persians* might seem to point to the earliest tragedy as having much more to do with historical events. There certainly were precedents in the work of Phrynichus, for example, but *Persians* was part of a group of four plays, the other three of which were all on mythological themes, *Phineus*, *Persians* (second), *Glaucus of Potniae* and a satyr play *Prometheus the Fire-Maker*. Frustrating as it may be, virtually nothing is known about the other three, so not even a conjecture can be made as to how this contemporary story fitted with the mythic others in the group.

Standing alone, *Persians* is still an intriguing and dramatic piece. It is set back in the Persian capital, Susa, close to the tomb of former King Darius, as news begins to filter through of the defeat of the expeditionary force. The chorus of Persian elders who open the play are initially full of patriotic rhetoric though they do utter a note of warning. They remain throughout the play, witnesses to and commentators on the destruction of a nation. Darius had died between the first and second invasions of Greece and the first leading character to enter is Atossa, the late king's wife, mother of Xerxes, the commander at Salamis. She has had a worrying dream, an omen and one of the ways in Homer by which the gods could make contact with human beings. The arrival of a messenger confirms her worst fears as, in a remarkable speech, he offers an eyewitness account of the naval battle which saved Athens. The only consolation is that Xerxes still lives. The dramatic effect is created from the context, the first confirmation of disaster for the play's characters, a rehearsal of a glorious moment in history for the entire audience. The

Athenian audience basked in their democracy, contrasted
with tyranny: Atossa asks the Chorus, 'Who shepherds
them? Their warlord – who?' and the Chorus Leader replies,
'Call them no mortal's slaves. They bow to none' (ll. 241–2).

The Queen, the text implies, is finely dressed and attended
on her first entrance. She leaves, to return alone and in
mourning and requesting that the Chorus conjure up the
ghost of her dead husband. He duly arrives as the play
becomes a series of complex images contrasting success and
failure, grandeur and degradation, life and death. Darius'
urgent questioning reveals a Xerxes who has brought the
catastrophe upon himself by his arrogant and insane
behaviour. 'God stole his mind,' says the Ghost before
advising the Chorus to ensure that Persia never again tries to
attack Greece. He instructs the Chorus to fetch clothes for
Xerxes' return: 'Defeat has tattered him,/ Beggared him,
ripped finery to rags' (ll. 836–7).

One last choral ode recalling the triumphs of the past gives
way to the bedraggled figure of the defeated king, who ends
the play with a litany of grief shared by the Chorus. Though
there might seem to be little action here, the graphic
illustration of the disaster has real power. The most striking
effect that Aeschylus contrives, though, is in the likely
reaction of the spectators. The Athenians did not initiate or
provoke either Persian expedition. They had to watch their
city set on fire. Marathon and Salamis were military
triumphs but there will have been people sitting in that
first audience who had lost brothers, sons, fathers – as had
Aeschylus, whose brother was mortally wounded at Marathon. There must have been many more who fought in that
battle and in the earlier engagement.

The Persian reaction to the loss of an empire will have
aroused more relief than grief in an Athenian audience. So
what lies beyond it? Perhaps there is a warning here, a
warning about the arrogance of power, that key word *hubris*,
the state of mind whereby the gods contrive the downfall of
those who acquire too great a sense of their own importance.
Xerxes is clearly held responsible for the downfall of the
state. That the Persians should have behaved like this was no
novelty to an Athenian audience. That they, the Athenians,

should learn about their own future conduct from the situation of their defeated enemies is a far more sophisticated message which Aeschylus seems to advocate and which, as Sophocles and Euripides were to bear witness, over the course of the rest of the century, their fellow countrymen consistently failed to heed.

Prometheus Bound

Of all the tragedies included here, perhaps of all tragedies, *Prometheus Bound* most has the aura of deepest myth. The other plays of Aeschylus are set in or around cities and deal with recognisable human beings, albeit in some strange guises. So unlike the rest of Aeschylus, both linguistically and thematically, is *Prometheus Bound* that a number of scholars believe it not to be by Aeschylus at all but by some other unknown playwright. Strongly as such revisionists argue their case, the arguments for Aeschylean authorship are cogent too. We know he wrote a tetralogy of plays about Prometheus; the ancient world believed that this was part of it; whoever did write this *Prometheus Bound* was a master dramatist; and there is no reason why, with such a small sample of Aeschylus for comparison, he should not have produced a play such as this which is quite unlike any of the six others which have survived. Nevertheless the metrics, vocabulary and other evidence suggest to some critics a later writer, possibly Aeschylus' son Euphorion.

Set high in the Caucasus, the play opens on a bare mountainside. Four characters enter, an Olympian god, Hephaestus, two personifications, Might and Force (*Kratos* and *Bia*), and Prometheus, a Titan, himself a god, perhaps the nephew of Zeus but implacably opposed to that god's harsh rule. The stubborn Prometheus is chained to a rock and left there to suffer, an immortal but part of some almost primeval struggle for supremacy in a world that is still striving to escape from chaos. Deserted though this mountain-top may be, the immobilised Prometheus receives a series of visitors, beginning with a chorus of the daughters of Ocean who will himself later arrive in person. If their lines are to be taken at face value, they fly in on a winged chariot. Perhaps, were we able today to conjure up that original production, a whole series of issues would be resolved about how early drama was staged. In *Prometheus Bound* we may have one of the earliest of all surviving plays. The fact that it appears to demand the staging resources needed for Wagnerian opera may well be an indication that what it actually received was not realistic production but the imaginative staging of an Adolphe Appia, the revolutionary Swiss designer who believed that Wagner should be presented in settings that hinted at the majestic and the primitive without trying to imitate them.

To a Greek audience, what could be presented through the medium of dance might have been quite sufficient to conjure up flight and it is probably most convenient to treat the whole play at its figurative and imagistic level. Prometheus is bound tight, his visitors are free, yet each faces restrictions of one kind or another. What Prometheus did, as an immortal, was to offer mortals knowledge: 'I planted seeds of thought/ Intelligence' (ll. 442–3). Prometheus gave mankind fire but fire as husbandry, writing, numeracy, skills and crafts, medicine, prophecy, metallurgy. Nor has he any reservations over what he has done, whatever the ultimate result. The Chorus are terrified that the opposition of Zeus and Prometheus is a threat to all stability. Their father, Ocean, arrives riding a winged horse, and advises Prometheus to compromise. Prometheus refuses and warns of the dangers of becoming associated with his notoriety. When Ocean has left Prometheus reveals his bargaining power, knowledge which he refuses to divulge but which could topple Zeus.

His next visitor is another victim of Zeus, or rather, of Zeus and his wife Hera. Io was seduced by Zeus and turned into a cow by Hera. She now roams the earth, pursued by a tormenting gadfly. He is fettered to his rock, she unable to stay in one place for more than a moment. She looks to Prometheus for relief but he can only forecast further pain. She threatens suicide: the immortal Prometheus seems to envy her for having such a choice. But he does reveal some of his secret. Zeus is destined to have 'a son mightier than his father' but only he knows who the mother might be. For Io he can offer no consolation but he does forecast the tale of

Danaus and his fifty daughters, forty-nine of whom murdered the husbands of their forced marriage, and whose story is told in one of Aeschylus' other surviving plays, *Suppliants*.

Io is replaced by the god Hermes but he is no more able to break Prometheus' resolve than had any of the others been. He warns the Chorus that they should leave, as an earthquake seems to consume Prometheus.

This may be a rare world of gods and primeval passions but for the discerning spectator there are messages too, messages about the dangers of offering democratic power to all and sundry; messages about individuality and individual action; messages about the nature of freedom itself. 'All tyrants are galled by the same disease:/ They dare not trust their friends' (ll. 222–3) has lost none of its validity over the centuries. Prometheus is a recognisable fanatic, stubborn and determined, glorying almost in the extremes of his deprivation as a means to exact the greatest recompense in due course. But it is he who has given mankind fire. In doing that he opts for progress but is a living demonstration of the price that progress may exact. Aeschylus, if Aeschylus was the author, was to move on to write the *Oresteia*, the only complete and connected trilogy to have been preserved. That views the progress of democracy in Athens at its most crucial turning-point, all in the story of the return home of the commander of the Greek army at Troy. The *Prometheia* in its entirety, which included the release of Prometheus, may well have held as compelling messages. Unearthly as the whole setting may be, there are ways in which Prometheus as archetype presents the human condition more closely and more uncomfortably than does many a more realistic play, even in the Greek canon.

Women of Trachis

Sophocles is often seen as a sort of stylistic halfway-house between the monumental world of Aeschylus and the new realism of Euripides. In fact his playwriting career covered such a length of time that he probably influenced both of them as well as being influenced by them. He competed with Aeschylus in 468 at the Great Dionysia, and beat him, though the plays have not come down to us. He and Aeschylus could have been competitors for the next ten years. The seven plays of Sophocles we have were all written during Euripides' working life even though *Oedipus at Colonus* was not performed until after the death of both dramatists. Were there any decent way of dating the work of each with any certainty, it would be fascinating to try and trace the cross-influences and, perhaps, the cross-references. The fact is, however, that each of Sophocles' plays has a wonderful singularity which removes it almost entirely from any temporal boundaries.

Women of Trachis is the least known and least often performed of all of Sophocles. No one knows when it was first produced but it makes no difference to our appreciation. It is a Heracles play, dealing not with any of his famous and infamous exploits, but with his death, brought about unwittingly by his wife Deianira. It is she who opens the play and who will, before Heracles even appears, have killed herself on discovering what she has done. When he does enter, in great pain and already dying, the play is three-quarters over. It is almost as though he were a secondary character. The title, *Women of Trachis*, referring to a Chorus who have fewer than 250 lines and do not directly affect the action, seems to be a kind of statement of neutrality.

It is, for all this, an extraordinarily poignant piece with several powerful scenes and an advanced sense of dramatic structure, more like that of Euripides than any other Sophocles play. It opens with a prologue, as do many of Euripides' plays including *Medea*, *Electra*, *Bacchae* and *Helen*. The prologue is quite like that in *Helen*, with Deianira lamenting her beauty and the trouble it has caused her. She married Heracles only after he had won her in a battle with a river god: but now she never knows where he is from one year's end to the next. Though the tone is less comic than in Euripides' *Helen* there is something very domestic lurking in the midst of all the savage surroundings. The juxtaposition is maintained in the central part of the plot. Many years ago a centaur, half-man, half-horse, had molested Deianira while carrying her across a river. Heracles had shot him with a poisoned arrow and the dying creature had advised her to preserve some of his blood, saying that this would work as a love-charm if ever Heracles started to stray. This he has constantly done: 'Do you think there haven't been others,' she asks Lichas, 'Other women in the life of a man like Heracles?' (ll. 459–60). This time is different.

She discovers that one of the captives sent on ahead before he returns is a princess for whom he has sacked a city. So Deianira decides to act and send him a robe imbued with the centaur's blood. The dying centaur, though, had been planning his revenge. The poison in the garment sticks to Heracles and begins to consume him. The similarity here between the death of Heracles and the death that Euripides' Medea contrives for the princess for whom Jason has deserted her would be difficult to overlook. Love is the killer, love that clings and burns and ultimately destroys. The difference between Deianira and Medea is one of intent. Medea has brewed up the poison herself, knowing exactly what the effect will be. Deianira is an innocent who believes she is doing the right thing. She goes so far as to tell the Chorus about it and say to them, 'I haven't done something stupid, have I?/ I think I'm right but if you don't agree I won't try it' (ll. 586–7). When the effect is, as their son Hyllus describes it, for the robe to burn itself into Heracles' flesh, she leaves without a word to kill herself. The Nurse's description of her farewell to house and marriage-bed before she drives a sword through her heart is all the more touching for being so credible, the only course of action left to the woman whose gentle nature dominates the first three-quarters of the play.

By contrast, the last scene is much harder to stomach, perhaps the reason for this play's comparative neglect. Heracles is carried in, in agony and dying. His son Hyllus is with him, himself remorseful now for having accused his mother of murdering Heracles. Heracles demands two things of him, binding him by an oath. He is to cremate his father alive, then to marry Iole, the girl who was the cause of the trouble in the first place. Oath or not, Hyllus is shocked at the prospect of doing either, but eventually he agrees. As it

happens it was not Hyllus who burnt Heracles on a pyre but
Philoctetes. For this, Philoctetes was given Heracles' famous
bow, possession of which is the key to the other Sophocles
play in the present volume.

Women of Trachis provides echoes and points of comparison to a number of other plays from the second half of the
fifth century, but more of them by Euripides than by
Sophocles. Perhaps this is simply because fewer plays of
Sophocles survive. Sympathy for the human condition is
strong in both. It is in Aeschylus, but reserved there mainly
for the heroic figures. Sophocles in this play looks at a
secondary figure, a woman, to whom things happen and who,
when she has choices of her own, makes the wrong ones. For
Sophocles, as for Euripides too, this can be the stuff of
tragedy.

Philoctetes

If the last quarter of *Women of Trachis* is focused on the
physical pain of Heracles, the whole of *Philoctetes* is
dominated by the eponymous hero's agony. That, and the
bow of Heracles which Philoctetes needs to keep himself
alive and which the Greeks need if they are ever going to
capture Troy, are almost extra characters in this strange and
uncompromising play. It is firmly dated to 409 when
Sophocles was apparently eighty-seven years old. The
group won first prize but there is no record of the other
plays to which this was a complement. *Philoctetes* certainly
contains enough unusual features to surprise those who think
there is a set formula for all Greek tragedy.

To begin with, the play is set on the otherwise uninhabited
island of Lemnos where Philoctetes has been marooned like
some prototype Ben Gunn in *Treasure Island*. He had been
part of the original expedition that set out for Troy but after
being bitten in the foot by a snake, his festering wound
proved so noisome and his cries of pain so unnerving that
nobody wanted him on board any longer. They abandoned
him on Lemnos, leaving with him only the bow that Heracles
had bequeathed to him in gratitude for lighting the funeral

pyre when Hyllus refused (cf. the ending of *Women of Trachis* above). The setting is a cave on the seashore where Philoctetes is living. It is described by Odysseus, who opens the play searching for him with the young Neoptolemos, son of Achilles, as having two entrances with a place to sit in between and a spring lower down. When he enters the cave 'up above', he discovers Philoctetes' bandages hanging out to dry. Realism of this sort is associated more usually with Euripides and raises intriguing questions about staging protocol. Two others of Sophocles' plays have unusual settings: *Ajax*, during the course of which the scene changes from outside the hero's tent to the seashore where he commits suicide; and *Oedipus at Colonus*, before the sacred grove of the Eumenides. Opinions differ wildly as to how representational the original set might have been.

Then there is the cast. It is small, only five speaking characters, four if, as some think, the Trader is Odysseus in disguise. The actors were all male but, out of the entire surviving Greek drama, tragedy and comedy, forty-six plays in all, this is the only one with an all-male cast. This may be no real surprise considering the situation but several other war, or fringe war plays, involve female characters either mortal or immortal. *Philoctetes* has no real god either, though Heracles does serve that function when he eventually appears *ex machina* to settle the ending.

The action revolves around the intrigues and deceptions that Odysseus and the young Neoptolemos are prepared to employ in order to trick Philoctetes. This provides a fascinating moral debate but at the end nobody dies and everyone is, if not happy, at least reconciled to the solution. This is a far cry from any notion of tragedy depending on the downfall and death of its leading character. Instead, *Philoctetes* raises the issue of military victory and its price. Does the end justify the means? It also shows a young warrior coming of age.

Odysseus persuades Neoptolemos to deceive Philoctetes in order to steal his bow. At first Neoptolemos lies and betrays his own nature, but then relents and returns the bow which Philoctetes has entrusted to him. Philoctetes then tries to shoot Odysseus, but Neoptolemos prevents him. Philoctetes

and Neoptolemos are about to sail home when the deified
Heracles appears to tell them that they must go to Troy.
Sophocles' genius is to show us Neoptolemos trying to
compromise his nature. Only after experience and reflection
does he see that the loss of self, or self-betrayal, is worse than
the loss of Troy. His dilemma is like Antigone's; his loyalty to
himself and to the ideals that constitute his character is finally
more important than loyalty to those in power, particularly
when his allegiance involves a loyalty to a higher truth.

The issue of truth versus falsehood is important here. In
The Iliad, Achilles, the father of Neoptolemos, says, 'As
hateful to me as the gates of Hades is a man who says one
thing while concealing another thing in his heart' (*Iliad* 9, ll.
312–13). Achilles lives a short life, and gains honour;
Odysseus lives a long life because of his lying. He is the
one Greek hero who is aware when it is in his own best
interest to be a coward. Sophocles renders the scene comic
with the blustering Odysseus running away after Philoctetes
regains his bow and tries to kill him. This is typical of
Odysseus. He is true to himself, and he is a survivor. Such
cowardice would have been unthinkable for Achilles.

Theme upon theme is repeated in Sophocles, as he
replicates Achilles in his strange majesty. Philoctetes and
Neoptolemos are like two sides of Achilles: one, the irascible
and wild nature of the devoted warrior, the other, his virtue
and integrity. When they are divided they lose; together,
they defeat Odysseus. Heracles brings about this powerful
fusion by forcing them back into the mythological track.
This may be one of the 'happy ending' tragedies, but it is
dragged to that ending 'kicking and screaming'.

The play offers, perhaps, the first *psychomachia* in drama.
Odysseus and Philoctetes fight to gain the soul of Neoptolemos. Neoptolemos ultimately opts for the truthful
Philoctetes, who most resembles his father. During the
course of the drama he matures. Older heroes generally
remain the same in Sophocles. This is a rite of passage for an
adolescent. As the only surviving tragedy with an entirely
male cast *Philoctetes* may have contained an important lesson
for a young citizen. Neoptolemos discovers, and is finally
true to, himself. He is a reverse Oedipus; instead of parricide,

Neoptolemos discovers his father Achilles in himself, and adopts his values which he sees as his own.

Philoctetes, like Prometheus and Io, suffers intermittently agonies sent to him by a divine source. He is representative of all those victims who suffer from chronic illness. The bow itself is a prominent and magical symbol. It never fails. It is both a provider of life, and a destroyer. Philoctetes says he cannot survive without it. The destruction that it will bring to Troy will also lead to peace. The bare island of Lemnos wonderfully represents the craggy hero Philoctetes. His description of the island he is about to leave shows that he loves it as much as he hates it. Both Aeschylus (*c.* 475 BC) and Euripides (431 BC) in their lost versions made it inhabited by Lemnians. Sophocles prefers the island deserted to point up his isolated hero.

This play has inspired many playwrights who found it offered philosophical or political commentary on their present situations. André Gide's *Philoctetes, or the Treatise on Three Ethics* (1898) shows the existentialist progression from love of one's country, to love of another, and finally the most valid of all: love of self. Heiner Müller's *Philoctetes* (1965, followed by another version, *Philoktet, Der Horatier*, 1968) offers an impassioned ideological critique of a man in power who seeks even greater power with no ethical restraint. His Odysseus is a soldier blindly following immoral orders. Müller offers a bitter Marxist critique of the misused worker who does not think for himself. Seamus Heaney's *The Cure at Troy* (1990) is based on *Philoctetes*, and deals with the Irish situation and people's persistence in nursing old wounds. His play proceeds from, and ends in, optimism. It is a version that truly urges and believes, and hopes 'for a great sea-change/ On the far side of revenge/ . . . that a further shore is reachable from here'. But all three of these plays minimise Sophocles' emphasis on honour, and a boy's loyalty to his own ideals.

Trojan Women

This is the greatest anti-war play ever written. From Aeschylus to Euripides there is a shift in focus. Aeschylus wrote with the glory of the Persian wars vividly in mind, but Euripides was overwhelmed by the horrors of the Peloponnesian War (431–404 BC), in which Greek fought Greek. The names of Marathon and Thermopylae are synonymous with Greek heroism, but the name of Melos is synonymous with the atrocity born of empire. Just before this play was produced (415 BC), the Athenians killed all the males and enslaved the women and children on Melos. This is vividly described by Thucydides, who reveals the Athenian *Machtpolitik* ('might makes right'). In the same year the Athenians made the disastrous decision to invade Sicily, the first step towards their final defeat in 404 BC. This play was strangely prophetic: a warning which was not heeded.

Though none of the other plays presented with *Trojan Women* has survived, the titles and some fragments of the two plays that preceded it, *Alexander* and *Palamedes*, lead one to speculate that Euripides may have written a connected trilogy: each title suggests someone connected with Troy and the Trojan War. Even the satyr play that followed these tragedies, *Sisyphus*, might be connected to Odysseus since Sisyphus has sometimes been mentioned in mythology as his father.

In the prologue of *Trojan Women*, the god Poseidon reflects on the destruction of Troy, his patron city. He enters into an unholy alliance with Athena, the former ally of the Greeks, now alienated by an act of sacrilege, and eager to change sides.

Hecuba, the former queen of Troy, is the pivotal figure. As her own tragedy unfolds, she has to face the murder of her daughter Polyxena; the rape of another daughter Cassandra; the murder of her baby grandson by the Greek army; and her daughter-in-law dragged away, as she will be, into slavery. Hecuba at the end is pure Hecuba: suffering has burned away her impurities.

There is brief comic relief when Menelaus meets Helen again, now a prisoner whom he has pledged to kill. She debates with Hecuba, in an attempt to justify herself, even laying the blame for the war on Hecuba for not killing her son Paris in the first place. The audience had just seen the *Alexander*, in which Hecuba and Priam, warned of the trouble their son will cause, expose the baby. Paris survives, as exposed babies in drama usually do, and, when grown up, is welcomed back as their son by Hecuba and Priam. Helen may have had a point. In the *Trojan Women*, by the end of the scene with Helen and Menelaus, it is clear enough, if not explicitly stated, that she has won over her former husband. Hecuba may have won the argument on intellectual grounds, but Helen emerges unscathed because of the passion she can still provoke. Her argumentation is reminiscent of the sophists, something that Aristophanes satirised in *The Clouds*. Arguing for the good or the true is irrelevant; it is only important that one argues well.

The play returns rapidly to the starkest horror as the desperate Hecuba has to face the death of her grandson, Astyanax. Talthybius, the Greek herald, carries the body of Astyanax over to Hecuba for her and the other women to prepare for burial. He carries him on his father's shield, the very object that was to protect him. This makes the burial all the more pitiable. Hecuba, who said earlier to Andromache that she should live because 'where there's life, there's hope', finally tries to kill herself by running into the flames of Troy. Her plight frames the play, which ends, as it begins, with her personal tragedy.

The Greeks, a thinly veiled portrait of the Athenians, are shown to be more barbaric than the defeated Trojans; they are cowards frightened of a child. They are afraid to leave a young boy alive in case he grows up to be an avenger. The shadow of Melos stretches over the play. This is Euripides at his greatest, savaging the conventional heroes, and showing the reality and sordidness of war. Besides this, it is hardly just to destroy a country for the sake of a woman, as the historian Herodotus points out.

Trojan Women is like Aeschylus' *Prometheus Bound* in that one character is on stage throughout, and others come and go. Both plays have been criticised for this and described as static, like their victimised heroes. But this staging can be seen as symbolic of their capacity to endure and adds to their stature. The play has to be seen for its tragic potential to be appreciated. There are two scenes of lamentation that leave only the rare person in the audience dry-eyed, and also an inner tempo and a shift of moods, from the lighter (the captured girls speculating on the relative merits of the places to which they may go; the debate between Helen and Hecuba) to the totally bleak (the burial of Astyanax; the final burning of Troy). One light after another is extinguished until there is darkness except for the fires of Troy in the background.

Like *Antigone*, *Trojan Women* is often performed, or rewritten, in the hotspots of the world, at times of crisis. Sartre's version, written in 1965, reflected the miseries of the Algerian War, at a time when he went so far as to encourage French troops to desert. Even in despair there may be hope for change, as the Greeks realised when they decided to kill Hector's infant son. As the Irish poet Brendan Kennelly puts it in his version of *Trojan Women*:

> There's nothing more dangerous to a winner
> Than one seed of hope in the heart of a loser.

Astyanax represented Trojan hope.

The message is as powerful as ever: earlier poets, like Homer, Aeschylus and Sophocles, focus on the glory of war, but Euripides shows us the suffering of women and children. This play is a play about sorrow: the grief of loss, particularly the loss that is irrevocable. In the Euripidean universe, chaos and malevolent gods rule and the human leaders imitate the brutality of the gods. Man's only recourse is to make an alliance with other men: here, women with women. This alliance goes by the name of *philia*, or love. Here the victims show a type of heroism in the way that they choose to live. The play is about grief, but it may offer a note of hope. Suffering burns away pettiness and purifies the soul. Perhaps the audience will experience a comparable transformation. The Greeks called that *katharsis*, and good art can bring about change.

Trojan Women is a play for all time. It is a plea for peace and understanding, besides celebrating life and its passions. It shows that it is never too late to take a step towards the light of peace, away from the darkness of brutal war; death will have no dominion over the heroism of these women.

Bacchae

Bacchae is, of all Greek tragedies, the most elusive and the most mysterious. It is a play in which odd things happen, things which the characters themselves cannot explain: where nobody is quite what they seem and truth and illusion overlap. The reason, though, is simple enough. *Bacchae* is about the god Dionysus and his attempt to receive recognition in the land of his birth. For the Greeks Dionysus was the god of the vine, the god of illusion, the god of the theatre. He was a latecomer to the Olympian hierarchy, introduced to account for the unaccountable, the god of wine, yes, but the god of the irrational too. The play poses questions at every turn about whom to trust, whom to take seriously and with whom to sympathise. If it is difficult to know where to post your allegiance, then the paradoxes that the play throws up are part of the purpose.

The opening prologue is delivered by Dionysus, who announces that he has arrived in Thebes 'disguised as a man'. At the end of the play he will return as Dionysus, a transformation that was presumably signposted in some clear theatrical manner. In between, in his disguise, he is simply a stranger, a threat to security, a foreigner, an outsider who arrives with a chorus of supporters who recognise him only as their leader but not as the god. The reason for his coming from Asia to Thebes is to install his religion and to redress a grievance. His mother, Semele, was loved by Zeus. Hera, Zeus's wife, gained revenge by telling Semele she would have no notion of her lover's real nature until he revealed himself to her as he really was. Semele exacted a promise before Zeus realised what she would ask. When he did appear as a thunderbolt she was blasted out of existence. Her embryonic son was plucked from the flames and sewn in Zeus's thigh, from which Dionysus was eventually born.

That, at least, is the story. That was the myth. The family don't believe any of it. Semele's three sisters – one of whom, Agave, is the mother of Pentheus, the young King of Thebes – reject Dionysus, 'proclaiming my godlike birth a trick/ Devised by Cadmus to save a harlot-daughter's face' (ll. 29–30). Dionysus is planning revenge and has sent the women of

Thebes mad, his aunts among them, to roam up on the mountains in a Bacchic frenzy. How much and whom to believe become issues in the play as Dionysus leaves the stage to his Asian supporters. Another theme is the nature of reason and of wisdom, attributes claimed by most of the main characters but hardly justified.

This chorus is one of the most graphic and exciting of any, a powerful riposte to those who might think that the chorus as a dramatic device is losing its appeal by the end of the fifth century. Their opening entrance offers a picture of the religion of Dionysus in all its forms, from the sweet and seductive to the threatening and ultimately destructive. Present for the rest of the play, their various interventions show them as a multiple embodiment of Dionysus himself.

The first Theban character to appear is Teiresias, the blind prophet, revered in other plays for his ability to reveal the truth. He has come to fetch Cadmus, the founder of the city and grandfather of the present king, so that they can go and worship Dionysus up in the mountains. But what are we expected to make of these two old men, one unable to see, the other hardly able to walk, when Dionysus has himself suggested that the religion is for women? They seem hard to take seriously especially when Teiresias goes off into a complicated linguistic explanation of how the story about sewing the embryo into the thigh was all a misunderstanding. Then Pentheus, the king, arrives, infuriated by what he has heard about the stranger and blaming the prophet for making his grandfather look foolish. What are we to make of Cadmus' conversion when he can suggest that his grandson pretend that Dionysus is really the son of Zeus because it will look impressive to have a god in the family?

The arrival of the first Messenger with a tale of the women going berserk in the mountains, ripping cattle to pieces and stealing children, makes Pentheus even stronger in his resolve and sets the scene for the first of the two confrontations between the cousins: for so they are if the stranger is really the son of Pentheus' late aunt.

The play progresses from here through its most dramatic scenes, the battle of wits between Pentheus and Dionysus which results in Pentheus imprisoning him; the earthquake unleashed by Dionysus to secure his escape – or is it simply a delusion inflicted on the Chorus of the sort he certainly admits to inflicting on Pentheus? The 'seduction' of Pentheus follows when he is persuaded through his own prurience to dress up as a woman to go and watch what the women are up to. Pentheus' own nature is subverted by Dionysus, released perhaps, to make him contribute to his own fate.

The final scenes, the death relayed by another shocked messenger, and the entry for the first time into the play of Agave, brandishing in her deluded state her son's head on her Bacchic wand, are as terrible as any scenes in the drama: not least for Dionysus' own detachment from what he has done. He was insulted, he claims, to which Cadmus howls his human response 'a god should not show passion like a man'. Dionysus may have demonstrated his godlike powers but he has shown himself incapable of compassion.

This play functions at so many different levels: as a grisly parable; as a myth from primitive times; as a family saga; as a revenge tragedy; as a black comedy; as sexual politics; as a philosophical tract on the nature of good, or rather, bad, government. What is extraordinary about it as a play from the fifth century BC is that it is a tragedy about the nature of theatre. Dionysus, the god of theatre, puts Pentheus in costume and lets him be the star of a drama where he would have preferred to be just a spectator. Dionysus insidiously harnesses an audience's own voyeurism to drive Pentheus to his own destruction. The lessons are frightening but they are wholly contemporary.

Marianne McDonald, University of California,
and J. Michael Walton, University of Hull,
2002

Transliteration of Greek words and, in particular, proper nouns, into English presents problems of consistency. These translations follow different conventions according to the volumes from the Classical Greek Dramatists in which most of them were first published. The Greek alphabet contains a 'k' rather than a 'c', a 'u' rather than a 'y'.

Line numbers alongside the text refer to the Greek originals rather than to these translations.

AESCHYLUS

Persians

translated by Kenneth McLeish and Frederic Raphael

Characters

QUEEN ATOSSA
MESSENGER
GHOST OF DARIUS
XERXES
CHORUS OF OLD MEN OF SUSA
ATTENDANTS (silent parts)

Before Darius' tomb, outside the palace doors of Susa.
Enter CHORUS.

CHORUS.
  You see trust. They trusted us,
  The Persians who marched on Greece.
  Seniority's office, our task
  Imposed by Xerxes,
  Darius' son: keep safe
  The royal gold, this seat of kings.
  Oh, when will our lord return?
  That swarm of men, gold-glittering?
  Drums of ill-omen beat,
  Beat in our hearts.   10
  Now Asia's might's afield,
  Our hearts all ache for him,
  Majesty.
  Why no message, no herald
  Galloping, galloping?

  From Susa's towers they swarmed,
  From Agbatana, from ancient Cissia:
  On foot, on horse, by ship,
  Brigades, battalions,
  Thronging for war.   20
  Their lords' names:
  Amistres, Artaphrenes,
  Megabates, Astaspes,
  Marshals of Persia,
  Kings loyal to one great king,
  Of one great force the pride.
  Master-bowmen, spearsmen, cavaliers:
  Fearful to see, more fearful far
  To fight: to dare their sole resolve.
  Artembares, chariot-lord,
  Masistres, Imaeus arrow-straight,   30
  Sosthanes horse-master,
  Pharandaces.
  More men wide Nile sends forth,
  Swirling, mother of mortals:

Susiscanes, Pegastagon Aegyptus' son,
Arsames, priest-prince of Memphis,
Ariomardus who holds mysterious Thebes in fee.
Marsh-Arabs, crafty oarsmen,
40   A host past numbering.
Soft Lydians; Ionians
Who fringe out continent,
Their generals Metrogathes,
Arcteus the Brave, kings in their pride.
From Sardis next:
Chariots thronging, a stream of gold,
Like javelins, three-horsed, four-horsed,
Terror to behold.
Next, sacred Tmolus' regiment,
50   All set to hoop Greeks for slaves:
Mardon, Tharybis, anvils of iron,
Mysian spearsmen. See! Golden Babylon
Mints sailors, a shoal, mints archers,
Their trust their bending bows.
All Asia's blades are drawn:
Crowding, thronging to answer
Their king's dread call to arms.
60   The flower of the Persian land is gone.
Their motherland,
Asia who mothered them,
Waits for them, weeps for them;
Families, wives,
Stretch fearful days upon the rack of time.

The crossing's made. The king's machine,
The city-smashing host, makes bridgehead
On alien shore. Now Helle's gulf
70   Stands cable-stitched, sea's neck
Bridged tight, road-yoked.

Lord Xerxes, teeming Asia's master,
Now view-halloos his pack against the land.
Stern generals, sure on sea, on land,
His confidence. Now, living gold,
80   He dazzles like the gods.
Dragon-eyes, iron looks,

A shoal of hands, of sails;
From hurtling chariot
He fires at spear-framed Greeks
Ares the war god,
Arrowing the foe.

A flood of men, a cataract!
Who'll face it down?
What weapons, what battle-cries
Can dam this sea?   90
Persia's army – Persians! –
Unstoppable.

Heaven's tricks and snares –
What mortal ever cheats them?
Quickfoot, high-leaping,
Who slips the cull?
Fate beckons, smiles,
Seduces:
You're trapped, you die.   100

God-sent, of old,
Our destiny since time began:
Tower-toppling war,
Hard-galloping,
City-sacking.

New knowledge now:
They scan the sea,
Wind-lathered, sacrosanct;   110
They tame it, bind it,
Swarm across.

Our hearts black-cloaked,
Fear-torn. O-ah!
Fear for Persia's marching might,
Fear for Susa
Widowed, stripped, unmanned.

From Cissia's proud citadel   120
Grief-cries, o-ah!,
Shrieks of women echoing,
Beat breasts,

Claw finery to rags.
Our army – knights, foot-soldiers –
Swarms from the hive,
130   Yokes continents,
Makes two lands one
And swarms across.

Empty marriage-beds, filled with tears.
All painful smiles,
They flung their men, like keen,
Hot spears, to war,
Themselves to widowhood.

CHORUS LEADER.
140   Come, Persians,
Here in this ancient place
Sit down, discuss, debate.
How fares lord Xerxes,
Son of Darius, king of kings?
Have our bowmen triumphed?
Have lance-thrusts, spear-casts
Given Greece the prize?

Enter QUEEN *attended.*

150   Look: like a god she comes,
Light to our eyes,
The Queen, his majesty's royal mother.
I bow.
In humble courtesy,
As is the law, I speak to her.

Majesty, of deep-gowned Persian womanhood the
    pearl,
Mother of Xerxes, our respects, Darius' worthy wife
Who shared the bed of Persia's god, and to a god
    gave birth,
Unless the luck has changed, for all our Persian host.

QUEEN.
Why else should I leave those gilded halls
160   Where Darius and I lay down, and come to you?
Care claws my heart. Thoughts haunt me. Friends,

I share with you secret fears. Is all our wealth
Now tramped to dust, our glory scattered
That Darius, with God's good help, raised up?
Two-pronged the thought unspoken in my heart:
What point in royal pomp if men be gone? What light
For manly muscle shines, unfed by power?
We're rich – look round! – but where's our guiding
   light?
A house is blind unless its lord is there.
Thus stands our case. Be then my counsellors: 170
Your age, your wisdom. Sirs, in this our state
I choose, and ground my trust in you.

CHORUS LEADER.
  Majesty, queen of all Persia, ask no more:
  You own the loyalty which now you ask.
  In word and deed our energies are yours.

QUEEN.
  Dreams haunt me.
  Night after night they come,
  Since my son drummed up his army,
  Marched on Greece. Dream after dream –
  And none so clear as in this last night.   180
  Two women came: well-dressed,
  One in Persian elegance, one Dorian.
  In bearing both belittled us today:
  In beauty flawless sisters;
  In race identical. Their native lands?
  One Greek, one ... not-Greek.
  Suddenly they quarrelled, the pair of them.
  My son separated them, calmed them,
  Tried to yoke them to his chariot.   190
  One stood quiet, obedient,
  Proud in her harness. The other
  Bucked, tore free the bridle, plunged
  Out of control, and smashed the yoke.
  My son stumbled. Darius came,
  His father, and wept for him. When Xerxes saw,
  He ripped his own clothes to rags.
  That was the dream. When morning came,   200

In running water I washed away the omen,
Ran to the altar, carrying in my hand –
This hand, the hand ordained –
Gifts to the gods to take all ill away.
Instead, an eagle, fluttering in fear,
Settled on Phoebus' holy hearth.
I watched. Mute with fear.
A hawk next. Swooped, perched – the talons! –
Raking, clawing its rival's head. Down, down,
The eagle cowered. Offered itself. No fight.
210   I saw this terror, saw as I tell you now.
Know this:
My son, successful, will dazzle every eye.
But if he fails, he'll not step down:
Long as he lives, this land is his.

CHORUS LEADER.
We answer, Mother. No fright in what we say,
And no false cheer. The gods, Majesty, the gods now
    need
Your supplication. Omens of evil in what you saw –
May the gods discard them, make them drop unripe.
May blessings rain on you, your son, your state,
Your friends. And next, libations pour
220   To Earth and the Dead below. In deference
Beg Darius your consort, whom you saw last night,
To send good things from Dark below to Light above
For you, for Xerxes, and snatch all evil down
To lie entombed. Pious advice! We offer it
In hope, in trust, that all may yet be well.

QUEEN.
My lord, your words, your reading of my dream
Show loyalty – to Xerxes, to the royal house.
God send it so! As you suggest, good prayers
To Heaven above, to those below who wish us well,
I'll offer up, inside. For now, one question more:
230   My lords, this ... Athens. Where on Earth – ?

CHORUS LEADER.
Far, lady. Where sets our lord the Sun.

QUEEN.
One town. Why should Xerxes want it so?

CHORUS LEADER.
If Athens falls, all Greece submits.

QUEEN.
Have they such soldiers?

CHORUS LEADER.
You know them, lady. They hurt the Medes before.

QUEEN.
What are they, archers, who bend the well-sprung bow?

CHORUS LEADER.
No! Spearsmen, hand-to-hand; their armour,
    shields.

QUEEN.
They're wealthy – ?

CHORUS LEADER.
They've silver, lady, springing from the earth.   240

QUEEN.
Who shepherds them? Their warlord – who?

CHORUS LEADER.
Call them no mortal's slaves. They bow to none.

QUEEN.
They nerve themselves to face the foe?

CHORUS LEADER.
They crushed Darius' heroes.

QUEEN.
Cold words for parents of our marching men!

CHORUS LEADER.
You'll know soon, Majesty. Clear words.
A soldier, look, running to bring us news.
Good words or bad, he'll tell them straight.

    Enter MESSENGER.

MESSENGER.
    Cities of Asia,

250   Land of Persia, fortune's anchorage,
      At a single stroke our good luck's gone,
      Our flower of glory withered.
      O cruel to bring first cruel news!
      I must, I must. Persians,
      The whole barbarian force is lost.

CHORUS.
      Pain stabs,
      Stabs sudden pain.
      Persians, hear and weep.

MESSENGER.
260   Our whole expedition wrecked.
      I never thought to see home again.

CHORUS.
      We've lived
      Too long, if these old ears
      Must hear such pain.

MESSENGER.
      I saw it all. No hearsay. Persians,
      I tell what these eyes saw.

CHORUS.
      O-toto-to-ee!
      In vain they marched,
270   That forest of weapons,
      From Asia to Greece, to death.

MESSENGER.
      Stiff corpses choke Salamis' sands,
      The dunes beyond.

CHORUS.
      O-toto-to-ee!
      Loved ones, bloated,
      Battle-cloaks their shrouds,
      Bobbing, bobbing on the sea.

MESSENGER.
      Their bows: useless. A whole army, crushed
      As ship impacted ship.

CHORUS.
> Shrill voices, weep   280
> Persians, cry.
> Gods heap disaster,
> Waste our men.

MESSENGER.
> Salamis, vilest of names!
> Athens! To say it is to weep.

CHORUS.
> Athens! Death to her enemies.
> Women of Persia,
> Husbandless, childless,
> We weep for you.

QUEEN.
> Blow on blow. I said nothing: 290
> What words can equal this?
> Yet when gods send pain,
> What can mortals do but bear it?
> Speak calmly. The whole disaster –
> Groan if you must, but tell it plain.
> Are any ... not dead? The princes,
> The high command? Are there ... gaps
> Among the leaders of the people?

MESSENGER.
> Lord Xerxes lives and sees the light.

QUEEN.
> Your words are dawn to this my house.   300
> Bright daylight shines from darkness.

MESSENGER.
> Artembares, who reined ten thousand horse,
> Rolls on the tideline at Salamis.
> Dadaces the chiliarch, speared
> Mid-jump from ship to shore;
> Lord Tenagon of Bactria
> Snags on sea-scourged rocks.

Arsames, Lilaeus, Argastes,
Below the cliff where rock-doves nest,
310   Swirl and butt, swirl and butt.
Allies from Egypt: Pharnuchus,
Arcteus, Adeues, Pheresseues,
All from one ship, all dead.
Matallus of Chrysa, myriarch:
Death scabs his black beard red.
Dead Magian Arabus; dead Bactrian Artabes,
Horse-lord, ruled thirty thousand men,
Now rules one narrow grave.
320   Amistris; Amphistreus, spearsman of death;
Brave Ariomardus, Sardis' woe; Seisames the
    Mysian;
Tharybis from Lyrna, handsome,
Who five times fifty ships deployed,
Death-wasted lies, his beauty spoiled;
Gallant Syennesis, Cilician king,
Swamped by enemies, dealt death and died.
So many leaders! So many names!
330   Disasters teemed for us; I name but few.

QUEEN.
Ai-ee! I scale the peak of pain.
Howl, shriek for Persia. Shame!
Begin again. These Greeks –
What swarm of ships had they,
To risk, to dare attack
Our Persian armada? Head-on? How dared they?

MESSENGER.
If numbers were all, we'd ride in triumph now.
For the Greeks: some ten times thirty sail,
340   With ten besides, crack warships.
For Xerxes: main fleet one thousand,
Fast galleons, two hundred and seven more.
The numbers are exact. We hardly failed
In numbers. Some power from the gods bore down;
Tipped scales; Fate cheated.
The gods it was kept Athens, Athene's city, safe.

QUEEN.
The city stands?

MESSENGER.
Its soldiers live. It stands.

QUEEN.
Tell how it began, the ships, their clash.   350
Who were first in line: the Greeks? –
My son, pluming himself on that great fleet?

MESSENGER.
Some demon, Majesty, some spite began disaster.
A man came to your son – a Greek, an Athenian.
Greek nerve would never hold, he said.
As soon as darkness fell, they'd leap on board,
Grab oars and row for their lives
In all directions. Xerxes believed him.   360
Why should he suspect the hand of God?
He sent word to all his captains. 'As soon
As the Sun withdraws his shafts that light the Earth,
As soon as darkness tenants the evening sky,
Action stations! Divide the fleet in three.
One group row round the island. The rest
Block access to open water. If any Greeks slip past,
If they trick any ships to freedom,   370
Your heads shall pay for it.' Proud orders:
How could he know what future gods had planned?
Our men, obedient, well-trained, ate dinner,
Then each sailor looped and tied his oar in place.
As soon as the Sun's bright light declined
And night crept in, each master-oarsman,
Each man-at-arms, embarked. The longships sailed.
Calling out to one another, they rowed
In line ahead across the strait. As ordered,   380
The captains kept them rowing to and fro
All night. All night –
And not one glimpse of Greeks!
Day dawned. White horses streaked the sky.
Light dazzled – and a huge Greek shout,
Crashing, echoing. We cowered: 390
Our plan had made us clowns.

These were no runaways, shrieking for safety;
These were fighters, nerving themselves for war.
The trumpet flamed and fired their ranks.
Their oars flayed sea to foam. Fast, fast they came,
Parading for battle: the right wing first,
400   The rest in good order. And all the time
From every throat, we heard their battle-cry:
'On, sons of Greece! Set free
Your fatherland, your children, wives,
Homes of your ancestors and temples of your gods!
Save all, or all is lost!'
On our side a roar, a tide of answering cries.
The fight began. Ship pounced on ship.
Bronze beaks stripped wood. First blood to Greece:
An Athenian warship rammed its prey,
410   A galleon from Tyre, sheared all its poop away.
Now, full ahead, ship skewered ship. At first
Our Persian fleet held firm. But soon
Ships choked the straits; no room to turn, to help.
Oars smashed; sterns caved in;
The bronze beaks bit and bit.
The Greeks snatched their advantage,
Surrounding us, pounding us.
Ship after ship capsized;
420   The sea was swamped with wreckage, corpses,
The beaches, dunes, all piggy-backed with dead.
Our ships broke ranks, tried one by one
To slip the line. The Greeks, like fishermen
With a haul of tunny netted and trapped,
Stabbed, gaffed with snapped-off oars
And broken spars, smashed, smashed, till all the sea
Was one vast salty soup of shrieks and cries.
At last black night came down and hid the scene.
430   Disaster on disaster. I could take ten days,
And not tell all. Be sure of this: never before
Have so many thousands died on a single day.

QUEEN.
Aiee! Destruction, wave on wave,
Breaks on us, our people drowned.

MESSENGER.
My news is scarce half told.
Ruin treads on ruin,
Sorrow beyond all bearing.

QUEEN.
What can you add,
What misery,
To tip the scale of grief?   440

MESSENGER.
Princes of Persia, who gave brave nature point,
The best in spirit and in blood the best,
In loyalty the King's own paragons,
Are dead. Ignobly, like common men.

QUEEN.
Lords! I tremble.
Speak, sir. Tell how they died.

MESSENGER.
There is an island, facing Salamis:
Small, too tight for ships.
On its rocky shore, God dances: Pan.
There Xerxes sent lords, picked men.   450
The enemy fleet gone down, he said,
Greeks would scramble there for safety.
Easy victims. Our enemies would die,
Our friends would live. He said.
But when the gods gave Greece the fight,
They noosed the place with warships,
A ring of bronze. Where could we turn?
Stones, arrows from springing bows,   460
Destruction. They streamed ashore,
Yelling, butchering. Life died.
No survivors. On the mainland,
Throned on a high headland,
Xerxes peered down on the killing-ground,
Saw everything. He tore his clothes; he groaned,
Sent word to his army: 'Break ranks and run'.
Disaster on disaster. Majesty, weep now.   470

QUEEN.

What demon spite cheats Persia's plans?
A bitter reckoning: brave Athens owed,
My Xerxes paid. Were they not enough,
The Persians who died at Marathon?
Lord Xerxes went to balance that account –
And paid, and paid.
Tell me: clearly, leave nothing out.
Some ships escaped? You left them – where?

MESSENGER.

480   Some ships survived. Their captains
Scrambled before the wind. No order.
The army, what was left of it,
Died on Boeotian soil, thirst-parched,
Gasping. A few of us reached Phocis,
Doris, the Melian gulf,
Rich farmland watered by sweet Spercheius;
The Achaean plain; the towns of Thessaly –
We were starving, they took us in;
490   Still many died, too weak to eat or drink.
We struggled on: Magnesia; Macedonia;
Across the Axius; the marches of Bolbe;
To Edonian territory, high Pangaeus.
That night, the gods sent frost, frost in autumn.
The river froze; soldiers who'd never prayed before
Fell on their knees, kissed Mother Earth,
500   Thanked God. Too soon. Our prayers all done;
We were on the ice, crossing the river,
Racing the rising Sun. We lost.
Its fire turned ice to water;
We jostled, choked;
Those who struggled least died soonest.
A few survivors. We staggered on,
510   Dragged ourselves through Thrace, a handful,
Home at last to Persia: motherland,
Widowland, stripped of all her sons.

A true tale, told – and a fraction, no more,
Of all the misery God spat on us.

    Exit.

CHORUS LEADER.
　　All Persia suffers. Heavy, hard to bear,
　　God's hard heel stamps us down.

QUEEN.
　　I weep for the army lost.
　　O my prophetic dream,
　　How clear it was, my lords,
　　How false your understanding.　　　　　　520
　　None the less, your advice is good.
　　I'll pray to the gods above,
　　Make offerings to Mother Earth
　　And the dead below:
　　Corn, honey, oil from the royal store.
　　What's done is done,
　　But still we can pray that all may yet be well.
　　My lords, it's in your hands.
　　Trusted counsellors! If Xerxes comes,
　　Speak to him, gentle him, bring him home.　　530
　　Let no more sorrow tread on sorrow's heels.

　　　Exit.

CHORUS.
　　Zeus, majesty, you took
　　Our army, swollen,
　　Teeming in its pride,
　　And smashed it;
　　Took Susa, Agbatana,
　　Shadowed them in tears.
　　See! Mothers' hands, soft hands,
　　Tear clothes for grief,
　　Beat breasts, cheeks drenched with tears.
　　Grief sisters all.　　　　　　540
　　New widows weep, young brides,
　　Drain wells of tears,
　　Their husbands lost,
　　Soft beds of happiness,
　　Sweet youth, all gone.

　　With tears we answer,
　　Tears for the dear dead, gone.

All Asia weeps, bereft,
Stripped of her men.
550   Xerxes took them, popo-ee,
Xerxes killed them, toto-ee,
Xerxes trusted to barges,
Freighted with doom.
No Darius he:
Prince of all archers,
Blameless, beloved lord.

Soldiers, sailors,
Sailed on wings of death.
560   Ships took them, popo-ee,
Ships killed them, toto-ee,
Ships splintered them.
But his majesty escaped,
We hear, slipped free,
Trod wintry paths,
Ice-plains, came home.

Too late for them,
A-ah!
Snatched to their deaths,
Ee-yeh!
570   They tassel the shore,
O-ah!
Fringe Salamis. Weep for them,
Bite lips, blood flow,
Till heaven hurts to hear.
O-ah!
Howl for them, howl.

Torn by sharp rocks,
A-ah!
Fingered by waves,
Ee-yeh!
Nibbled, nibbled,
O-ah!
By wordless mouths in clean, clean sea.
580   Weep for them, parents,
Children, wives bereft,

O-ah!
Hear how they died, and howl.

Who in Asia now
Will knuckle to Persian rule,
Pay tribute, crook the knee?
Who'll hug the ground?
Royal power is dead.   590

Keep guarded tongue?
No longer. Freedom's born,
Lifted the yoke of power.
That bloodsoaked soil
Of Salamis, sea-sprayed,
Holds what was Persia once.

    Enter QUEEN.

QUEEN.
Friends, seas of misery we sail.
Only one thing's sure. When disaster breaks,
We wallow in terror; when fair winds blow   600
We think our luck will last forever.
Now, for me, all's dark.
The gods have turned away.
Terror, not triumph, roars in my ears.
Fear flutters in my heart.
So I return alone. On foot. No ... majesty.
In my own hands I bring him offerings –
Darius, my son's royal father –
Peace-offerings. The dead need sweetening.
Here's milk, from purest beast expressed;
Honey, flowers distilled;   610
Here's water from sacred spring;
Wine, Mother Earth's most cherished gift;
Olive oil, pungent, pale;
Plaited flowers, Earth's progeny.
Sing, friends. For the dead,
For Darius, his majesty below.
Call his name. Summon him.   620
I'll slake the ground with offerings,
Due honour to the powers who rule below.

CHORUS LEADER.
Royal lady, Persia's queen,
Pour offerings to those who sleep below.
We'll beg the nether powers,
Despatchers of the dead,
To smile on us.

CHORUS.
Great powers, powers of the Underworld –
Mother Earth; Hermes; Majesty of Death –
630   Send his soul from dark to light.
Some remedy he knows, perhaps,
Knows ruin's cure. Alone of mortals, knows.
Perhaps, perhaps he'll speak.

Can he ever – happy that he is,
Divinity, our lord –
Hear our wretchedness,
Pain's litany?
Must we cry again, again?
640   Down there, can you hear us, Majesty?

Mother Earth, lords of all below,
Free him, all praise, our king:
Loud-trumpeted,
Susa's son, divinity.
Release him to us, whose equal
Persian soil never yet embraced.

Dear, dear he was, and dear his tomb,
Dear the qualities that it enshrines.
Lord of the Underworld,
Surging power is yours –
650   Let him come up, our god, our king.
Ee-yeh!

No warriors of ours he killed,
War-mongering insanity;
Divinity we called him,
Wise as god,
Sure pilot of his men.
Ee-yeh!

Sire, sire of old,
Come up, be here!
On tomb's high mound
Saffron sandal step,   660
Royal diadem display.
Evil's antidote, Darius, come!
O-ee!

Hear it now, the pain,
Your people's pain.
Lord of our lord, be here.
Hell's dark boils over us.
Our young are gone, are gone.   670
Evil's antidote, Darius, come!
O-ee!

Ai-ee, ai-ee.
We wept, your friends, wept and wept your death.
Why is this happening, dear lord, dear lord?
Whose is the blame?
They're gone,
The galleys, gone,
Unshipped, no ships at all.   680

The GHOST *of Darius appears.*

GHOST.
Lords, trusty of the trusty, whose youth was mine,
Old men of Persia, our state's distracted – why?
It groans; it's scarred; it's crushed. Our land!
Her Majesty, here by my tomb:
I tremble; I accept her offerings.
You, sirs, crowding, chanting.
'Rise up, rise up'. I heard; I woke.
Hard, hard to find the way. The powers below
Would sooner keep us there than let us go.   690
Only my majesty unbarred me. I am here.
But waste no time. My lease is short.
What evil weighs Persia down?

CHORUS LEADER.
Majesty. How can I look,

How speak? My lord.
Old fears return.

GHOST.
Up I came, up, drawn by your spells.
Time's short. What would you say to me?
Spare reverence. Speak up.

CHORUS LEADER.
700   Such things. Even to friends,
I'd shrink to speak.
How can I tell my lord?

GHOST.
Since antique fear still strikes them dumb,
You, lady, who shared my bed and now are old,
Stop wailing, dry these tears. Tell me.
What else is human life but pain?
Sea brims with sorrow; it stalks the land,
Haunts mortals, more every day they live.

QUEEN.
You, of all mortals, knew the happiest fate.
710   Each day you lived, you saw the Sun,
Your life was blessed. All Persia called you god.
I envy you in death, who died before the fall.
Hear all of it, Darius, in one brief moment hear.
We're ruined, lord. All Persia's ruined. All.

GHOST.
Some epidemic? Civil war?

QUEEN.
In Greece. Our army perished there.

GHOST.
Which of my sons their general?

QUEEN.
Xerxes, wild Xerxes, who now rules empty sand.

GHOST.
This march, this madness – land, or sea?

QUEEN.
  Two-pronged attack; twin force.   720

GHOST.
  They crossed the sea – such thousands?

QUEEN.
  He yoked the waves, and walked across.

GHOST.
  He tamed the Bosphorus?

QUEEN.
  God helped.

GHOST.
  God stole his mind.

QUEEN.
  Even so. And this is what he did.

GHOST.
  What of his men, who cause these tears?

QUEEN.
  Destroyed at sea; on land destroyed.

GHOST.
  The king's whole army – speared?

QUEEN.
  Why else should Susa weep?   730

GHOST.
  O popo-ee! Our strength, our rock –

QUEEN.
  Our Bactrians, gone. Not a pensioner remains.

GHOST.
  The flower of our allies, scythed!

QUEEN.
  Alone, they say, Xerxes, a handful of men –

GHOST.
  Died? How? Or are they still alive?

QUEEN.
— by luck reached the bridge that yokes two lands.

GHOST.
And crossed? Are they safe? Are you sure of that?

QUEEN.
The report's confirmed.

GHOST.
O-ee, how soon the oracle comes true:
740   Zeus hurls it on my son. God's purposes!
I hoped for longer. But when
We mortals lose control, the gods fall in with it.
The spring overflows. Death gushes on all I love.
My son, the brainless boy, crowned folly king,
Shackled the Hellespont, God's property,
Changed sea to land — against all nature! —
Fettered the waves and made men march across.
750   A mortal playing god to gods! My son
The fool, the fevered mind, possessed.
Now all the gold, the power I worked to win
Lies free for all. It's vulture's meat.

QUEEN.
Bad company he kept, and listened to,
Wild Xerxes. You won your sons much gold,
They told him. Your mighty spear. How weak he
    was,
They said, who puffed himself at home, who spent
But never earned. So they said, and said again —
Until he planned this march, this strike, on Greece.

GHOST.
And so what's done is done, and done to us.
760   The worst. Complete. A mockery forever.
Our city, derelict! Our land, unmanned!
Unheard-of, since Zeus decreed this privilege:
One man to rule all Asia, her fertile flocks,
His sceptre all-determinant — as Medus proved,
First warlord. Next, Medus' son
Capped all his father's work, steered prudent course.

Then third came Cyrus, favourite of the gods,
Blest king of peace for all who loved his rule.
All Lydia, all Phrygia he won, 770
Ionia. God loved him: right ideas made man.
Next, Cyrus' son commanded, fourth in line;
Fifth Mardus, who fouled his fatherland,
Soiled its ancient throne. A palace coup,
Artaphrenes its leader, strong friends,
Loyal hands, did him to death. Lots cast,
Who should be king. The luck was mine:
Campaigns I fought, proud armies led – 780
And brought no blight on this our state.
Now Xerxes rules. My son. He's raw. Raw his ideas,
No mind for all I taught him. My lords,
Who were young with me, be clear on this:
Of all the kings who held this throne,
Not all of us together did such harm.

CHORUS LEADER.
What now, Darius, lord? It's done, it's done.
Where steer a reasoned course?
Your Persians – how can we now survive?

GHOST.
Don't tangle with Greeks in Greece. 790
You may outnumber them,
But the land itself fights for them.

CHORUS LEADER.
How, fights?

GHOST.
Starvation sends, to kill huge armies.

CHORUS LEADER.
A small force then, hand-picked?

GHOST.
Not even those still left in Greece today,
Rags of our men, will win safe passage home.

CHORUS LEADER.
Not cross the straits?
Not march from Europe, home?

GHOST.

800   A few of many. God's oracle. Trust it,
    Exact so far in all that's happened here.
    There's more. His hand-picked force,
    Left with such swagger, such empty hope,
    Is doomed. Where the plain grows lush and green,
    Where Asopus' stream plumps rich Boeotia's soil,
    The mother of disasters awaits them there,
    Reward for insolence, for scorning God.
    As they tramped through Greece, shameless,
        shameless,

810   They plundered images, sacked shrines,
    Uprooted altars, junked, defiled, debased.
    Such sacrilege breeds pain.
    They'll pay and pay. Who'll cap
    The well of grief? It spouts and spouts.
    See! Bloody slaughter scabs Boeotia's soil;
    Greek spears pile dead; heaped corpses send
    Voiceless messages – to us, our children,
    Our children's children.

820   'You're mortal. Don't plume yourselves.
    When vanity flowers,
    Its fruit is pain, its harvest tears.'
    See what they did; their punishment;
    Remember Athens, Greece, each time
    You think today's good luck not good enough.
    Each time you play for more, you'll lose:
    Zeus comes down hard on those who grow too
        proud.

830   You're wise, sirs. Use your wisdom.
    Teach Xerxes – explain to him –
    He must end his pride, his arrogance,
    Must not provoke the gods.
    As for you, Majesty, mother of my son:
    Go in, fetch clothes to welcome him.
    Your child. Defeat has tattered him,
    Beggared him, ripped finery to rags.
    Speak kindly. Gentle him.
    Your voice is the only one he'll bear.
    Now I return, to the dark below the Earth.

My lords, farewell. In all this grief   840
Enjoy what you have, still have: your life.
Pomp, honour, wealth, are nothing to the dead.

The GHOST *disappears.*

CHORUS.
To hear poor Persia's pain,
Pain now, to come. It hurts!

QUEEN.
God tramples us. Grief swarms.
But worst of all, it stings
To hear how my son, my prince,
Wears tatters, rags.
I'll go, find royal robes.
I'll smile for him.   850
My darling!
I'll not betray him, come what may.

Exit.

CHORUS.
O popo-ee, how great, how good the life
In peaceful times enjoyed!
The days when our old king,
Great governor, who worked no harm,
Allowed no war, our king of kings,
Godlike, Darius ruled this land.

How glittering our armies then!
Our laws high battlements,
Our state steered straight.   860
Home then from foreign wars,
Unscared, unscarred,
Our men marched home to happiness.

Oh, the cities he stormed!
He never quit his native land,
Never crossed its boundaries,
Cities on Strymon's banks,
Achelous' mouth, the towns of Thrace,
Acknowledged him.   870

All called him king:
Mainland towns, high-towered,
Far from those lagoons;
Seaside towns, by Hellespont,
By intricate Propontis,
At Pontus' mouth.

880   The islands too, sea-scoured,
Buckled against our shore:
Lesbos, Samos olive-rich,
Paros, Naxos, Mykonos,
Tenos, Andros close to land.

890   Limnos, where Icarus fell,
Rhodes, Cnidos, the cities of Cyprus,
Paphos, Soli, Salamis,
Daughter of that Salamis
Who brings us such tears today.

Ionia, teeming, rich, he ruled,
900   Did as he pleased.
Tireless strength was his –
Elite guards, native regiments,
A wall of warriors.
But now the whole world knows
What God has done to us:
We're crushed, we're smashed, we drown.

Enter XERXES.

XERXES.
Yoh!
Unlucky! I! Spit fate,
910   No hiding, mine!
It bites, it feasts,
Eats Persia,
Pain on pain.
O senators, so old, so wise,
My strength is water.
Zeus! Let me lie with them,
The dead ones.
Death shroud me, close my eyes.

CHORUS.

    O-toto-ee, Majesty! Good army,
    Proud Persia's high renown,
    Squadrons   920
    Scythed down, made straw!
    Earth cries for her sons,
    All dead, for Xerxes dead.
    You crammed Hell's jaws with them:
    Rank on rank they marched,
    Their country's flower,
    Master-bowmen, rank on rank,
    Ten thousand, a million, gone.
    Ai-ee! Who'll guard us now?
    Our land, our Asia, Majesty,
    Shame! Shame!
    Is humbled, on its knees.   930

XERXES.

    O-ee. I did it. Our race,
    Our land, our fatherland,
    I blighted them.

CHORUS.

    How can we greet you home?
    Our words are bruises,
    Our whirling cries.
    Take them, all stained with tears.   940

XERXES.

    Cry. Shriek. Wail.
    Burst ears. Now Fate
    Falls full on me.

CHORUS.

    We cry, shriek, wail.
    Defeat demands. The ships:
    Sea drums on them, death drums.
    Cry grief, cry pain.

XERXES.

    Greeks did it, Greeks,   950
    Their ships their armour,
    Ares their armourer,

Sculling that midnight sea,
That dreadful shore.

CHORUS.
O-ee, o-ee, o-ee. Cry out,
Ask all the questions.
Where are they, where, our sons?
Where those who stood by you?
Pharandaces,
Susas, Pelagon, Agabatas,
960   Dotamas, Psammis, Sousiscanes?

XERXES.
I left them. All,
Spilled from Tyrian ship,
Lurching against the shore,
Hard Salamis, pulped
On unyielding rock.

CHORUS.
O-ee, o-ee, o-ee. Where now
Pharnuchus, where
Brave Ariomardus, Seualces lord,
970   Lilaeus, Artembares,
Memphis,
Tharybis, Masistras,
Histaechmas? Account for them!

XERXES.
Yoh yoh mo-ee,
Athens, mouth of hell,
They saw, in one last gasp,
E-he! E-he!
They choked on it.

CHORUS.
Was it there, was it there you saw
Your eye plucked out,
Alpistus, Eye of Majesty,
Who counted them out, your men,
980   Your thousands, Batanochus' son?
Parthus, son of Sesames,
Great Oebares, Megabates' son —

Did you dump them there,
Oh, oh, oh, da-yohn,
Unmanned great Persia there?

XERXES.
  You name my friends,
  My dear companions.
  Accursed, accursed,   990
  Bo-a-ee, bo-a-ee, tear the heart.

CHORUS.
  More we need to know. The Mardians,
  Their marshal Xanthes,
  Anchares Ares' liege,
  Diaexis, Arsaces horsetamer,
  Lythimnas, Egdadatas,
  Tolmus, spearlord who strode in blood —
  We name them in tears.
  Where are they, where?   1000
  Why not here,
  Your Majesty's loyal retinue?

XERXES.
  They're gone, our warlords, gone.

CHORUS.
  Gone, o-ee, no more.

XERXES.
  Yay, yay, yoh, yoh.

CHORUS.
  Yoh, yoh, great powers,
  Fate glared, we fell.
  Ruin! How could we know?

XERXES.
  Whips bite and bite.

CHORUS.
  It hurts.

XERXES.
  New lash. New pain.   1010

CHORUS.
Greeks of the sea,
We chanced on Greeks.
Defeat, disaster, pain.

XERXES.
Our army, gone.

CHORUS.
Great Persia, down.

XERXES.
All's tatters.

CHORUS.
Rags.

XERXES.
1020   This quiver –

CHORUS.
You kept it, why?

XERXES.
My strength, my treasure.

CHORUS.
So much before, so little now.

XERXES.
No help. We're naked.

CHORUS.
Greeks stood their ground.

XERXES.
I watched. I saw. Disaster.

CHORUS.
When the warships ran?

XERXES.
1030   I ripped my robes.

CHORUS.
Papa-ee, papa-ee.

XERXES.
Papa-ee, yet more.

CHORUS.
Whips bite and bite.

XERXES.
We mourn. They gloat, our enemies.

CHORUS.
Our strength's sliced off.

XERXES.
I'm naked. Guards, lords, gone.

CHORUS.
Drowned all we love.

XERXES.
Weep, weep, the grief.
Go in and weep.

CHORUS.
Ai-ee, ai-ee, again, again.

XERXES.
Cry out, echo tears with tears.   1040

CHORUS.
A sorry gift for sorrow's sorry sire.

XERXES.
Sing sorrow. Cry my pain.

CHORUS.
Ototo-toto-ee.
It weighs on us;
Your grief, our pain.

XERXES.
Beat, beat your breasts.
Your sobs are my relief.

CHORUS.
All tears are we.

XERXES.
Cry out, echo tears with tears.

CHORUS.
Our voices are yours. We weep.

XERXES.

1050   Lift your voices. Cry.

CHORUS.
Ototo-toto-ee.
Black bruises speak,
Give voice to pain.

XERXES.
Beat breasts. Cry. Howl.

CHORUS.
Pain, pain.

XERXES.
Rip hair from beards. White hair.

CHORUS.
Claw, tear.

XERXES.
Howl.

CHORUS.
We howl.

XERXES.

1060   Tear clothes. Robes. Tear.

CHORUS.
Pain, pain.

XERXES.
Rip hair from head. For them!

CHORUS.
Claw, tear.

XERXES.
Flow tears.

CHORUS.
Tears flow.

XERXES.
Cry out, echo tears with tears.

CHORUS.
O-ee, o-ee.

XERXES.
Home, home in tears.

CHORUS.
Yoh, yoh, each step is pain. 1070

XERXES.
Yoh-ah, down every street.

CHORUS.
Yoh-ah, yoh-ah.

XERXES.
Walk softly. Sob.

CHORUS.
Yoh, yoh, each step is pain.

XERXES.
Ee-ee, ee-ee, the trireme men.
Ee-ee, ee-ee, they drowned, they died.

CHORUS.
Home now. We lead you home in tears.

Exeunt.

AESCHYLUS

Prometheus Bound

translated by Kenneth McLeish and Frederic Raphael

Characters

PROMETHEUS
HEPHAESTUS
MIGHT
FORCE (silent part)
IO
OCEAN
HERMES
CHORUS OF OCEAN'S DAUGHTERS

Deserted mountainside. Enter HEPHAESTUS, MIGHT
and FORCE, *with* PROMETHEUS *in chains.*

MIGHT.
   No further. This is Scythia. End of the world.
   No exit. No tracks. No ... life.
   Hephaestus, our father's orders: obey them now.
   Spike that criminal, here on these crags.
   Iron pegs, steel chains. No breaking.
   Your flower he stole, your fire,
   Spark of all knowledge. To give to mortals!
   That was his crime. His punishment: whatever
   The gods demand. He must turn his face
   From mortals, and learn to love lord Zeus.   10

HEPHAESTUS.
   Might, Force, you *are* the word of Zeus.
   He orders; you obey; you are fulfilled.
   But I – how can I bring myself
   To bind a kinsman here in this wintry place?
   I must. To ignore Zeus' word is no careless thing.
   Prometheus, noble-hearted son
   Of Themis the counsellor,
   Not I, not you, chose this.
   I'll spike you here on this hill.   20
   No mortals to hear, to see. Sun's rays
   Will scorch you, wither you. You'll cry
   For starry-mantled Night to douse the fire –
   And cry again, when next day's Sun
   Scatters the dew and renews your pain.
   Forever. No blunting the tooth of pain.
   Your rescuer's unborn, does not exist.
   You chose it. Mortal-lover! Chose it yourself.
   A god, you laughed at gods. You gave
   What was theirs to mortals. Free choice!   30
   Now brood on that, here on this rock.
   No rest. No sleep. Limbs locked with cramp.
   You'll groan. You'll curse. You'll shriek.
   You'll not move Zeus. All new-throned kings are
     harsh.

MIGHT.
Time-wasting! Weeping! All in vain.
Why love the god all gods detest?
He gave your pride to mortals.

HEPHAESTUS.
But kinship ... fellowship ...

MIGHT.
40   Zeus speaks, and you ignore.
Do you dare? Are you not afraid?

HEPHAESTUS.
You're made of stone. No pity.

MIGHT.
For him? Sing dirges? Save your breath.
You've work to do.

HEPHAESTUS.
I curse my skill –

MIGHT.
Why? Bluntly,
Did your skill bring him here?

HEPHAESTUS.
Perhaps someone else –

MIGHT.
Who? All are slaves, feel pain.
50   All creation. Only Zeus is free.

HEPHAESTUS.
How can I argue?

MIGHT.
Hurry, then. Chain him,
Before Zeus spots you hesitating.

HEPHAESTUS.
The manacles are here.

MIGHT.
Round his wrists. Hammer. Hard!
Peg him to the rock.

HEPHAESTUS.
No hesitation now.

MIGHT.
Harder. Wedge tighter.
He'll snatch any chance to wriggle free.

HEPHAESTUS.
He'll not work this arm loose.   60

MIGHT.
The other one. Hit hard! He's clever:
Teach him Zeus is cleverer.

HEPHAESTUS.
It's done. Only he could blame me now.

MIGHT.
Spike him. Beak of steel drives
Through flesh and bone and bites the rock.

HEPHAESTUS.
Prometheus, I weep for your pain –

MIGHT.
Still crying for Zeus' enemies?
Be careful. You may be next.

HEPHAESTUS.
You see a sight that tears the eye –

MIGHT.
A criminal getting what he's earned.   70
Tight round his ribs.

HEPHAESTUS.
I know my orders. Save your breath.

MIGHT.
I'll tell you in detail, exactly what to do.
Go lower. Hoop his legs. Hit hard.

HEPHAESTUS.
It's done. It was easy: look.

MIGHT.
Tighter. Hammer harder. The foreman
Who'll inspect this work is hard.

HEPHAESTUS.
You're hard, too. Looks, voice ... hard.

MIGHT.
You be soft. I don't give way.
80   I'm what I am. I'm not to blame.

HEPHAESTUS.
It's done. He's chained. Let's go.

MIGHT (*to* PROMETHEUS).
There. Now defy the gods. Plunder,
Squander their gifts on mortals.
Will mortals ease this pain?
Prometheus, 'Farsighted'. What a name!
Be farsighted now. See how
To wriggle out of this!

Exeunt MIGHT, FORCE *and* HEPHAESTUS.

PROMETHEUS.
Day-brightness, winds on beating wings,
Rivers, waves of the myriad-laughing sea,
90   Earth mother of all, bright Sun,
See me, a god.
See how gods treat god.
See my agony:
I must wrestle eternity,
Gnawed by this pain.
His doing! The new one,
Tyrant of the blessed –
See what he found for me.
A-ah! A-ah! Pain now,
Pain then, unending pain.
I weep for them.
100   What end will he ordain for them?
Far-sighted! I know them all.
No stranger-pain will come.
This is my fate, and I must bear it.
No struggling. Destiny:
What power can master it?
Shall I tell my fate? Not tell?

Both hard. I gave a gift
To mortals, and in that giving
Yoked myself to fate – to this!
I filled a hollow reed with fire,
Stolen from heaven. I gave it
To mortals. It sparked them,
Taught them cunning, filled their need.   110
For that, now, I pay this price,
Chained, staked, wide open to the sky.

Ah! E-ah!
Sound. Smell. No words.
God-sent? Mortal? Demigod?
Has it come to creation's edge
To gape? What would it see?
A god in chains, accursed,
The enemy of Zeus, despised   120
By all who throng his court.
Prometheus, mortal-lover. Here I am!

Birds. I hear a flock of birds.
Wings whisper in the air.
Whatever is coming, I fear it.

    Enter the CHORUS *of* OCEAN'S
    DAUGHTERS.

CHORUS.
Fear nothing. We are your friends.
Swift wing-beats bring friends,
Here to this cliff   130
On the chariot of the winds.
From our sea-cave far below
We heard iron ring on iron.
At once, barefoot –
No meek-eyed modesty –
We mounted our chariot of wings
To weep with you.

PROMETHEUS.
A-ah! A-ah!
Daughters of fertile Tethys
And of Ocean whose tides   140

Unsleeping gird the Earth,
Look, see me nailed,
Chained, here
On the eyebrow of this hilltop,
Keeping watch,
A vigil no one envies.

CHORUS.
We see you, Prometheus.
Our eyes blur with tears,
With fear, to see you
Chained to this rock.
A new pilot steers Olympus:
150   Young king, young laws,
No precedent.
The glory of the past,
The might of yesterday –
Who remembers them?

PROMETHEUS.
If he'd hurled me down,
To Tartarus beyond escape,
Chained me there
Far below Hades' kingdom of corpses,
I'd have borne it.
Who'd have mocked me then? Which god?
Which . . . other? Instead, look!, I hang here,
The wind's plaything,
Joy to my enemies.

CHORUS.
160   Which enemies? Which gods
Are so rock-hearted as to laugh?
Who finds no tears
To echo such suffering? None but Zeus.
He'll not bend. He'll break
The children of Sky, not rest
Till he gluts his heart
Or someone comes with tricks
To snatch that throne of his.

PROMETHEUS.
    My time will come. Racked, enfettered,
    Still I know this: his lordship,
    Immortal king, will send for me
    To tell him the secret I know,   170
    The plan to snatch his power, his rank.
    When that day comes, he can fawn on me,
    Honey my ears with soft persuasion,
    Threaten me faint with fear;
    I'll still keep silent. Let him crawl;
    Let him break these chains, pay recompense
    For all my suffering. Then I'll speak.

CHORUS.
    Brave words. Your spirit chafes
    At suffering, and will not yield.
    But you go too far.   180
    Fear arrows my heart.
    You drift in a sea of pain –
    What harbour, then, is set for you?
    Zeus, Kronos' son, is harsh.
    He'll not be persuaded.

PROMETHEUS.
    His highness thinks
    That justice is his alone.
    But one day he'll melt:
    Ice-heart will thaw,   190
    He'll run to me, smile for smile,
    With friendship in his hands.

CHORUS LEADER.
    What caused his anger? Tell us.
    What crime deserved such punishment,
    Such injustice? Tell us,
    Unless telling, too, is dangerous.

PROMETHEUS.
    If I speak, I suffer. Silence, too, brings pain.
    All's misery. No escape.

When civil war began in Olympus,
200 Two factions split the gods. Some chose
To topple Kronos, snatch his throne for Zeus.
The rest were hot that Zeus should never rule.
I went to the Titans, children of Earth and Sky,
Offered them strategy. They laughed me down;
Their muscles promised strength would win.
I said, 'Our mother – Themis, Earth,
She has many names –
210 Foretold the future.
Fate's decree. Not strength
But guile will win.'
Deaf ears; they turned away.
I took my mother's words to Zeus. My gift,
Freely given freely taken. By my plan
Tartarus' deeps enfold the Titans,
220 Kronos and all his army. Zeus is king,
By my plans – and pays me with these pains.
All tyrants are galled by the same disease:
They dare not trust their friends.

But you asked my guilt, what crime deserved
This agony. I'll tell you.
He was not yet warm on his father's throne
When he began rewarding his acolytes,
230 Granting each god new powers, new privilege.
Humans he ignored. No word, just loathing.
Stamp them out and start again.
In all Olympus only I said no. I dared.
I held off the thunderbolt, saved the human race
From Hades' halls – and for that he spiked me here,
Tormented, racked, an abject sight to see.
240 I pitied humans; who now pities me?
This punishment, this agony, dishonours Zeus.

CHORUS LEADER.
Iron-hearted, carved from stone, Prometheus,
Are those who see your suffering, and find
No tears to shed. Unwilling witnesses,
We see you now. Your anguish wrings our hearts.

PROMETHEUS.
Friends at least can look on me, and pity.

CHORUS LEADER.
Was there more guilt? Is there more to tell?

PROMETHEUS.
My mortals feared the future. I ended that.

CHORUS LEADER.
What cure did you find for that disease?

PROMETHEUS.
Hope, planted in their hearts. Blind hope.   250

CHORUS LEADER.
A generous gift for creatures born to die.

PROMETHEUS.
One other thing I gave them: fire.

CHORUS LEADER.
The creatures of a day have fire? Bright fire?

PROMETHEUS.
And with it knowledge: yes.

CHORUS LEADER.
And for this crime lord Zeus –

PROMETHEUS.
Torments me and will never set me free.

CHORUS LEADER.
No end is fixed?

PROMETHEUS.
Until he chooses, none.

CHORUS LEADER.
Why should he choose? How can you hope for that?
Can't you see your sin? What other name   260
Can I give it, sweeter to say, to hear?
Think up some way to escape your pain.

PROMETHEUS.
It's easy to gush with good advice
From outside the snare. 'You're trapped. Do this.
    Do that.'

I knew what would happen, from the start.
I chose. I chose. I'll not deny it.
By helping mortals, I condemned myself.
But how could I foresee such punishment?
Chained to this giddy rock,
270   Alone in this wilderness, left to rot?
Don't waste your tears on the suffering you see.
Come closer ... step down ... and hear the rest,
The future. Do as I ask. Do as I ask.
Share my sorrow. Pain's a restless wanderer,
Settles now here, now there.

CHORUS LEADER.
Prometheus, we hear and answer.
Light-footed – look! –
We step from chariot,
280   Step down from Sky,
Stand here on stony ground.
Tell all your grief:
We're listening.

Enter OCEAN.

OCEAN.
Prometheus, I've travelled fast and far
To see you, beyond the boundaries.
My steed needed no bit, no bridle:
My will sufficed to guide him.
I weep for what has happened.
290   Kin-duty – and more than that,
Warm friendship. We need
No flattery, you and I:
Tell me the help you want,
It's yours. You'll never say
You've a truer friend than Ocean.

PROMETHEUS.
Ocean! Have you too come to gape?
Have you brought yourself to leave
300   The waters called after you, the caves
Self-hollowed? Here, to this iron land,
To drink my misery, to weep for me?

Look, then. I was Zeus' friend,
I set him up in power;
This rack is my reward.

OCEAN.
I see, Prometheus, and I offer good advice –
Hear it, for all your cleverness.
Know yourself. New ways: accept them.
A new king rules the immortals.   310
Fling bitter words, sharp as knives,
He'll hear, for all his throne is far away,
And your present throng of pain
Will seem like a children's game.
Poor friend, control your anger,
Look for a way to earn release.
Old advice, but still the best.
You were proud before, Prometheus.
Words vaulted from your tongue,
Earned you this – and still you refuse   320
To bend, pile pain on pain. Listen.
Learn from me. Don't kick the goad.
Our ruler's hard, does as he likes,
Accountable to none. Let me go to him,
Work on him to free you.
Meantime, bite your tongue, lie quiet –
Or is the only thing you've never learned
That foolish talk earns sharpest pain?

PROMETHEUS.
So lucky! To share with me, to dare,   330
And still stand free of punishment!
Stay clear. Don't meddle. He won't
Be wooed; you'll not persuade him.
Look out for yourself. There's danger here.

OCEAN.
Always good advice for others,
None for yourself! I take my cue
From what you do, not what you say.
My decision's made. Don't stop me.

I know, I know lord Zeus will grant
The favour I ask: to set you free.

PROMETHEUS.

340   Such loyalty! Such eagerness!
I'm grateful. But give up now.
You'll fail. You'll put yourself out, and fail.
Do nothing. Stay away from it.
How will it help my suffering
To share it with all my friends?
I weep for my brother-Titans: Atlas,
Far in the west, who bears

350   The pillar of the universe, a weight to strain
endurance.
Hundred-headed Typhon, who left his lair
In the caverns of Cilicia to topple Zeus.
His jaws hissed terror. His eyes
Flashed gorgon-glances. Still he fell.
Zeus' thunderbolt, unsleeping fire,

360   Blasted his boasting, scorched his strength.
Witless now, shapeless, limp,
He lies by the narrow sea,
Pinned under Etna, while on the peak above
Hephaestus perches, smithying.
One day rivers of fire will gush from there,
Gulping green Sicily,

370   As Typhon vomits rage, torrents of rock
Spewed, red-hot, from thunder-ash.
Why do I tell you this? You know it.
Save yourself. I'll bear my fate,
Endure it to the end – till Zeus relents.

OCEAN.

Can't you understand, Prometheus?
Soft words are anger's antidote.

PROMETHEUS.

If the time is right, if the heart is soft.

380   If not, they rub it raw.

OCEAN.

You say I'm over-hasty.
What harm in that?

PROMETHEUS.
Wasted labour ... fatuous –

OCEAN.
Let me be fatuous, then. A healthy sickness,
To mask good sense in foolishness.

PROMETHEUS.
I'd be foolish to let you try.

OCEAN.
Your advice is clear: 'Go home' –

PROMETHEUS.
Or you'll earn hatred too.

OCEAN.
From his new high lordship?

PROMETHEUS.
Watch out for him. Do nothing to rouse his rage.   390

OCEAN.
Your suffering, Prometheus, teaches that.

PROMETHEUS.
Go, then. Before you change your mind.

OCEAN.
Your words find no deaf ears.
Already my steed is fretting the sky
With eager wings. He longs to settle
And relax in his own familiar stall.

   Exit.

CHORUS.
We cry your fate, Prometheus,
Your bitter fate.
Gentle eyes well tears;
Rivulets
Stain soft cheeks.   400
Oppression. Tyranny.
Zeus hardens his heart,
Makes laws unchallenged
To trample powers of old.

Earth cries your fate, Prometheus,
Cries out your fate.
Powers, principalities,
410   Long-honoured,
Weep for you now.
Mortals of Asia, proud
In ancient land, groan
With your groaning,
Pine with your pain.

In Colchis, Amazons
Who fear no fight.
In Scythia, hordes
By the waters of Lake Maeotis,
Brink of the world.

420   In Arabia, the flower
Of warriors,
High in the hills,
By Caucasus, baying for battle,
Bristling spears.

One other, one only,
Is yoked to such punishment:
Atlas, straining age-old strength
To heft the whole world's weight
430   And sky above.

Waves roll on empty sea,
Furl, crash, roar. Groan for you
Chasms, caverns, the gulf of hell.
Quicksilver water-springs
Weep bitter tears.

PROMETHEUS.
Stiff-necked you think me? Too proud to speak?
Not so. Shame gnaws my heart,
Rage at the outrage done to me.
It was I – you know it – I and no other
440   Who handed these gods their power. No more
Of that. But hear how it was with mortals.
Blank minds. I planted seeds of thought,

Intelligence. No shame to them in this:
I tell it to show how good my gift.
They had eyes but saw nothing, ears
But could not hear. Like dream-people
They blundered from birth to death.
They built no houses, from brick or wood: 450
Termites, they scrabbled underground
In runs and hollows, sunless.
They knew no seasons – winter, flowery spring,
Abundant summer passed them by.

Life without reason. Then I helped them.
I showed them the stars' elusive movements,
Rising and setting. I taught them numbers,
Skill of skills, and writing,
All-memory, mother of arts.   460
I tamed wild animals, yoked them
To drudge for mortals. Horses I broke
And harnessed, trained to draw
The glittering chariots the wealthy love.
I gave them ships, sail-carts
With wings to ride the sea.
These were my gifts to mortals –   470
Who now can find no cleverness to help myself.

CHORUS LEADER.
Heart's grief. Mind-sick.
You're rudderless,
A sickly doctor
Who dare not dose himself.

PROMETHEUS.
Apt words, when you hear the rest,
The other skills and ways I found for them.
Greatest of all: when they fell ill
They had no remedy. No drugs,
No ointments. They withered and died,   480
Until I taught them to mix soothing herbs,
Defence against all disease.
I showed them the paths of prophecy:
How to unravel dreams and oracles,

Interpret meetings on a journey,
Read the flight of hook-toed birds –
490 The luck each movement meant, each cry,
When they flocked or fought.
Secrets of sacrifice I showed them: the gloss
Of entrails, what colour pleased the gods,
Delicate spectrum of liver and heart.
I taught them to wrap thighs in fat, to burn
The long shank-bone, what signs to seek
In smoky altar-fires. I dazzled them
With star-patterns, before unknown.
What more? Who found for them
500 Wealth hidden in the ground: iron, copper, gold?
I did: admit it, all who believe in truth.
It's briefly told: whatever mortals know
They learned from me –

CHORUS LEADER.
You gave them everything.
You've nothing left to give yourself.
But still we hope.
One day you'll be free.
510 You'll rival Zeus.

PROMETHEUS.
Not yet. Ten thousand agonies
I must endure, then break these chains.
There's no escape:
Necessity outmatches skill.

CHORUS LEADER.
Who steers Necessity?

PROMETHEUS.
The trinity of Fates, the watchful Furies.

CHORUS LEADER.
They outmatch even Zeus?

PROMETHEUS.
Even Zeus is prisoner to Fate.

CHORUS LEADER.
What is his fate? Eternal rule?

PROMETHEUS.
Don't ask. That secret stays.   520

CHORUS LEADER.
A dreadful secret, if you hide it so!

PROMETHEUS.
Ask something else. I'll not tell that.
Not yet. I'll hide it, clutch it close –
My secret, the knowledge I hold
To smash these chains and set me free.

CHORUS.
May Zeus all-powerful never
Set his might against my will.
May I untiring pay the gods
Due sacrifice, hecatombs   530
By Ocean's unfailing stream,
Never sin in words.
Precepts fixed for me, pillars
Beyond erosion.

Sweet, sweet, to fatten long life on hope,
Banquets of joy, soul-feasts.
I see you ragged-raw,   540
Ten thousand pains,
See you and shudder.
Prometheus, free spirit,
You championed mortals,
Refused to cringe to Zeus.

You gave – what recompense?
What help from them? Strengthless,
Creatures of a day, dream-beings
Impotent, blind, death-bound.
How could such puniness –
Why could you not see? –
Ever smudge the pattern, tear   550
The web of Zeus' law?
This song today, Prometheus,
Pain-song, tear-song,
Flies from our lips,

Not like that other song we sang,
Wedding-song, bath-song, bed-song,
When you wooed Hesione,
Your fellow-Titan, took her
560 For consort, bedmate, queen.

   Enter IO.

IO.
What land? What people? Who
Fettered here to rock,
Enduring?
What guilt? Such punishment!
Tell, where
Pain drags me, here on Earth.

A! A! E! E!
Stings, again, gadfly,
Spectre of earthborn Argus.
Alyoo, Ah Dah! I fear him,
The shepherd, the thousand eyes.
570 Crafty-looker, stalker, dead,
Sprouted again from Earth,
From inner gulfs, hunting-dog
Yapping me down lonely, hungry shore.

Reedpipe drowses:
Lullabies, cicada-songs.
A-ah! A-ah! Where
Am I wandering, wandering, ah?
Zeus son of Kronos, why, what guilt
Yokes me to this pain?
E! E!
580 Gadfly, sting, afraid,
Worn witless, why?
Cinder me, smother me,
Bait me for sharks,
I pray, I pray,
O hear me, lord.
Wandering, wandering,
Learning, but still no way

To end this pain.
Lows the cow-horned maid. D'you hear? D'you
    hear?

PROMETHEUS.
    Io's voice: Io, daughter of Inachus,
    Whose love flamed Zeus' heart.   590
    Now, gadfly-stung, she lopes the world
    Endlessly, hopelessly, nagged by Hera's hate.

IO.
    Io, daughter of Inachus. You say my name.
    Speak to my wretchedness.
    Who are you? How do you know   600
    My punishment, God's plague,
    How it stings, it goads, it gnaws?
    E! E!
    Bounding, loping, starving
    I pelted here,
    Twisted by Hera's rage,
    Her jealous rage.
    Who, E! E!,
    In all creation's agony
    Has ever known pain like mine?
    Tell me, true,
    What suffering more? What cure,
    What medicine to end this pain?
    If you know it, speak.
    Asks the wanderer, the sufferer. Speak, oh speak!

PROMETHEUS.
    I'll tell you. All.
    No riddles. A friend's duty,   610
    To open the mouth to friends.
    You see Prometheus, who handed mortals fire.

IO.
    Prometheus – ah! Beacon of blessing you shone
    For creatures of day. Why this reward?

PROMETHEUS.
    I've told my tale of tears.

IO.
But not to me. I beg you, grant me –

PROMETHEUS.
Ask.

IO.
Who punished you? Who nailed you here?

PROMETHEUS.
Lord Zeus' orders. Hephaestus' hands.

IO.
620   What crime earned such a punishment?

PROMETHEUS.
The one I told you. Nothing more.

IO.
One other thing. Tell me:
The length, the limit of my wandering.

PROMETHEUS.
Better not to know –

IO.
Don't hide my agony.

PROMETHEUS.
I don't begrudge you.

IO.
What, then? Tell!

PROMETHEUS.
I hesitate to hurt.

IO.
You spare me more than I spare myself.

PROMETHEUS.
630   If you insist, I'll speak.

CHORUS LEADER.
Not yet. Grant us a favour too!
First let her tell what caused
Her sickness, her wandering.
Then you reveal the suffering still in store.

PROMETHEUS.
    Tell them, Io. Ocean's daughters,
    Your father's sisters!
    Tell them: shared grief,
    A tale of tears well told
    To willing ears, is easier to bear.

IO.
    Should I trust you? Distrust you? Hear   640
    The tale you asked for, briefly told.
    And yet ... god-storms, disfigured innocence.
    I blush to speak.

    Night-phantoms jostled round my maiden bed
    And whispered,
    'Why still virgin?
    Lucky girl, who could give yourself to power.
    Zeus burns to sleep with you.
    To sleep with you – lord Zeus!   650
    Don't spurn him. Go to Lerna,
    Where sheep and cattle browse
    In your father's grassy meadows.
    Ease Zeus there.'
    The same dream, night after night, tormented me.
    At last, in desperation, I told my father,
    And he sent messengers to Delphi and Dodona
    To ask what he should do or say to placate   660
    The gods. They brought back riddles,
    A tangle of oracles and prophecies,
    Impossible to unravel. Then at last,
    Like a piercing ray of light, Apollo spoke
    Clearly and simply. I was to be banished,
    To roam the fringes of creation,
    Exiled from all I loved. If my father refused,
    God's fire-faced thunderbolt would kill us all.
    Apollo's oracle. My father wept; I wept;   670
    But Zeus' goad bites deep.
    I went. They slammed the gates behind me.
    Looks and mind contorted,
    Horned as you see me,
    Gadfly-stung, I bucked and ran

By Cerchneia, sweet to drink,
By Lerna's spring.
Argus, Earthborn, herded me:
Rage, a thousand eyes, tracking, tracking ...
680   Fate stole his life, when least he looked for it,
Leaving me, god-scourged, the gadfly,
Goaded, ends of the Earth. O Prometheus,
If you know what else I must suffer,
I beg you, tell me now. Don't pity me,
Don't comfort me with lies:
False words are germs. They breed, they kill.

CHORUS.
Ah! Stop! Ee-ah!
690   Unheard-of! Hear, see, shudder.
Agony. Stab, goad,
Soul-freeze. Yoh! Yoh! Fate.
We hear, and cringe.

PROMETHEUS.
Too soon. These wails, these shudders.
Save tears till you hear the rest.

CHORUS LEADER.
Speak, tell. It soothes to know
How long the pain, what suffering remains.

PROMETHEUS.
700   Your first prayer I granted:
To hear her tell how suffering began.
Now hear the rest: pain planned for her,
Ordained by Hera.
Io, daughter of Inachus,
Store my words, hear your journey to the end.
Turn first to the rising Sun.
Tread empty sand.
You'll see nomads, Scythians who live
710   In wicker houses built on ox-carts:
Archers, whose arrows kill from far.
Avoid them.
Keep to the coast that hems their country.

Surf, wave-roar.
On your left, iron-working Chalybes.
Savages, harsh with strangers. Pass them by.
Hybristes next. Insolence: a river aptly named.
If you try to cross, you'll drown.
Follow it instead:
Up, up, where it spurts from highest peaks
On Caucasus, ceiling of the world. Climb here,   720
Rock-pinnacles beside the stars, then down,
South, where Amazons live, women warriors
Who scorn all men, whose home one day will be
Themiscyra, round Thermodon, beside
Salmydessus, cursed by sailors,
Ship-swallower, whose rocks bite sea.
Guides, Amazons, will take you to Cimmeria,
The isthmus, the gateway. Glad-hearted,   730
Pass over, cross the seaway. Ever after,
Mortals will call it after you:
Cow-crossing, Bosphorus.
Out of Europe, into Asia.

   To the CHORUS.

You see his arrogance, the gods' new king?
All crushed alike. He lusted for her, god
For mortal, dizzied her with wandering.
A harsh seducer, Io. All I've said   740
Is hardly the beginning of your pain.

IO (*lowing and bucking*).
   Yoh! Mah! E! E!

PROMETHEUS.
   Yes, moan, low, cry. What will you do
   When I tell you the suffering still to come?

CHORUS LEADER.
   There's more? More suffering still to tell?

PROMETHEUS.
   A sea. A storm.

IO.
Why do I go on living? I could climb
To the lip of the precipice, dash myself down
And be quit of all my troubles.

750   Better once to die
Than to drag out each day in misery.

PROMETHEUS.
And what of me?
How would you bear my pain?
Immortal: no death-hopes comfort me.
No end to misery, so long as Zeus is king.

IO.
So long – ? His power will end?

PROMETHEUS.
You'd smile to see it?

IO.
He tortures me!

PROMETHEUS.
760   His power will end.

IO.
Who'll end it?

PROMETHEUS.
Himself. His brainless majesty.

IO.
How? Tell, if tell you can.

PROMETHEUS.
He'll make ... a union.

IO.
With god? With mortal? Speak!

PROMETHEUS.
That answer is forbidden.

IO.
His ... partner will take his throne?

PROMETHEUS.
She'll bear a son, mightier than his father.

IO.
Has he no way to save himself?

PROMETHEUS.
Only my release.   770

IO.
Who'll free you? Zeus forbids it.

PROMETHEUS.
A descendant of yours, the Fates decree.

IO.
My descendant will set you free?

PROMETHEUS.
Three generations, three and ten.

IO.
A riddling prophecy. Unguessable.

PROMETHEUS.
Then ask no more about yourself.

IO.
You offer favours, then snatch them back.

PROMETHEUS.
Two stories. I'll tell you one of them.

IO.
Which? Tell me. Let me choose.

PROMETHEUS.
Your sufferings, every detail still to come,   780
Or who it is who'll set me free. Now choose.

CHORUS LEADER.
Two stories, one for her and one for us.
Tell her her wanderings, us your saviour's name.
A favour: grant it. We long to hear.

PROMETHEUS.
Since you're so eager, I agree. I'll tell.
First, Io. Your tearful wanderings:
Write them in your mind.
You'll cross the sea that divides the continents,   790
Tread deserts scorched by Sun's bright eye,

Along booming shore to Cisthene's plains
Where monsters live. Phorcys' daughters,
Swan-women old as the stars.
One eye they share, one tooth.
Their like no sun, no moon, has seen.
Not far away their sisters: Gorgons,
Winged, snake-haired, implacable
800 No mortal looks on them and lives:
I tell you this for your own protection.
There are fiercer guardians to hear of:
Wolf-vultures, Zeus' hunting-pack,
Beaked, fanged, silent; one-eyed Arimaspians,
Horse-warriors, who live where Pluto's stream,
Gold-laden, bubbles from the ground. Avoid them.
On to a distant land, black people, who live
By the river Aethiops, birth-spring of the Sun.
810 Follow it as far as the mountains of Biblus,
The waterfall where holy Nile is born.
Its waters, pure to drink, will lead you
To the Delta, distant home decreed by Fate
For you and your descendants forever.
Io, your future. If there are riddles left,
Ask. I'll explain. Time hangs on my hands.

CHORUS LEADER.
If she has more weary wandering to hear,
820 Tell her. If you've told them all, remember
And grant that favour you promised us.

PROMETHEUS.
I've told her all her wandering. Its end.
To prove, now, that what I say is true,
No invention, I'll tell what she endured
Before she came here. A crowded tale. I choose
The last stage only, these last days.
You came to the plains of Molossus, Io,
830 To Dodona, Zeus' shrine, where talking trees
Miraculously utter oracles.
Clearly, no riddles,
The voices greeted you: 'Hail, majesty,
Consort of Zeus that shall be'.

Do you smile at that?
Next, gadfly-goaded, down to the coast,
To the Gulf of Rhea. Storms drove you back,
But that sea will bear your name: Ionian, 840
Reminding mortals forever of your wandering.
I tell you this to prove how I can see
Further and deeper than is revealed.

To the CHORUS.

The rest I tell to you and her together.
I pick up the tale where I broke it off before.
In Canopus, settlement at creation's edge,
The Delta, where Nile pours silt to clog the sea:
There Zeus will come to you, restore your wits –
Tenderly, gently, touch that brings no fear. 850
You'll bear a dark-skinned son: Apis, bull-king,
Who'll reap wherever Nile waters fertile soil.
His descendant Danaus, in the fifth generation,
Will fly with fifty daughters from there
To Argos, saving them from rape
By their own cousins. Hot for them,
Hawks for doves, the cousins will swoop.
Forbidden prey: the gods will cheat them.
Argive earth will swallow them, 860
Deathstruck, outwomaned, murder in the dark.
Each daughter's blade will run with one man's life –
If only my enemies could find such love!
One man, one only, will be saved.
His girl will smile on him as he sleeps.
Desire will blunt her purpose, stay her hand.
She'll choose
To be called coward not murderer;
Her descendants, dynasty of kings,
Will rule in Argos. To cut it short, 870
A hero, a famous archer, born of her line,
Will set me free. This is my future, Io,
Foretold by Themis, Mother Earth
As old as time. But how it will happen, when –
Too long to tell, no profit to you to know.

IO.
> Eleleu! Eleleu!
> Madness! Brain bubbles, burns.
880 Gadfly goads, sharp steel
> Forged in no fire.
> Heart bucks for fear,
> Eyes roll. Mist,
> Whirlwind, driven.
> Tongue raves,
> Words jostle, spate,
> River of madness, storm of fate.

> *Exit*.

CHORUS.
> Wise, wise who first
> Established, first proclaimed this law:
890 Seek no relationship above yourself.
> Let not those who work with hands aspire
> To marry into families
> Flaunting wealth or ancestry.

> Never, never see
> Us, long-lived Muses, share Zeus' bed,
> Unite with lover from the stars.
> Io's fate we see, and shudder:
900 Virgin blighted by Hera,
> Ravaged unravaged, wandering.

> Marriage equal-matched,
> No threat. Fasten
> No god's hot eye on us. Fight no-fight,
> Love no-love: we fear it.
> What could we do?
> Zeus raging – how escape?

PROMETHEUS.
> Almighty Zeus! Stiff-necked and obstinate,
> Still he'll fall one day. The match he's planning
910 Will topple him from power forever.
> As his father Kronos was driven into exile
> He cursed his son – and that curse lives on,
> And will soon be carried out. Only I

Of all immortals, only I can tell him
How to escape destruction. Let him rule!
Let him perch on his throne, hug thunderbolts!
Not even they will save him, shield him
Against disaster, dishonour, a fall
Beyond endurance. His adversary – monstrous,   920
Unstoppable – will outface his lightning,
Deafen his thunder, smash Poseidon's spear
That shakes the land, stirs up the sea.
Zeus will trip and fall, and in his falling learn
The gulf between ruling and being ruled.

CHORUS LEADER.
  These are wishes, not threats, to hurl at Zeus.

PROMETHEUS.
  His fate, my wishes. All will be fulfilled.

CHORUS LEADER.
  You say a power will arise, and outmatch Zeus?   930

PROMETHEUS.
  Will give him grief more than I suffer now.

CHORUS LEADER.
  You dare him with words. You should be afraid.

PROMETHEUS.
  Of what? An immortal – what have I to fear?

CHORUS LEADER.
  He'll send you sharper grief than death.

PROMETHEUS.
  He'll not surprise me.

CHORUS LEADER.
  Wiser to bow to fate, accept necessity.

PROMETHEUS.
  You grovel! Kiss dust at Zeus' feet.
  He's less than that dust to me.
  He has a little moment of ruling left:
  Let him enjoy it! He won't rule heaven long.   940
  Oh look. His page-boy,

His jumped-up majesty's step-and-fetch.
What fearful message is he bringing us?

Enter HERMES.

HERMES.
Word-spinner, insult-monger,
Who pedestalled mortals above the gods,
Fire-thief, hear me. Our father's orders:
This marriage you boast will topple him.
Name it, now. No riddles. Tell everything.
950   Prometheus, I'll not come twice.
Chains, spikes, pain –
Hard proof that Zeus is not to be talked down.

PROMETHEUS.
Big threats, big boasting. Lapdog of the gods!
New gods, new powers.
You think sky-battlements beyond all threats.
But so did Kronos, once.
I've seen two tyrants fall; I'll see a third,
Fastest and furthest. What, must I flatter,
960   Fawn on that upstart? Run away. Run home
Your journey's wasted. Answer is refused.

HERMES.
We've heard such insolence before.
It berthed you here. Self-chosen agony.

PROMETHEUS.
I look at this. I look at you.
Torment or slavery? I wouldn't change.

HERMES.
You'd change. What? Slave to this rock,
Or personal messenger to father Zeus?

PROMETHEUS.
970   Upstart for upstart. Pleased with yourself?

HERMES.
Aren't you? Taking pride in pain.

PROMETHEUS.
I long to see one day
My enemies so proud, so gratified. You.

HERMES.
You blame me too?

PROMETHEUS.
All gods. I hate them all.
I put them where they are. They put me here.

HERMES.
You're sick. Deranged. No cure.

PROMETHEUS.
It's sick to hate my enemies? I'm sick.

HERMES.
If you were well, how would we cope with you?

PROMETHEUS (*a cry of pain*).
Aaah!

HERMES.
Cry on. But remember: Zeus is deaf.   980

PROMETHEUS.
Time passing will unstop his ears.

HERMES.
Time passing. Was it that made you so wise?

PROMETHEUS.
How, wise, and squander words on crawlers?

HERMES.
You'll tell our father nothing?

PROMETHEUS.
In spite of all his kindness –

HERMES.
You treat me like a child.

PROMETHEUS.
You are a child, a babe in arms,
If you expect an answer. Nothing –
No rack, no ... instrument devised by Zeus
Will make me speak. Until he sets me free.   990
Whirlwinds of fire, ice-storms, thunder-roars
To engulf the Earth. Hurl! Churn! Destroy!

Let him do what he likes. Until I choose
He'll not know who it is who'll topple him.

HERMES.
Think, Prometheus. What will you gain by this?

PROMETHEUS.
I've all eternity to think.

HERMES.
Fool! Learn from this pain.
1000 Change your mind while still there's time.

PROMETHEUS.
Lecture the tides. You'll not change me.
What? Whimper to the one I hate,
Wheedle, palms upwards,
Like a woman,
Till he slips these chains?
I'm far from that.

HERMES.
I'll waste no more words. I've treated you
Respectfully, generously – and failed.
You're like a newly broken colt
1010 Wrestling the reins, bolting, bucking the bit.
So clever! So confident! So weak! Mistake
Self-confidence for wisdom, you'll fall.
You won't be persuaded? Listen then:
This storm, this sea of suffering,
You call down on yourself. No hiding.
First, our father's thunderbolt
Will split this mountain, splinter it.
Rock-tomb, rock-womb. You'll lie engulfed
1020 For an eternity. When you do see light again,
Spewed to the surface, Zeus' hunting hound,
His eagle, blood-beaked, ravenous, will strip
Your flesh, tear titbits from your liver.
Day after day after day:
A feast of agony; no end
Till some other god accepts your pain,
For your sake visiting the darks
Of Hades, gulfs of Tartarus below.

Take thought for that. I spin no idle threats.   1030
Mouthpiece of Zeus. Exact. He speaks; it is.
Look round you. Think.
D'you still put stubbornness
Ahead of common sense?

CHORUS LEADER.
Good advice, Prometheus.
Give up your anger, seek out common sense.
Do as he says.
You're wise. You're wrong. Give way.

PROMETHEUS.
No word he yaps is new to me.   1040
I'm at war, I'm wounded: no disgrace.
Let Zeus hurl lightning-spears,
Rockets, knives of fire.
Shake air, tear sky,
Tornadoes splinter Earth,
Uproot, convulse.
Boil sea, dissolve the stars.
Lift me, break me, hurl me,   1050
Black deeps of Tartarus,
Whirlwinds of fate.
Do all he likes, I'll never die.

HERMES.
Mad thoughts, mad words.
Slip rein, hard galloping,
Insanity's race is run.

To the CHORUS.

You pity him, show sympathy.
Go! Now. Stay here,   1060
Thunder-bellows, too,
Will stone your wits away.

CHORUS LEADER.
Try another tune! New words!
Not this advice. You tempt,
You preach disloyalty.
How dare you? We stay,

We bear what he bears.
1070 This we know, we learned from him:
We spit on those who betray their friends.

HERMES.
Remember, then, I warned you.
Don't snarl at the fate that traps you.
Zeus is not to blame:
You chose it. No secret.
You knew,
You saw Fate's net, and jumped at it.

Exit.

PROMETHEUS.
1080 No more words. It's happening.
Earth writhes.
Thunder bellows from the deep.
Fire-tendrils, lightning-flares.
Hurricanes hug dust,
Death-dervish-dance.
Wind leaps on wind,
Howling, tearing.
Sky drinks sea.
Zeus did this. His storm.
1090 Themis, mother!
Sky-wheel that turns the stars!
See how unjust my suffering.

Exeunt.

SOPHOCLES

Women of Trachis

translated by J. Michael Walton

Characters

DEIANIRA, wife of Heracles
NURSE
HYLLUS, Heracles' and Deianira's son
MESSENGER
LICHAS, Heracles' herald
AN OLD MAN
CHORUS OF LOCAL WOMEN OF TRACHIS
IOLE (non-speaking)
WOMEN CAPTIVES (non-speaking)

Before the house of HERACLES, *in Trachis.*

Enter DEIANIRA, *wife of* HERACLES, *and a* NURSE.

DEIANIRA.
It's a long-established saying amongst men
That no one knows his fate before his death,
Nor how his life will turn out, good or ill.
Well, I know mine. It will not take my dying
To recognise my life as ill-starred, full of grief.
When I was still in my father Oeneus' house
I first acquired a desperate fear of sex,
Worse than any unmarried girl in Aetolia.
It was a river asked father for my hand,
I mean, of course, Achelous, who had three forms.   10
First he would come as a raging bull and then
In the shape of a wriggling snake, or else
In the form of a beef-faced man with a sooty beard
Spewing out water like a river in spate.
With the threat of a lover like that confronting me
I prayed for death to release me once and for all
From the horrors of this monster's marriage-bed.
And, in the nick of time, to my relief,
The son of Alcmena and Zeus came to the rescue,
Great Heracles, who made a formal challenge   20
To try and set me free. What kind of battle they
    fought
I can't say. I didn't see it. If you want to know
You'll have to find someone who dared to watch.
I cowered there, paralysed with fear,
The fear that beauty like mine can only lead to
    misery.
Zeus decreed that the fight should end happily.
Happily, I suppose. But since I've been Heracles'
    wife
I've worried about him ceaselessly, night and day.
Fear breeds fear. Night follows lonely night,
Dispelling some fears, creating others, worse.   30
We've had a family but he sees them no more often
Than a farmer visits his boundary field,

Once to sow it, and then again to reap it.
He's hardly set foot in the house and he's off again.
That's his life, always at someone's beck and call.
But now he's finally completed all his labours
I'm even more frightened than I was before.
Since he killed the powerful Iphitus,
I've stayed here in Trachis, living on charity,

40   In a stranger's house, an exile from my home.
Where he's taken himself off to, who can say?
I'm here without him, left to suffer alone.
I can't help feeling something terrible's happened.
It seems an age since he went away this time,
Ten months now and more, add another five to that,
And not a word from him. Yes, something terrible.
He left behind an oracle when he went. Here's its
      message.
I hope and pray my anxiety's unfounded.

NURSE.
Deianira, my mistress, many's the time

50   I've seen your face all tear-stained just like now,
Sorrowing for your absent husband, Heracles.
If you'll accept the right of a slave to advise
Someone freeborn, listen to what I have to say.
You're not short of sons.
Why not send one of them to go and find him?
Hyllus would be my choice, if he's prepared to do it.
He'd soon find out how his father fares abroad.
I can see him now, hurrying towards the house.
If you are prepared to follow my advice,

60   This would be a good moment to tackle him.

      Enter HYLLUS.

DEIANIRA.
Hyllus, my son, please wait. Sometimes the lowborn
Can give us good advice. This woman here
Has given me 'free' counsel, though she's a slave.

HYLLUS.
Really? You'd better tell me, mother, what I'm to
      hear.

DEIANIRA.
  She pointed out that you've never once inquired
  Where your father is and she finds that wrong, she
    says.

HYLLUS.
  I know where he is, or where they say he is.

DEIANIRA.
  If you know, Hyllus, why don't you tell me?

HYLLUS.
  He spent last season, at least, this is what I heard,
  Serving some Lydian woman as her slave.   70

DEIANIRA.
  If he could sink to that, anything's possible.

HYLLUS.
  I've also heard that he's freed himself of her.

DEIANIRA.
  And do your sources suggest he's alive or dead?

HYLLUS.
  They say he's making war, or he's about to,
  Against the city of Eurytus on Euboea.

DEIANIRA.
  He left behind an oracle, did you know that too,
  With some prophecy that relates to Euboea?

HYLLUS.
  I know nothing about that. What does it say?

DEIANIRA.
  It says that he will either end his life
  Or, if he can complete one final labour,   80
  He'll find peace and live to a serene old age.
  I'm sure his fate lies in the balance as we speak.
  Please, Hyllus, will you go and help him, if you can?
  I don't know how we'd survive your father's death.
  For better or worse our fate is tied to his.

HYLLUS.
  Of course I'll go. If you hadn't kept these prophecies
  So close, mother, I'd not have stayed till now.

He's always been a lucky man in the past, you know.
90   I saw no reason for your being so concerned.
But now I do understand and will not spare
Myself in finding out the truth, the whole truth.

DEIANIRA.

Do go, Hyllus, go now. However late it comes,
Once we hear it, good news is always welcome.

Exit HYLLUS. *Enter* CHORUS.

CHORUS.

Sun-God, oh Sun,
To whom starry night gives birth as she dies
And at twilight kills you in turn,
Tell me, I beg, please tell me,
Where may I find Alcmena's noble son?
Sun-God, oh Sun,
100   Whose shining eye brings everything to light,
Do the twin continents hold him fast?
Where is he? Is he there still?
Or driven through the sea-straits restlessly?

Deianira,
Like a bird which dare not face its fate,
Piteous, her mind awash with tears,
With eyes that can weep no more.
Poor battle-prize, Deianira.
Deianira
110   Feeds on fears for her roaming husband,
Lonely, ever hoping fearfully,
Ever fearing what she hopes,
Like a widow, Deianira.

The winds of heaven
Swirl and storm, South and North,
Toing and froing, restless as the waves.
So struggles Heracles,
Always against the odds,
Fighting the currents of his laboured life.
120   And yet, there is a God,
Some guardian God, it seems,
Who keeps him from Death's premature embrace.

So I can chide you,
Lady, though with respect.
Why do you choose to disregard your faith?
The Lord of Heaven decrees,
Despite your suffering now,
That no one's life be wholly free from pain.
As the Great Bear revolves
Across the starry heavens,   130
The scale of good and evil balances.

And as the darkest night
Will always yield to day,
In poverty or wealth,
In happiness or grief,
'This too will pass'
Is always true for men.
So you must never court despair,
But ask yourself, as I do now,
When did Zeus ever abandon one of his sons?   140

DEIANIRA.
I suppose you must have heard of my distress
And that's why you've come. I hope you never face
The depths of anguish into which I am sinking.
The young grow up cherished in their own home,
Protected like hothouse plants from too much heat
    or shade,
And neither storm nor gale will trouble them.
A girl can live a sheltered life and be quite happy.
But marriage changes that.
A woman now, she faces nightmare fears
For her husband, and, if not for him, for her children.   150
Unless you're married yourself you can't
Understand how weighed down I feel with anxiety.
I've put up with so much already,
But nothing to compare with this. Let me tell you.
When Heracles went away on this last occasion,
He left behind a tablet with an inscription.
The tablet was old, one I'd seen before,
But he would never tell me what the writing meant,
However daunting his enterprise. He always left

160   Like a hero, not someone facing death.
      This time was different. He read me his will,
      Disposing of his effects as though he were a dead
          man,
      Something for me and a share of his land for each
          child.
      He set a fixed time, one year and a further three
          months.
      When that had passed, from the moment he left the
          house,
      Then he must face death. But if he proved able to
          survive
      This crisis, all would be well and he could expect
      To live his life out in tranquillity and peace.
      The Gods themselves had decreed it, so he told me.
170   Heracles' troubles were to be resolved, one way
      Or another, according to Dodona's priestesses,
      Interpreting what Zeus' holy oaks had whispered.
      And now this is the hour, the very hour in time,
      When we shall see this prophecy fulfilled.
      You can hardly be surprised, dear friends, that I
          should
      Start from my sleep, terrified at the thought of
          finding myself
      A widow, parted from the finest man the world has
          known.

CHORUS.
      That's enough now. Hush. Look, that man coming
          this way.
      Is garlanded. He must be bringing good news.

      Enter MESSENGER.

MESSENGER.
180   Deianira, my mistress, let me be the first
      To free you from your fears. Alcmena's son lives.
      He has won a great battle and with the spoils of war
      He'll soon return to give his country's gods their
          share.

DEIANIRA.
Is it true? Tell me, old man. Is this the truth?

MESSENGER.
It's true enough. Crowned with victory. Trium-
phant.
Your much-respected husband will soon be home.

DEIANIRA.
Who told you this? A citizen or a stranger?

MESSENGER.
Lichas, the herald, is broadcasting it to the world,
Down in the summer pasture. I heard him
And hurried here to be the first to let you know   190
And win your thanks, perhaps even a small reward.

DEIANIRA.
If all is really well, why doesn't Lichas come himself?

MESSENGER.
He's finding it difficult to go anywhere,
My lady. The whole of Trachis, so it seems,
Surrounds him, asking questions. He can hardly
move.
Everyone wants to hear the news. They won't release
him.
Whatever he wants, they must hear what they want.
You'll see nothing of him until he's satisfied
Their curiosity. Then, I'm sure, he'll come.

DEIANIRA.
Oh Zeus, God of the uncut fields of Oeta,   200
Praise be that after so much time you bring me joy.
This news is the more welcome taking me by
surprise.
Sing out in chorus, women, sing it indoors and out.
Sing all of you how day has dawned when least
expected.

CHORUS.
Rejoice and sing
From hearth and home.
Come, girl, come,

Sing and rejoice.
Join with the men,
210   As they sing the praise
Of Lord Apollo,
Bowman, protector.

And raise our song
For the maid of Ortygia,
Apollo's sister,
Oh my sisters,
Joined with the nymphs,
Singing the praise
Of Lady Artemis,
220   Torch-bearer, huntress.

I am losing my mind, the flute commands my soul.
Watch me, see me spinning out of control.
The twining ivy makes me Dionysus' slave.
Look, lady, how my joy takes living shape in song.

DEIANIRA.
I am looking, dear friends, and I can also see
A group of people who seem to be coming this way.

   Enter LICHAS *with a group of* WOMEN
   CAPTIVES.

DEIANIRA.
Herald, you're welcome, especially if the news
You bring, though long delayed, is worth the waiting
   for.

LICHAS.
A friendly greeting, madam, and suitably so,
230   Considering my news. A civilised reception
Should always reward a man who does his best.

DEIANIRA.
First, dear friend, first you must tell me please
Whether I shall welcome my Heracles home alive.

LICHAS.
Of course you will. When I left him he was
   flourishing,
Alive, certainly, thriving, bursting with health.

DEIANIRA.
   But where is he? Is he still abroad? You must tell me.

LICHAS.
   On Euboea, the coast of Euboea, setting up an altar
   Where he can dedicate the first-fruits to Cenaean
      Zeus.

DEIANIRA.
   Is he fulfilling a vow or was there some oracle?

LICHAS.
   It was a vow he made when he first declared war   240
   Against that country, whose women you see here
      before you.

DEIANIRA.
   Who are they? And whose property, god help them?
   I can't pretend I don't feel pity when I look at them.

LICHAS.
   After Eurytus' city had been sacked by Heracles,
   He picked out this lot for himself or for the gods.

DEIANIRA.
   Was it in order to capture that city that he
   Stayed away – heaven knows how long?

LICHAS.
   Not a bit of it. Much of the time he was detained
   In Lydia, involuntarily, so I hear,
   Sold into slavery. It would hardly be fair,   250
   My lady, to blame him for something Zeus ordained.
   He had to undergo a year, as he told me,
   In submission to the barbaric Queen Omphale.
   He was so ashamed of this and so incensed
   That he swore an oath, promising himself
   That when he was free, he would enslave in turn
   The man responsible and his wife and child.
   He's a man of his word. No sooner had he atoned
   For his crime than he raised an expeditionary force
   Against Eurytus, whose fault he thought it was   260
   Beyond all others, for what he'd had to endure.
   He had come to Eurytus' house as a former guest,

A friend of long standing, but was greeted with
  reproaches,
Pure malice from a poisoned mind. Saying things
  like
'You think you can't miss with those arrows of yours.
My sons are better archers than you ever were.' Or
  again,
'Listen to the broken slave talking like a freeman.'
Once, Heracles got a little drunk at dinner
And Eurytus threw him out the house. That's why
270   When Heracles encountered Iphitus, Eurytus' son,
Tracking horses on the slopes above Tiryns,
He was so incensed he grabbed the distracted boy
And hurled him headlong over the towering cliff.
Our lord and master, Zeus, father of Olympus,
Was angered by the violence of this act.
Implacable, he sent Heracles to be sold
For killing the young man so treacherously.
If the fight had been fair, then Zeus would have
  judged his case
A just one and pardoned him for any offence.
280   But gods, like men, have no fondness for arrogance.
So, all that overweening, loud-mouthed crew are
  now
First citizens of Hades, down to the very last man.
It's a slave city. These women that you see here
Are finding how high estate can quickly change to
  low.
They're all yours. Your husband charged me to
  deliver them
And that's what I've done, exactly as he prescribed.
He will, of course, be here himself the moment
He's fulfilled his holy vows to father Zeus
For his victory. Of all the news I bring you,
290   This, I'm sure, must be by far the most welcome.

CHORUS.
You must be so happy, lady, hearing
What has happened and what you can look forward
  to.

DEIANIRA.
    I am happy, of course I am. Isn't it natural?
    Good fortune for my husband means the same for
        me.
    Come what may, our fates are linked by Destiny.
    All the same, those who take a balanced view of fate
    Will know and fear how ill luck stalks prosperity.
    I can't help the pity that wells up in me, dear friends,
    Seeing these unhappy women here before us,
    Bereft of parents, home and country, desolate.   300
    Maybe their fathers were free men until recently.
    Now they're condemned to a life of slavery.
    You, the god who turns the tide in war, please, Zeus,
    Save me from the sight of any child of mine so
        doomed.
    Or, if it has to happen, let me be dead before it does.
    The sight of these poor women is terrifying.
    Tell me – you look so unhappy – who are you?
    Do you have a husband, a child maybe? Looking at
        you,
    I doubt it. You're a child yourself and nobly born.
    Lichas, who is this girl   310
    Who was her mother? Tell me. What's her father's
        name?
    Well? I feel the greatest pity looking at her.
    She seems the only one who's aware what's
        happening.

LICHAS.
    How should I know? No use asking me. I suppose
    It's possible she has more breeding than the rest.

DEIANIRA.
    Royal blood? Did Eurytus have a daughter?

LICHAS.
    I have no idea. We never cross-examined her.

DEIANIRA.
    And you never heard the others call her by name?

LICHAS.
  Never. There was a job and I did it. With my mouth
    shut.

DEIANIRA.
320   Poor girl, please tell me what your name is.
  It distresses me not to know who you are.

LICHAS.
  If you get a peep out of her it will be a miracle.
  Up to now, I assure you, she hasn't uttered a word,
  Not a single word, good or bad, to anyone.
  She does a lot of weeping. Most of the time she's
    spent
  Lamenting her misfortunes from the moment she left
  Her windswept homeland. Poor thing. It's hard on
    her.
  But that's the way it's taken her. Make allowances.

DEIANIRA.
  Let her be. Let her go indoors now.
330   Whatever she pleases. I wouldn't want to be
    responsible
  For adding to her present load of misery.
  Enough's enough. We'll all retire indoors.
  I'll not waste your time if you have things to do,
  While I make my domestic preparations.

          Exeunt LICHAS *and the* CAPTIVES.

MESSENGER.
  If you've a moment ... I can actually tell you
  Privately who those women are you've welcomed.
  No one has said anything to you, but I think you
    ought to hear
  Exactly what's going on.

DEIANIRA.
  What do you mean? You're standing in my way.

MESSENGER.
340   Wait a moment. Hear me out. The news I brought
    before
  Was worth listening to. And, so, I think, is this.

DEIANIRA.
  I'd better call the others back again, shall I?
  Or is this only for me and these women here?

MESSENGER.
  Just us, I think. Better forget the rest.

DEIANIRA.
  Very well then. They've gone. So, what do you want
    to say?

MESSENGER.
  He's not telling the truth, not strictly anyway.
  Either what he just told you is a fabrication,
  Or his previous report to us was inaccurate.

DEIANIRA.
  What do you mean? I want to know what's going on.
  I can't follow these insinuations.   350

MESSENGER.
  He said before – I heard him say it myself
  And there's no lack of witnesses – that this girl
  Was the sole reason Heracles made war on Eurytus
  And razed the walled city of Oechalia.
  The God of Love's the only one responsible
  For the hostilities. No Lydians. No slaving for
    Queen Omphale.
  No punishment for throwing Iphitus off a cliff,
  But Love – that had no part in Lichas' version of
    events.
  The fact is that Heracles, finding a father
  Loath to sanction his daughter's illicit affair,   360
  Manufactured some excuse to pick a quarrel
  And brought an army to attack the land
  Of which, as Lichas said, Eurytus was the king.
  And Heracles did kill the girl's father, razing
  His city. Now, madam, as you see, she's joined your
    household,
  Casually sent ahead, but don't delude yourself.
  She's not here as a slave. He has other plans for her,
  As you might expect, with him so fired by passion.
  I felt I had to tell you everything, madam,

370   As I chanced to hear it from Lichas himself.
There was no lack of witnesses in the market-square,
People of Trachis, who heard the same as I did
And will testify to it. I'm deeply sorry
If what I've said upsets you. But it is the truth.

DEIANIRA.
Oh no. What can I do? What have I done?
What canker have I welcomed into my home
Without realising? What a fool I am.
How could I think her of no account, anonymous,
As her escort claimed, when she's so beautiful?

MESSENGER.
380   She's famous, all right. Eurytus was her father.
They call her Iole. If Lichas can't tell you that,
It can only be because he never asked her.

CHORUS.
A curse on everyone like that, a curse especially
On deceivers, stirring up trouble, stealthily.

DEIANIRA.
What am I to do? Help me, friends, help me.
All this I've heard, I'm going out of my mind.

CHORUS.
Go and ask Lichas. Perhaps it will all become clear
If you confront him and make him tell the truth.

DEIANIRA.
Yes, you're right. I'll go and fetch him.

MESSENGER.
Do you want me to stay? What do you want me to
390   do?

DEIANIRA.
You can stay. We won't have to summon him.
Here he comes from the house of his own accord.

Enter LICHAS.

LICHAS.
My lady, what message do you have for Heracles?
As you see, I'm leaving. So tell me now.

DEIANIRA.
Leaving? You took long enough to get here. Now
You're taking off before we've had a proper talk.

LICHAS.
I am still here if there's anything you want to ask.

DEIANIRA.
Do you think of yourself as a truthful sort of man?

LICHAS.
Certainly, as God's my witness. As far as I know.

DEIANIRA.
Who's the girl, the one you brought just now?   400

LICHAS.
Some Euboean. Who her parents are I can't say.

MESSENGER.
Listen, you. Who do you think you're talking to?

LICHAS.
May I ask what right you have to speak to me like
    that?

MESSENGER.
I'd advise you to answer if you have any sense.

LICHAS.
I am prepared to answer any questions put to me
By Deianira, Oeneus' daughter and lord Heracles'
    wife.
She's my mistress unless I'm much mistaken.

MESSENGER.
Right, I'm glad to hear you admit it.
You're in service to Deianira, agreed?

LICHAS.
                                        I said so.

MESSENGER.
Well then. What sort of punishment would you   410
    deserve
If you were found out and proved a hypocrite?

LICHAS.
A hypocrite? I don't know what you mean.

MESSENGER.
Don't you? You're the one who's been mincing words.

LICHAS.
I'm off. I was a fool to listen in the first place.

MESSENGER.
Not until you answer one question. It's a brief one.

LICHAS.
If you're so fond of the sound of your own voice, fire away.

MESSENGER.
That prisoner you sent into the house,
You know who I mean?

LICHAS.
I know whom you mean. What about her?

MESSENGER.
Didn't you say that this girl you can't identify
420   Was Eurytus' own daughter, Iole?

LICHAS.
When did I say that? Who to? Where's your witness?
Who ever heard me say anything like that?

MESSENGER.
Plenty of witnesses down in the town. There was a great crowd
Heard you announce it in the public square in Trachis.

LICHAS.
They can say they heard it. They can say anything they like.
But hearsay report is hardly evidence.

MESSENGER.
'Hearsay report' is it? Didn't you swear an oath
That you brought this girl as a bride for Heracles?

LICHAS.

    Bride, do you say I said? Dear lady, for God's sake,
    Who is this man? I've never even met him.   430

MESSENGER.

    I was there. I heard you. I heard your whole story,
    How a city was sacked all for the love of this girl –
    Lust rather, but nothing to do with the Lydian
       queen.

LICHAS.

    Send the fellow packing, madam. He must be sick.
    There's no point listening to a madman.

DEIANIRA.

    No. By Zeus who hurls his thunderbolts across
    The tree-lined slopes of Oeta, I want the truth.
    You are not addressing some craven creature,
    Nor someone ignorant of human nature.
    I realise that affections may not remain constant.   440
    Only a fool would oppose the God of Love.
    To take on Eros would be mere shadow-boxing.
    He numbers gods among his victims. Me too.
    And if me, why not any other woman like me?
    To blame my husband for succumbing to this disease
    Would put me as much at fault. Sheer foolishness.
    Or to treat the poor girl as though she were the cause.
    She's done nothing wrong. I can't say she's wronged
       me.
    It's not like that. But if you've learnt deception from
       him,
    For both pupil and teacher the lesson is unjust.   450
    If self-taught, then I must tell you straight,
    However well-meaning, what you did was wrong.
    Tell me the truth. Hold nothing back. The real
       disgrace
    Is for a free man to have himself branded a liar.
    That you could get away with it is inconceivable.
    There are quite enough people you talked to who
       will tell me.
    If for some reason you're afraid, there's no need.

Not knowing the truth upsets me, I'll admit,
So what harm in knowing? Do you think there
   haven't been others,
460   Other women in the life of a man like Heracles?
But never has one of them received a reproach from
   me,
Not a word of blame. Neither shall this girl here,
Even if she was consumed with passion for him.
When I first saw her all I felt was pity.
Nothing can so destroy a life as beauty.
She would not willingly have seen her country
   overrun,
Poor thing, her people sold as slaves. What's past is
   past,
Water under the bridge. For the present though,
However you may treat others, don't play me false.

CHORUS.
470   You should obey her. Her advice makes sense.
If you take it, she'll thank you, and so will we.

LICHAS.
Now that I realise, madam, your humanity,
Your sympathy for human weakness,
I'll tell you the truth, holding nothing back.
He's right. Everything's exactly as he said.
The desire for the girl which overwhelmed Heracles
Was uncontrollable. Because of it, because of her,
Her home, Oechalia, was flattened to the ground.
And, in his defence, I must point out
480   He neither tried to hide it, nor told me to.
That was my fault, madam, mine alone, from
   concern
In case you might find the truth upsetting.
If trying to protect you was wrong, then I was
   wrong.
But now that the whole story is out in the open,
For both your sakes, his no less than yours,
I think you should bear with her and honour
The reception you gave her when she arrived.

Your husband may be the best man-at-arms in the
      world,
But he met his match when he fell for this girl.

DEIANIRA.

I think you're right. I'll do as you suggest.   490
What point is there in inflaming his desire
By challenging the gods? We'll go inside now.
I want to write a letter, which you must take
Along with presents in exchange for his,
Gift for gift. It wouldn't be right to take nothing
      back,
And return empty-handed when you brought so
      much.

      Exeunt all but the CHORUS.

CHORUS.

The power of Aphrodite is irresistible.
No need to talk
Of Gods' affairs,
Still less Zeus' own: 500
No mention of Hades dark as the pit,
Nor of the earth-shaker,
Lord Poseidon.
Shall I not sing instead
Of two mortal champions,
Rival suitors for one bride,
Raining blows, raising the dust, antagonists?

The power of one of them was a river's power,
A power horned
As well as hooved,   510
Shaped like a bull,
Achelous of Oeneadrae:
And opposite to him
Lord Heracles,
Supreme with bow and club,
From Dionysus' Thebes.
Rivals fighting for one mate,
With referee and marriage-broker, Aphrodite.

The twang of a bow,
520   The blow of a fist,
Locking of horns:
Grapplings and batterings,
Contortions and groanings,
As they clash head to head.
And a gentle girl,
So fair of face,
Sits on the hillside waiting for a husband.
The battle rages
While, scarcely weaned,
530   The girl-prize waits.

Enter DEIANIRA *with a box.*

DEIANIRA.
My friends, while Lichas is in the house as our
      guest,
Talking to the captives until it's time to leave,
I've come outside to share a secret with you.
I want to tell you what I've been working at.
After all I've been through, I hope you're
      sympathetic.
This girl – this mistress would be more appropriate –
I've taken her in, like a captain who takes on a cargo
Despite the fact he fears it. I must be going mad.
Now we are to lie here waiting for him, two lovers
540   In the one pair of sheets. That is what Heracles,
My kind and faithful Heracles as I used to call him,
Offers me in return for all my years of service.
And yet I can't bring myself to be angry with him.
It's a sickness with him and he's been sick like this
      before.
But how can I share my home with another woman,
Share a marriage with her, share the same bed?
I look at her and she's young. Her beauty's just
      blooming,
While mine begins to fade. It's the flower that
      catches the eye.
When it's past its best, a man's footsteps start to
      wander.

What frightens me is that Heracles, my husband,   550
May call me wife, but the young one will be his
   woman.
However, as I say, a wife has to be sensible.
Anger will get me nowhere. And here, dear friends,
I have the answer. Let me show you my deliverer.
A long time ago, when I was young, Nessus the
   Centaur,
A wild shaggy creature, presented me
With a gift that I kept in a bronze container,
A cupful of blood from his wound as he lay dying.
He used to act as ferryman on the Euenus.
He needed neither oar nor sail, not even a boat,   560
But carried people for money, straight through the
   rapids.
He carried me, when I first left home
To go with Heracles as his new bride.
I was riding on his shoulders when in mid-stream
He started to fondle me. I screamed.
Heracles turned
And planted an arrow straight into his lungs,
Right through the chest. As the creature lay dying,
He gasped out these words: 'Daughter of ancient
   Oeneus,
Pay heed to what I say and this shall be your reward   570
For being the very last of all my passengers.
Scoop up the blood congealing round my wound,
There where the poison on his arrows, drained
From the Lernaean hydra, has discoloured it.
Keep it and it will serve you as a charm
For Heracles, to make sure he never looks at
Another woman, preferring her to you.'
I thought of this just now, my friends. Since the
   creature's death
I've kept the stuff safe, hidden away in the house.
Before he died he told me how to anoint   580
A tunic with the blood. Here it is. I've done it.
I've never taken even calculated risks,
Nor could I ever learn to. I hate those who do.
But as for a love-philtre to work on Heracles,

I'll defeat this child by a charm if I have to.
Anyway, it's done. I haven't done something stupid,
  have I?
I think I'm right, but if you don't agree, I won't try
  it.

CHORUS.
If you're quite sure it's going to work,
I can't see the harm in it. Your reasoning is sound.

DEIANIRA.
590   I can't guarantee it will work. It's never been tried.
I've no reason to doubt how powerful it may be.

CHORUS.
You'll only find out by using it, that's for sure.
Anything else can only be guesswork.

DEIANIRA.
We'll find out soon enough. Here comes Lichas.
He'll be leaving shortly.
Only keep this to yourselves, will you, please?
If what I do is shameful, I don't want my shame
  public.

        Enter LICHAS.

LICHAS.
Have you any instructions, daughter of Oeneus?
Tell me now. I've delayed too long already.

DEIANIRA.
600   While you've been talking to those women indoors,
This is what I have been doing, Lichas,
Preparing a full-length tunic for you to take
As a present for my husband from his wife's own
  hand.
Make sure he receives it and tell him without fail
That no one else must try it on.
On no account must it be exposed to sunlight
Nor to the light or heat from a sacred hearth
Until he stands up in full view of everyone
On a sacrificial day, to show the Gods.
610   I promised myself as soon as I should see him

Back home, or at least hear that he was safe,
To dress him in this tunic, put him on display
In the glorious robe, an offering to the Gods.
I'll put my seal to the lock, impress it with my signet,
So he'll know the box was sent by me.
Away you go now and make sure you take care this
    time
Not to let your tongue exceed your authority.
That way he will thank you and so will I,
And you will have earned double thanks.

LICHAS.

  Hermes, god of messengers, attend me.   620
  If I follow his craft as I should, I will serve you
    truly,
  Delivering this casket exactly as it is,
  And faithfully repeating your message, word for
    word.

DEIANIRA.

  You may go. I presume you are aware
  Of how things stand, domestically.

LICHAS.

  I am, yes, and I'll tell him all is well.

DEIANIRA.

  And you know, because you saw it, about the girl.
  How I received her and welcomed her here.

LICHAS.

  I was delighted, madam, as well as surprised.

DEIANIRA.

  That's it then. Is there anything else to tell him?   630
  I'm wary of saying how much I want to see him
  Before I find out if he still wants me.

    Exeunt severally LICHAS *and* DEIANIRA.

CHORUS.

  All you who live your lives
  By the warm springs and the rocky sanctuary
  Of Oeta,
  By the Malian gulf

And by the shoreline of the golden-bowed Artemis,
There where the Council meets,
Famed throughout Greece,

640   The mellifluous flute
Will soon enough be heard again amongst you,
Not sombre,
But lyrical, lyre-like.
Heracles, the son of Zeus and Alcmena,
Brandishing trophies,
Is coming home.

Twelve months we have waited,
Enduring his absence,
The drifter adrift.

650   While at home and lamenting,
Grief doubling and redoubling,
His poor wife was wasting
Till, moved at last, Ares
Has freed them from misery.

Let him come. Let him come.
Hurry, you great ship
With your rows of oars,
Don't stop till you've brought him here,
Leaving his sacrifice behind

660   At the island altar,
Driven by the passion
From the Centaur's magic charm.

Enter DEIANIRA.

DEIANIRA.
Listen, all of you, I'm frightened. I may have gone
    too far.
I'm afraid I shouldn't have done what I just did.

CHORUS.
Deianira, whatever has happened?

DEIANIRA.
I don't know. But I'm afraid that with the best
    intentions
I may have triggered some catastrophe.

CHORUS.
You don't mean with the gift you sent to Heracles?

DEIANIRA.
I do, yes. To rush blindly into action
Without knowing the consequences is so stupid.   670

CHORUS.
But what are you afraid of? Tell us, if you can.

DEIANIRA.
Something just happened. If I tell you as friends,
You'll know I never expected anything so strange.
I used a tuft of wool, a good piece, white,
To smear the tunic that I sent him to wear.
It's disappeared.
No one indoors got rid of it. It simply disintegrated,
Shrivelled up by itself where I dropped it on the
     flags.
I'll tell you the full story, hold nothing back.
Everything that the Centaur gasped out to me   680
As he lay with the arrow in his ribs
I remembered, precisely as he told it,
Indelible, as though engraved on bronze.
I followed those instructions in every detail.
I was to keep the charm out of harm's way
Where heat could not reach it from fire or sunlight.
That way it would stay fresh till I needed it for him.
So I did. The time came. Just now I pulled out
A handful of wool from one of the palace sheep
And took it to my room, privately. I anointed the   690
     robe
Carefully, my special present for him, folded it
And put it safely in the strong-box as you saw.
But as I was returning indoors, I saw something,
     maybe an omen –
I don't know how to tell you – something
     inexplicable.
I happened to have thrown the piece of wool,
The piece I smeared the tunic with, down where the
     sunlight

Fell full upon it. As it grew warm, then hot,
It dissolved,
Till all that was left was a little heap of something
700   Like nothing so much as sawdust, lying there.
But from the ground on which it had fallen
There started to ooze up bubbles, a mass of bubbles,
Frothing like the blue-black juice when grapes
Have been picked from the vine and crushed
    underfoot.
I don't know what to do. I think I'm going mad.
What I've seen tells me I've done something
    monstrous.
Why ever should I think that some wild creature
Would look on me kindly when I had caused his
    death?
Of course he didn't. He must have been tricking me
710   To get his own back on the man who shot him.
Too late. I see it all now. But it's too late.
Unless I am deceiving myself yet again,
I've killed my own husband, God help me, single-
    handed.
The arrow that killed Nessus would have killed any
    creature
Who touched it, I know that. It wounded Cheiron
And he was a God. How could I ever think
That the black blood which seeped from Nessus'
    wound
Would not kill Heracles? It must. I know it will.
Well then, I'm resolved that if he is destroyed,
720   I won't live to see the consequences.
For any woman who truly values virtue,
To live branded evil would be unbearable.

CHORUS.
There's no escaping the fear of disaster,
But don't abandon hope before you know the
    outcome.

DEIANIRA.
To someone who has made the wrong decision
Hope is a luxury to keep up the spirit.

CHORUS.
　But when it's a mistake, as in your case,
　The victim's anger is usually moderated.

DEIANIRA.
　That's easy for you to say – you're innocent
　Of complicity – harder for me who has to live with it. 　730

CHORUS.
　You'd be advised to say nothing more at present.
　Unless you want to say it to your son.
　You sent him to look for his father. Here he is back.

　　Enter HYLLUS.

HYLLUS.
　I would want one of three things for you, Mother.
　Your death. Alternatively,
　That I was someone else's son. Or failing that,
　That you were wholly changed from what you are.

DEIANIRA.
　Hyllus, what is it? Why do you hate me so?

HYLLUS.
　Your husband, Heracles, my father, are you
　　listening?
　Today, you killed him. 　　　　　　　　　　　　　740

DEIANIRA.
　What do you mean?

HYLLUS.
　I mean that it's inevitable.
　What's done cannot be undone.

DEIANIRA.
　How can you say this, Hyllus? Who told you
　That I was responsible for this dreadful business?

HYLLUS.
　I saw the whole terrible thing, Mother,
　With my own eyes. No one told me.

DEIANIRA.
　Where did you find him? Were you with him when it
　　happened?

HYLLUS.
If you must know, then I must tell you everything.

750   When he had sacked the famed city of Eurytus,
Laden with trophies and the spoils of victory,
He came to Cenaeum on the wave-washed shore
Of Euboea. There he marked out the space to
     dedicate
Altars and a sacred grave for his father Zeus.
I was so relieved to see him.
He was planning a multiple sacrifice
When Lichas arrived, his herald, come from home.
Bringing your gift to him, that lethal cloak.
Heracles put it on, as you had prescribed,

760   And proceeded to the sacrifice, killing first
A dozen perfect bulls. Altogether
He sacrificed a hundred beasts of various kinds.
At first light-hearted, revelling in the splendour
Of the robe, he began to pray, poor man.
But when the flames from the sacrifice began to flare,
Bloody and hissing from the pitchy pine-logs,
His skin began to sweat. The tunic was
Sticking to his body, all over him,
As though a craftsman had glued it.

770   A stinging pain tore at his body, bone-deep.
Like snake-venom, it began to feed on him.
He called out for Lichas, poor Lichas,
Who had nothing to do with the suffering you had
     caused,
Demanding to know what he'd plotted, bringing the
     tunic.
The wretched fellow knew nothing except that
The gift was yours. You sent it, he delivered it.
While Heracles listened, a spasm shot through him,
Agony clawing at his lungs.
He grabbed Lichas by the foot where the ankle
     bends at the heel,

780   And smashed him against a rock jutting out of the
     sea.
And where the skull was broken, hair and blood,
Brains beginning to dribble through, whitely.

Everyone present cried out in horror
At one man suffering, the other who'd lost his life.
No one dared come anywhere near Heracles.
He was writhing on the ground, then stretching full-
    length.
He was screaming. He was shrieking. The cliffs
    echoed,
From the headlands of Locris, round the heights of
    Euboea.
Then the pain passed, but now in his misery
He cast himself to the ground, grieving, lamenting,   790
Reviling the calamity of his marriage
To a malignant wife, meaning you, won as a bride
From Ceneus, to his irrevocable destruction.
He caught sight of me through the swirling smoke,
Fixed me with his eye as I stood there in the crowd,
Tears streaming down my face. Distracted with pain
    he called out
'My boy, come here. Don't run away when I'm in
    trouble
Even if it means your sharing my death with me.
Take me away from here, take me to where
No mortal man can witness what is happening.   800
At least, for pity's sake, take me away,
Away from this land, now. I don't want to die here.'
So he charged me. We found a ship and laid him on
    the deck,
And headed for home, back to this land, still
Groaning and writhing. Soon you will see him,
Just alive, or just dead.
That, Mother, is what you planned against my father,
And that is how successful you've been. May Justice
And an avenging Fury pay you out. That is my
    prayer,
If such a prayer can be right. But it must be right,   810
Since you have cast right to the winds by slaughtering
The finest man who ever lived, whose like we'll
    never see again.

Exit DEIANIRA.

CHORUS.
Why do you creep away in silence? Don't you see
That silence will be taken for a confession?

HYLLUS.
Let her creep away. As long as it's out of my sight,
She can creep wherever she wants.
How could she still deserve a mother's name,
When there's nothing of the mother in what she's
    done?
Creep off. What a triumph. And may she inherit
820   The self-same blessing she visited on my father.

    Exit HYLLUS.

CHORUS.
It closes in.
Watch, sisters,
How the ancient prophecy
Suddenly comes true.
'The twelfth month of the twelfth year
Shall see an end to the labours
Of Zeus' great son.'
It all ties up.
For how can a man who's lost his life
830   Be asked to serve amongst the dead?

Necessity,
Pain-dealing,
Wraps about his ribs the Centaur's
Bloody winding-sheet,
Steeped in poison, bred by Death,
Stewed in the long-dead hydra-juice.
How shall he see
Another dawn?
Black-maned, sly-speaking, the Centaur
840   Drives him, gnawing at his nerve-ends.

How much of this did the poor woman know?
She knew nothing,
Saw a threat to her marriage,
Her rival a novelty.

The remedy was destructive, but only through her
    blindness.
Her grief is real enough,
Real the flood of tears
That wets her cheeks.
What's happening brings treachery to light,
Impending doom.   850

And now our tears are flowing. Heracles,
His sickness spreading,
Pitifully faces pain
No enemy could inflict.
Alas for the black spear which won him his battle-
    bride,
Too hasty a marriage
To his bride from steep
Oechalia.
Now the real cause is revealed,
Secret work by   860
Aphrodite.

SEMI-CHORUS A.
    I think I hear –
    Fancy maybe –
    Someone crying in the palace.
    What did I tell you?

SEMI-CHORUS B.
    There, clearly.
    Something terrible inside.

      Enter NURSE.

SEMI-CHORUS A.
    Look, the old woman,
    Bowed down, down-cast.
    Something has happened.   870

NURSE.
    Oh, my dears, what a shock of troubles
    In the gift she sent to Heracles.

CHORUS.
What are you talking about that we don't already
know?

NURSE.
She's left us. Deianira's set out
On the final journal that you take stock-still.

CHORUS.
Not dead. Please, not dead.

NURSE.
You heard me.

CHORUS.
Poor woman. Dead?

NURSE.
Again, then. Yes, she's dead.

CHORUS.
Poor, poor woman. Can you tell me what happened?

NURSE.
The way she chose was awful.

CHORUS.
Tell us anyway.
880   Tell us the worst.

NURSE.
She killed herself.

CHORUS.
What possessed her? What made her do it?

NURSE.
Impaled herself . . .

CHORUS.
How could she heap another death on death?
And all alone?

NURSE.
On the sharp point of a sword.

CHORUS.
Did you see this mad act?

NURSE.
I saw it. I was standing close by.

CHORUS.
Did anyone ... ? How did she ... ? Tell me the
details.

NURSE.
She did it by herself, all by herself.   890

CHORUS.
Do you expect us to ... ?

NURSE.
It's the truth.

CHORUS.
That bride, that brand-new bride
Has given birth already,
Given birth to a Fury in this house.

NURSE.
A Fury, yes. And had you been there to witness
What Deianira did, you could only have pitied her.

CHORUS.
But could a woman set her hand to such a deed?

NURSE.
Oh yes, terrible as it seems. I'll tell you. I was there.
When she came indoors she was by herself.   900
She caught sight of her son, Hyllus, getting ready
A litter, hollowed out, for carrying his father home,
And went to hide where nobody would see her,
Throwing herself down, inconsolable, by the altars
Soon to be neglected for ever. And she wept.
She wept as she touched the furniture, things she
    used,
Rushing here and there, all over the house.
Catching sight of servants she was fond of,
She would stare at them, poor thing, and burst into
    tears,
Weep at her own ill-starred destiny   910
And her house condemned to lose its children.
After that she said no more and I saw her run

Suddenly to Heracles' bedroom.
Hidden where she couldn't see me, I watched her
Take bedclothes and throw them down.
She was making Heracles' bed.
And when she'd finished she threw herself on top of
    it,
Cowering there in the middle of the bed she'd made,
Tears streaming down her face. And she talked to it:

920   'Dear bed, goodbye. Goodbye, bedroom,
A long goodbye.
This is the last time that you'll welcome me to sleep.'
That was all she said. Resolutely, she raised her hand,
Undid her dress at the brooch over her breast,
Laying her left side bare
And her left arm to the elbow.
Then I ran, ran as fast as my strength allowed
To tell Hyllus what she was planning to do.
But in the time it took to find him and get back,

930   She took a double-bladed sword, as we discovered,
And stabbed herself through the ribs straight to the
        heart.
Hyllus screamed when he saw her. He knew, the
        wretched man,
That his anger was responsible.
By now he'd found out from the others in the house
That she was a mere instrument in the Centaur's
        plan.
But too late. Poor boy, he's overcome with grief,
Comfortless, sobbing over her body,
Kissing her, hugging her,
Lying there, crying out

940   That it was he had killed her with his accusation,
And now, all in one day, found himself orphaned,
Deprived of both his father and his mother.
So, there you have it. Only a hare-brained man
Banks on tomorrow or what comes after tomorrow.
There never was, there cannot be tomorrow
Until today is safely yesterday.

    Exit NURSE.

CHORUS.
>What grieve for first?
>What griefs crowd next?
>Help me, my judgement falters.

>What's there in the house,   950
>What's coming,
>What's here, what threatens, which worse?

>Oh for a whirlwind
>To pick us gently up
>And take us away from here.
>I'm frightened
>That the sight of our illustrious hero
>May be too much for me.
>They say he's coming home,
>Wracked, tormented,   960
>Shocking to see, shocking beyond belief.

>Now it's upon us,
>The sorrow that I sensed
>In my song, like a nightingale.
>A procession
>Of foreigners heading this way. Will they manage,
>Shuffling like pall-bearers,
>Escorting a friend?
>Unconscious or dead?
>Asleep, or have we already lost him?   970

>*Enter* HYLLUS, *an* OLD MAN *and* ATTEN-
>DANTS *with* HERACLES *on a litter.*

HYLLUS.
>I mourn for you, father,
>Mourn for your pain, for my suffering.
>God help me, what can I do?

OLD MAN.
>Hush, boy, don't excite
>Your tormented father's agony.
>He's alive, just.
>Hold on, bite your lip.

HYLLUS.

Did you say he's still alive?

OLD MAN.
Don't wake him,
Don't provoke him, don't stir up
980   That fearful frenzy, boy.

HYLLUS.
I can't bear it.
I'm losing my mind.

HERACLES.
Oh God,
Where am I? Who are all these people?
I don't know them. Watching me suffer.
Ahh. That hurts.
The fearsome thing gnaws at me.

OLD MAN.
I told you to keep quiet.
I told you not to rouse him,
990   Chasing the peace of sleep from his eye and mind.

HYLLUS.
I couldn't help myself.
I couldn't stand so terrible a sight.

HERACLES.
So this is my reward
For all the sacrifices
Made at Cenaea's altar-steps
This is how you treat me, is it, Zeus?
Would that I had never set eyes on Cenaea,
Or had to face such pain.
Such exquisite, maddening pain.
1000   Is there any sorcerer,
Any surgeon, skilled enough
To free me from the scourge, but Zeus?
To find one would be a miracle.
Ah! Let me be.
Let me sleep,
My final, desperate sleep.

Don't touch me. Where are you putting me?
That kills me. You're killing me.
It was calming down. You've roused it again.
Here it comes. It snatches at me.   1010
You're the vilest of Greeks, if Greeks you really are.
I slaved for you, cleaned up your high seas and your
    forests.
And is there no one will fetch me fire or a sword
To free me from my suffering?
Will none of you
Cut the head from my body?
Damn you all.

OLD MAN.
Come boy, this task is greater than I can manage.
I haven't the strength. Give me a hand here.
You're fitter to help him than I am.   1020

HYLLUS.
I've got him.
But offering relief from pain,
Out here or indoors, is beyond my power.
This is God's will.

HERACLES.
Hyllus, where are you?
Hyllus? Support me.
Here, here, lift me up. Oh God.
It's savage, savaging me again,
Mercilessly clawing at me,
Murderous, incurable.   1030
Ah Athena, Athena, it's eating me alive.
Pity, Hyllus. Be merciful to your father.
Take your sword – you won't be blamed for it –
And thrust it here into my throat,
The only way to free me
From this agony your godless mother
Has inflicted on me.
May she suffer the same
And may I watch,
Watch her die as I am dying.   1040

Sweet death, brother of Zeus,
Rest me, free me from this torture.
One stroke, quick, sharp, then peace.

CHORUS.
I shrink with horror, dear friends, to hear
How such a man could be so driven by pain.

HERACLES.
These hands, this back, have suffered in the past
Hard work, heated endeavours, evil, truth to tell.
But never like this. Not when Zeus' wife, Hera,
Confronted me, not at the hands of wretched
    Eurystheus.

1050   Nothing to match the way the daughter of Oeneus,
Two-faced Deianira, has entangled me,
Murdering me, stuck in a Fury's clinging web.
It clings to me, consuming my very innards,
Invading till the breath drains from my lungs,
Guzzling on my fresh blood to the last drop.
My body's wasting away – there'll be nothing left –
Imprison'd in her unspeakable embrace.
No enemy spear could do this on the battlefield,
No earth-born giant, no wild beast,

1060   No Greek, no foreigner anywhere I roamed,
Purging the land as I went. But she did.
One woman, acting as a woman, nothing like a man,
Has downed me, single-handed without even a
    sword.
Hyllus, you must act now as your father's son
And pay no respect to your mother's name.
I want her. Fetch her yourself from the house
And deliver her into my hands. I need to watch you
While she is suffering to see which grieves you most,
Her pain or mine.

1070   Come on, boy, be brave. I need compassion from
    you.
Others feel pity enough when they see me howling,
And weeping like a girl. There's no one alive
Can say they saw the like of this before.
Whatever I suffered, I suffered without a murmur.

But this. I've lost my manhood.
Come here. Come on, stand by your father.
Take a good look at this suffering, brought about
By mischance. Off with the coverings. I'll show
    you.
Now look, all of you, look at this poor body.
Feast your eyes on this miserable, pitiful sight.   1080
Ah, damned pain.
It shoots straight through me.
Through my chest. Consuming pain.
Will it never leave me?
Death take me, I beg you.
Demolish me, Zeus,
With a thunderbolt.
Strike me with lightning, my father. Please.
It's breaking out again, flaming, devouring
My hands and my back, my chest and my arms: 1090
Arms, which overcame the indomitable lion
None of Nemea's herdsmen could stand up to,
Yet you subdued it. The Lernaean hydra too.
And that savage Centaur pack, half-horse, half-man,
Lawless and overbearing, vicious crew that they
    were.
And the Erymanthian boar and from Hades
Beneath the earth the triple-headed hound,
The whelp of Echidna. What a monster that was.
Irresistible. And at the far end of the earth,
The dragon, guardian of the golden apples.   1100
These and a hundred others I overcame.
No one took me on and then set up a trophy.
Now look at me, with no use left in my limbs,
A shredded thing, blind Fate's whipping-boy,
Me with a mother well-born enough,
My father Zeus himself, lord of the starry heaven.
But this I swear to you. I may be nothing now,
Unable so much as to crawl, but let me
Get my hands on who's responsible. Let her come
    here
And I'll show her, show the whole world,   1110
In death, no less than in life, I pay evil back.

CHORUS.
Poor Greece. With the loss of such a man as this,
What grief, what mourning you must undergo.

HYLLUS.
You have spoken, father. Now you're silent.
I know how ill you are, but listen to my response.
I ask nothing else for you but what is right.
Be true to your real self, before you were consumed
With fury from the grinding pain. There's no point
Glorying in revenge for what you have suffered.

HERACLES.
1120 Say anything you like, so long as it's clear.
I'm too sick to play word-games.

HYLLUS.
I have to tell you about mother,
How she is – how she did what she did in error.

HERACLES.
You little wretch. How dare you speak of her,
A murdering mother who has killed your father?

HYLLUS.
I can't keep silent about what I know.

HERACLES.
Nor should you after the crimes that she's
committed.

HYLLUS.
What she's done today, you mean?

HERACLES.
Go on then. But take care. You may condemn
yourself.

HYLLUS.
1130 You have to know. She's dead. A short while ago.

HERACLES.
Who killed her? Strange. I don't like the sound of
this.

HYLLUS.
By her own hand. She killed herself.

HERACLES.
Too soon. I ought to have killed her myself.

HYLLUS.
Even you would soften, if only you knew.

HERACLES.
An odd thing to say. Knew what?

HYLLUS.
Briefly. She did wrong. But she meant well.

HERACLES.
'Meant well', did she, damn you, when she
      murdered your father?

HYLLUS.
She thought she was giving you a love-charm.
It was a mistake. She'd seen your brand-new wife.

HERACLES.
Who in Trachis could have given her a love-charm? 1140

HYLLUS.
Ages ago the Centaur, Nessus, told her
She could rekindle your love by using a charm.

HERACLES.
Nessus. Ah, Nessus, damn him. I might have known.
I'm finished. Done for. Out goes the light.
Now I know. I see it all.
Come here, my boy, come. This is the end of your
      father.
Go and fetch your brothers, all the family,
Alcmena too, poor Alcmena, loved by Zeus –
What a waste. My parting words to you
Shall be prophecies I know and you must hear.   1150

HYLLUS.
Your mother's not here. She went to the coast,
To Tiryns. That's where she lives now.
Some of the boys are with her. She looks after them.
And I have to tell you some of us live in Thebes.
Those of us who are here, father, will follow
Your instructions as thoroughly as we can.

HERACLES.
    Listen then. Listen carefully. The time has come
    For you to show whether or not you're any son of
      mine.
    It was prophesied by my father long ago
1160   That no man alive would cause my death,
    But some resident of Hell, a dead creature.
    The Centaur was that creature. It all turned out
    According to God's word. The dead kill the living.
    There was another oracle following on the first.
    Of course. They match, the first, then this.
    Up in the mountains where the Selli live
    And sleep on the ground, I heard my father's
      prophecy,
    Delivered in the rustling of the oak-groves.
    I wrote what he said, that in due time
1170   I'd find release from all the labours that oppressed
      me.
    That time is now.
    A happy release is what he meant, not happiness.
    The dead are free from labour.
    It's obvious, Hyllus, that's what's happening.
    And you have a part to play. You must help me.
    No hesitating. Don't provoke me now.
    You alone can do what we have to do.
    Remember this rule as golden. Obey your father.

HYLLUS.
    What you say worries me, father. I don't know
1180   What you have in mind but I'll do it. I'll obey.

HERACLES.
    Give me your right hand.

HYLLUS.
    Why do you need such a promise?

HERACLES.
    Don't cross me. Your hand. Quick.

HYLLUS.
    It's all right. Here.

HERACLES.
  Swear. On the head of my father, Zeus. Swear.

HYLLUS.
  Swear what? Aren't you going to tell me?

HERACLES.
  That you'll do what I tell you to do.

HYLLUS.
  As Zeus is my witness. I swear.

HERACLES.
  And a curse on your head if you withdraw.

HYLLUS.
  That isn't necessary. I'll do it. Oh, very well.   1190

HERACLES.
  Right. You know the highest peak on Oeta, sacred to
    Zeus.

HYLLUS.
  I know it. I've sacrificed up there many times.

HERACLES.
  You must carry my body up there, yourself,
  With help from your friends, if you need it.
  Then cut down wood, lots of it,
  Mature oak with deep roots, wild olive,
  Then you must lay my body on top,
  Light a pine torch and set it on fire.
  No weeping, not a single tear.
  Dry-eyed, I'll have no signs of mourning.   1200
  That's if you really are a son of mine.
  If you don't do it, I'll come back and haunt you.

HYLLUS.
  Father, what are you saying? That's a terrible thing,
    you're asking.

HERACLES.
  It has to be done. And if you refuse,
  Don't call me father. I disown you.

HYLLUS.
  Dear God. You're asking me to murder you.
  Polluted. Parricide, that's what they'll call me.

HERACLES.
No. No. My doctor. The means, the only means
By which my suffering can be cured.

HYLLUS.
1210   How can I cure your body by burning it?

HERACLES.
If you're afraid of that, at least do everything else.

HYLLUS.
I'll carry you there. Of course.

HERACLES.
And build the pyre, just as I said.

HYLLUS.
As long as I don't actually have to lay my hands on it.
I'll do everything else. You needn't worry about that.

HERACLES.
All right. I'm satisfied. There is one thing.
One extra favour on top of all you've done.

HYLLUS.
You've only to ask, whatever it is.

HERACLES.
You know that girl, Eurytus' daughter?

HYLLUS.
1220   Iole, you mean?

HERACLES.
Oh you do know her. Well, my son, this is my
    request.
It's to do with her. When I am dead – remember
You did swear an oath to do whatever I said –
I want you to marry her. Now, don't let your father
    down.
I slept with her. Iole. She's lain by my side.
I don't want anyone else to have her
Except you, my boy. Take her as your bride.
Please. Do as I say. All these great things you've
    agreed
Will be cancelled out if you won't humour me in this.

HYLLUS.
  How can I be angry with someone so sick?   1230
  But who could tolerate a thing like that?

HERACLES.
  Does all that muttering mean you won't?

HYLLUS.
  How could anyone agree? That's the girl who single-
      handed
  Caused my mother's death and the state you're in.
  I'd have to be possessed to marry her.
  Father, to die alongside you would be better
  Than to live in the same house as our enemy.

HERACLES.
  So, this fellow, it appears, will not respect
  A father's dying request. God's curse awaits you
  If you fail to keep faith with everything I said.   1240

HYLLUS.
  Calm yourself. You'll have a relapse if you're not
      careful.

HERACLES.
  It's your fault, stirring up my sleeping demon.

HYLLUS.
  Damned. I'm damned, whichever way I turn.

HERACLES.
  Because you won't listen to what your father fairly
      asks.

HYLLUS.
  Fairly? You've only wickedness to teach me.

HERACLES.
  How can it be wicked if it's what I want?

HYLLUS.
  Are you sure it would be right to do what you say?

HERACLES.
  Of course it would be right. The gods are my
      witnesses.

HYLLUS.
I'll do it. With the Gods' approval,
1250   I'll not hold back. Anything's better, father,
Then appearing to break my word to you.

HERACLES.
At last. Thank heaven. Now, quick as you can,
Pick me up and take me to the fire
Before another spasm overtakes me.
Lift me. Hurry now.
Peace at last and an end for Heracles.

HYLLUS.
There's nothing to stop me, father,
Obeying your orders now. You force me to it.

HERACLES.
On then. Be resolute, my soul.
1260   Before the pain floods back,
Lips set like stone, steely, muzzling,
Muffling the scream,
Grudging but the end is triumph.

HYLLUS.
Raise him aloft as you carry him.
Forgive me my complicity.
The Gods, not men, are the true cause,
Of everything that happens,
Claiming a father's respect
But overlooking all our suffering.
1270   No mortal man can see the future,
The present's bad enough.
For all this suffering here,
The cruellest fate that any man endured,
The Gods should be ashamed.

You too, women of Trachis, away from this house.
For you have witnessed strange and terrible deaths,
Horrors never seen before.
Zeus' fault. All of it. The fault of Zeus.

    Exeunt.

SOPHOCLES

Philoctetes

translated by Kenneth McLeish

Characters

ODYSSEUS
NEOPTOLEMOS
PHILOCTETES
TRADER, a disguised servant of Odysseus
HERACLES
CHORUS OF SAILORS FROM NEOPTOLEMOS' SHIP

This translation of *Philoctetes* was performed by Cheek by Jowl at the Donmar Warehouse, London, and on nationwide and world tours in 1989. The cast was as follows:

ODYSSEUS	Charlie Roe
NEOPTOLEMOS	Paterson Joseph
PHILOCTETES	Keith Bartlett
TRADER	Trevor Baxter
HERACLES	Duncan Duff
CHORUS	Peter Darling
	Duncan Duff, Michael Jenn, Lloyd Owen, Cecilia Noble, Dale Rapley, Timothy Walker

Directed by Declan Donellan

A seashore. In the background, a cave.

Enter ODYSSEUS *and* NEOPTOLEMOS, *with a*
SERVANT.

ODYSSEUS.
    This is the coast of Lemnos, a barren island
    In the midst of empty sea. No one lives here.
    Look, Neoptolemos, son of Achilles, son
    Of the noblest of the Greeks; this is the place
    I chose to maroon him, years ago –
    Philoctetes of Malis, son of Poias.

    I was obeying orders from our generals.
    His foot was festering, oozing pus
    From a foul wound. Even at festivals
    We hardly dared touch the wine or meat:
    He gave us no peace; day and night, he filled   10
    The whole camp with groans and curses, cries
    Of ill omen that spoiled the sacrifice.

    But no more of that now. If he hears us,
    If he finds out we are here, the plan
    I have made to capture him will fail.
    Your part is to help me. Look around
    Till you find a cave with two entrances –
    Two suntraps to sit in when it is cold,
    And a passage between them, to sleep in
    In summer, cooled by the breeze. Below it,
    On the left, you should find a spring   20
    Of fresh water, if it has not dried up.
    Go quietly. Signal if he is there.
    Then I'll tell you what we must do next.

NEOPTOLEMOS.
    Odysseus, sir! This *is* the right place.
    I think I see the cave you mean.

ODYSSEUS.
    Where is it? Above you, or further down?

NEOPTOLEMOS.
    Up here. Deserted, silent. No one is here.

ODYSSEUS.
30   Look inside. He may be inside, asleep.

NEOPTOLEMOS.
It's empty. There's no one about.

ODYSSEUS.
Does anyone live there? Are there signs of that?

NEOPTOLEMOS.
Yes: a bed of leaves, where someone sleeps.

ODYSSEUS.
Is there anything else? Go further in.

NEOPTOLEMOS.
A cup, roughly carved from a block of wood –
Not by a craftsman. And twigs, for a fire.

ODYSSEUS.
This must be the cave. He must live here.

NEOPTOLEMOS.
Look! Bandages. The rags he wears to bind his
wound.
Rolled carefully – but foul with pus.

ODYSSEUS.
40   This is the cave. He can't be far away.
A sick man, crippled by that old wound –
He couldn't get far. He's gone foraging,
For food, or some soothing herb he knows.
Leave your servant up there to stand on guard,
In case Philoctetes takes us by surprise.
He'd like to catch me, more than any Greek alive.

        Exit SERVANT.

NEOPTOLEMOS.
He's gone further up. He'll guard the path.
Now, lord Odysseus, what must we do next?

ODYSSEUS.
50   Son of Achilles, I'm asking you
For courage first, and then obedience.
Whatever I tell you, however strange,
You must do it at once. That's why you came.

NEOPTOLEMOS.
   What must I do?

ODYSSEUS.
   You must cheat Philoctetes,
   And tangle his soul in a net of words.
   He'll ask who you are, where you are from.
   Begin with the truth: you are Neoptolemos,
   Son of Achilles. Then say you are sailing home,
   Away from the Greeks, in a furious rage:
   They begged you, persuaded you to go to Troy;   60
   Only then, they said, could they hope to win.
   But when you asked them for your father's arms –
   The armour of Achilles, yours by right –
   They refused, and gave it to Odysseus.

   Tell him that. Call me any names you like.
   Spare me no insults. He must believe you,
   Or else you bring ruin on all the Greeks.
   For we must have his bow;
   Without it, you'll never capture Troy.

   Are you surprised that he'll believe *you*,
   Trust *you*, rather than me? This is the reason.   70
   You took no part in the first expedition;
   You are your own free man; you are not bound
   By oaths of loyalty; you sailed with us
   Of your own free will. For me, none of that
   Is true. If he sees me, and has the bow,
   He'll kill us both. The bow gives him power
   That no one else can match. Force is useless.
   That's why you must trick him, and steal the bow.

   My dear boy, I know how unused you are
   To this talk of stealing and trickery.   80
   But the prize is worth it – the fall of Troy!
   Take the risk. The future will prove us right.
   For one little day, for one dishonest hour,
   Do as I say. When it is done, your life
   Can be the noblest the world has ever seen.

NEOPTOLEMOS.
My lord Odysseus, even to talk of it
Is painful. How can I ever do it?
I am Achilles' son, noblest of Greeks —
How can I cheat and steal to get my way?
90   I'll conquer by force, not trickery.
The man is outnumbered, a poor cripple —
If he fights, he'll lose. I know
I was sent to help you, to obey you;
But with respect, my lord, I'd rather
Fight fair and lose than cheat and win.

ODYSSEUS.
So like your father! When I was a young man
I was just like you: action, not argument.
But now I have learned from experience
That blows sometimes miss; words always win.

NEOPTOLEMOS.
100   Have you more orders — or is lying enough?

ODYSSEUS.
Your orders are these — play a trick, and win.

NEOPTOLEMOS.
And if I persuade him without a trick?

ODYSSEUS.
You won't. Persuasion, just like force, will fail.

NEOPTOLEMOS.
Is he so dangerous? Has he such power?

ODYSSEUS.
He has arrows of death that never miss.

NEOPTOLEMOS.
To speak to him at all is dangerous.

ODYSSEUS.
Not if you trick him. There is no other way.

NEOPTOLEMOS.
But ... to lie! How can you approve of that?

ODYSSEUS.
If we lie, we're safe. I approve of that.

NEOPTOLEMOS.
I must look him in the face, and lie to him?   110

ODYSSEUS.
It's for your own good. Remember that.

NEOPTOLEMOS.
What good will it do me, if he comes to Troy?

ODYSSEUS.
With his bow, and his arrows, Troy will fall.

NEOPTOLEMOS.
The oracle said that I would capture Troy.

ODYSSEUS.
Using his weapons, yes. Without them, no.

NEOPTOLEMOS.
We must take him, then. There is no other choice.

ODYSSEUS.
Do it, and you'll win a double prize.

NEOPTOLEMOS.
What prize? Tell me. I might not still refuse.

ODYSSEUS.
To be called noble and wise: that is the prize.

NEOPTOLEMOS.
Very well. I refuse no longer. I agree.   120

ODYSSEUS.
You understand clearly what you have to do?

NEOPTOLEMOS.
It's clear enough. I understand.

ODYSSEUS.
Stay here, then, and wait for him. I'll go:
He must not see me with you. Your servant
Up there must come back to the ship with me.
If things go slowly here, I'll send him back
Disguised as a ship's captain, to help the trick.

130   We'll find some clever tale for him to tell –
       And whatever he says, go along with it,
       Make use of it. I'll go now, back to the ship.
       The rest is up to you. And may Hermes
       God of trickery guide us, with Athena,
       Goddess of victory, who watches over me.

         Exit ODYSSEUS, *enter the* CHORUS *of*
         SAILORS.

A SAILOR.
    Sir, we are strangers, in a strange land.
    If we meet that sharp, suspicious man,
    Tell us what to hide, and what to say.

ANOTHER.
    Princes, who rule in Zeus' name,
    Are gifted more than other mortals:
140   They're subtle, they decide, they know.

ANOTHER.
    Sir, you are a prince, with royal power
    Inherited from kings of long ago.
    Tell us your orders. We will obey.

NEOPTOLEMOS.
    Look around now: he's not here.
    This is his lair, on the island's edge.
    Look your fill. But when he comes back,
    The outlaw, the castaway,
    Keep hidden and watch, in case
    I signal suddenly for help.

FIRST SAILOR.
150   Sir, we'll protect you, keep an eye
    On you, as we have always done.
    Your safety's our first concern.

SECOND SAILOR.
    Tell us this first: where does he live?
    Where should we look? We must take care:
    He may be hiding, waiting to attack.

THIRD SAILOR.
> Show us his haunts, his tracks,
> His lair. Does he sleep rough,
> Or under cover? Tell us where to look.

NEOPTOLEMOS.
> Look, up there: a nest in the rock,
> Two entrances –   160

FIRST SAILOR.
> Poor wretch. Is he inside?

NEOPTOLEMOS.
> He'll be out hunting,
> Shuffling in pain along these paths,
> Shooting deadly arrows:
> Soul-sick, they say, with pain,
> With gnawing agony
> No one will cure.

SAILORS.
> We pity him.
> He is alone, and full of pain.   170
> There is no one
> To talk to him or care for him.
> He is eaten with pain,
> Baffled by each new day.
> How can he bear it?
> He is mortal: his fate
> Was chosen by the gods.
> Weep for the miseries of mortals.
> Whose burden is endless pain.

> Was he rich?   180
> A nobleman's son, perhaps,
> Second to none?
> Now he's nothing: alone
> With the beasts of woods and hills.
> He is starving,
> Twisted with pain,
> How can he bear it?
> No one hears his bitterness:

Only Echo, chuckling in the hills,
190   Answers his cries.

NEOPTOLEMOS.
His sufferings are nothing strange.
I know they were sent by the gods.
He was marooned here alone
To soothe the savage rage
Of Chryse, and fulfil the plans
The gods made for Troy. His arrows
Are deadly: no one can escape.
When the time comes, Troy will fall
By them – and it is Heaven's will
200   That until then, he must stay here.

FIRST SAILOR.
Listen!

NEOPTOLEMOS.
What is it?

FIRST SAILOR.
I heard a groan,
The cry of a man in pain.
From this side. No, this.
There it is again. A man
Dragging himself along,
Moaning with pain. A sick man,
A cripple. It's plain enough.
My lord –

NEOPTOLEMOS.
210   What is it?

FIRST SAILOR.
Think what to do:
He's nearly here. Listen:
This is no shepherd
Whistling as he goes along –
It's a man in torment,
Groaning, stumbling
His way on an empty shore.

Enter PHILOCTETES. *He carries a bow.*

PHILOCTETES.
　Strangers!
　Who are you? Where have you come from? Why   220
　Have you put in here, to this empty place?
　There is nothing here: no shelter, no people.
　What country are you from? What people?
　From your clothes, you look like Greeks,
　The most welcome sight in all the world.

　If only you'd speak. Don't be afraid.
　I look like a savage beast, more than a man.
　Pity me. An outlaw, a castaway.
　Alone, in pain. If you mean me no harm,
　If you're my friends, speak to me. Answer,   230
　Please answer. I ask for nothing else.

NEOPTOLEMOS.
　Of course I'll answer. And first of all,
　The words you most hoped to hear: we are Greeks.

PHILOCTETES.
　No words are more welcome in all the world.
　Greeks! After all these years ... and you are Greeks!
　My boy ... my dear boy ... why have you come
　　here?
　Is there something here you want? Something you
　　need?
　Or were you blown off course, in a lucky storm?
　O my boy, answer me. Tell me who you are.

NEOPTOLEMOS.
　I come from the island of Scyros.
　I am sailing home. My name is Neoptolemos,   240
　Son of Achilles. There: you know it all.

PHILOCTETES.
　Achilles' son? I was his dearest friend.
　I loved Scyros. I knew your guardian, too,
　When your father left for Troy. But why
　Have you come here? Where did your journey start?

NEOPTOLEMOS.
　In Troy. I am sailing home from Troy.

PHILOCTETES.
How can that be? You were not with us then,
Years ago, when our army left for Troy.

NEOPTOLEMOS.
When our army left . . . ? You mean *you* were at Troy?

PHILOCTETES.
Don't you know me? Don't you recognise me?

NEOPTOLEMOS.
250   How could I recognise a man I've never met?

PHILOCTETES.
Have you never heard my name? Never heard
Of the wrongs I suffer, the pain I bear?

NEOPTOLEMOS.
No. Every word you say is new to me.

PHILOCTETES.
O gods! Is there more? More misery to bear?
Ten years twisted with pain – and no one knows
How I suffer, no one in the whole of Greece!
My wound feeds and grows stronger every day –
Is it still a secret, a private joke
To the criminals, cursed by the gods, who left me
    here?

260   Neoptolemos, son of Achilles:
I think you have heard of me. I am the man
Who was made master of the bow of Heracles –
Philoctetes, son of Poias. I am the man
Our generals and Odysseus of Ithaca
Banished to this empty place, the man gnawed
By a vicious sickness, marked out for death
By the murderous fangs of a deadly snake.

They left me to endure it: here, alone.
They sailed away and left me. We had come
270   From the island of Chryse – a hard voyage
In stormy seas. I was exhausted,
And fell asleep in a cave here on the headland.
At once, overjoyed, they seized their chance
And sailed. Oh, they left me a supply of rags,

Beggar's rags, and a little store of food.
God curse them! God send them the same one day!

Can you imagine what it was like to wake up
And find them gone? Can you imagine my tears,
My despair? The warfleet I took to Troy,
Stolen away; its captain marooned, alone,   280
A helpless cripple racked with pain. I looked
For a living soul to help. I searched the island.
There was no one. Nothing. All I had was pain.

So the years passed: season after season.
No one came. I am the master; I am the slave.
I just keep alive. When my belly needs food,
The bow provides it: birds, shot on the wing.
The arrows never miss, but whatever I shoot   290
I have to fetch myself, crawling, dragging
This foot. Sometimes in winter the pools freeze:
If I want water to drink, I must light
A fire. Then I must crawl to fetch wood,
And if the old embers are dead, strike flint
On stone to unlock the secret spark.
Shelter, and fire. I keep alive. What more
Do I need, but an end to my endless pain?

My boy, do you know what this island is like?   300
No sailors land here by choice. Why should they?
There are no harbours, no markets, no towns.
A sensible traveller keeps well away.

But now and then, as the years pass, crews put in
   here
By accident. When they do, they pity me –
Or so they say. They leave me charity:
A little food, say, or some cast-off clothes.
But that other thing, when I mention it –
To be taken home – they never give me that.   310

A living death. I have been here ten years.
I pine, I starve, only my sickness thrives.
This is the handiwork of the sons of Atreus
And of proud Odysseus. May the gods above
Punish them one day with suffering like mine.

FIRST SAILOR.
Like everyone else who comes here
I pity you, Philoctetes, I pity you.

NEOPTOLEMOS.
The sons of Atreus! Proud Odysseus!
320   Every word you say is true. I know
Their arrogance. Their evil has touched me too.

PHILOCTETES.
They are evil men, cursed by the gods.
How have they harmed you? What debt do they
    owe?

NEOPTOLEMOS.
A debt of suffering they will pay in full.
Mycenae and Sparta will learn, one day,
That Scyros, too, breeds fighting men.

PHILOCTETES.
Well said, boy! Good. But why do you hate them?
Tell me. What lodged such fury in your heart?

NEOPTOLEMOS.
I'll tell you, hard though it is: how I came
330   To Troy, and how they mocked and insulted me.
When Fate decreed Achilles had to die –

PHILOCTETES.
What? Achilles, dead? Tell me clearly:
Achilles son of Peleus, your father, is dead?

NEOPTOLEMOS.
Yes, he is dead – and by no mortal hand.
They say Apollo killed him, the archer god.

PHILOCTETES.
His will be done. And now, Neoptolemos
Son of Achilles, what should I do? Listen
To your story, or weep for your father's death?

NEOPTOLEMOS.
Already you have cause enough to weep
340   For your own sake. You need not weep for him

PHILOCTETES.
    What you say is true. I accept it. Tell me, then:
    How did those noble lords insult you?

NEOPTOLEMOS.
    They came to fetch me from Scyros, in a ship
    Fluttering with flags: noble Odysseus
    And Phoinix, my father's old guardian.
    They said – and it could have been true or false –
    That with my father dead, the gods had decreed
    That I, and only I, was to capture Troy.

    That was their story. They soon persuaded me
    To sail with them. There were two reasons. First,
    My father, the father I had never seen.   350
    His body was laid out for burial:
    I wanted to touch him and weep for him.
    And second, I was flattered. To think
    That I, and I alone, was to capture Troy!

    So we set sail. Wind and the sailors' oars
    Brought us in two days to cruel Sigeum.
    I went ashore. The soldiers crowded round
    To welcome me. 'He's Achilles!' they said,
    'He's Achilles come to life again!'
    But Achilles my father was dead, laid out
    For burial. I mourned him as custom demands.   360
    Then I went to the sons of Atreus, my friends
    (Or so I thought), and asked for my father's arms
    And whatever else was his. For answer
    They laughed at me, laughed in my face, and said,
    'The arms of Achilles! Everything else
    Is yours to take. But his arms have been given
    To another man: to Odysseus, Laertes' son.'
    Tears of fury burned my eyes. I leapt up,
    Blazing, and shouted at them. 'How dare you?
    How dare you give my arms to another man
    Without my leave? How dare you insult me so?'   370
    At that Odysseus said – he was standing by –
    'Now, now, my boy. The arms are mine by right.
    I earned them when I saved your father's life.'

I was furious. I cursed him. I called down
Every insult I knew. That he should steal my arms
He's a mild man, but at last I stung him
Into answering. 'Your place was here with us,
Fighting the Trojans – and you stayed away.
380   Insult me how you like, boast how you like,
You'll never sail home and take those arms.'

So, insulted and mocked, empty-handed,
I am sailing home. Odysseus took from me
What was rightly mine. The lord Odysseus!
Lord of deceit. And what of them, the generals,
The commanders, the sons of Atreus?
As a city looks to its king, so men
In battle look to their generals to lead them well.
If the slave's corrupt, the master is to blame.

That's my story. Whoever hates
The sons of Atreus is my friend,
390   And the gods' friend, for evermore.

SAILORS.
Mother Earth,
Mother of Zeus himself;
Queen of the wide river,
Pactolus of golden sands;
You ride in majesty,
Your chariot drawn
400   By a team of hunting lions.

Earth-mother, Queen,
I called you to witness then,
When the sons of Atreus in their pride
Over-ruled this man,
When they gave his father's arms,
A wonder of the world,
To Odysseus, Laertes' son.

PHILOCTETES.
Neoptolemos, you bring a convincing tale
Of lies and insults. Everything you say
Fits what I knew of them, the sons of Atreus
And Odysseus lord of deceit, who bends

His tongue to any lie, any trick
Right or wrong, that will bring him what he wants.
I know them: I'm not surprised. But where   410
Was Ajax? He is an honest man: he
Could have stopped them. Why didn't he speak up?

NEOPTOLEMOS.
Ajax is dead. If he'd been still alive
I'd not have been robbed; I'd have the arms.

PHILOCTETES.
Ajax, dead? Have the gods taken him as well?

NEOPTOLEMOS.
Yes he's dead. He lies in the underworld.

PHILOCTETES.
Why should he die, and not those criminals?
Diomedes son of Tydeus, Odysseus –
Why don't they die? They should never have lived.

NEOPTOLEMOS.
They live and thrive. They are princes of men,
The glory of all the fighting-men of Greece.   420

PHILOCTETES.
And Nestor, King of Pylos – what news of him?
He was an old friend, a good, honest man.
His wise advice often stopped their wickedness.

NEOPTOLEMOS.
He too has suffered. He has lost his son,
Antilochus, who sailed with him to Troy.

PHILOCTETES.
Antilochus too! You have told me of the deaths
Of two good friends. What is left for us now,
What can we hope for, if Antilochus
And Ajax, who should have lived, are dead,
And Odysseus, who should be dead, still lives?   430

NEOPTOLEMOS.
He's a skilful wrestler, who has survived
Till now. But even skilful wrestlers fall.

PHILOCTETES.
In god's name, Neoptolemos! Was Patroclos
Not there to help you? Your father's dearest friend.

NEOPTOLEMOS.
He too is dead. And it is always so,
Philoctetes – the wicked never die
In war, except by chance. Only good men die.

PHILOCTETES.
In that case, give me news of one wicked man:
That vile creature with the clever tongue,
440   So expert in arguing. Is he alive?

NEOPTOLEMOS.
I don't understand. Do you mean Odysseus?

PHILOCTETES.
Not Odysseus, no. There was another one.
His name was Thersites. No one could stop him
Talking and arguing. Is he still alive?

NEOPTOLEMOS.
I don't know him. I've not heard he is dead.

PHILOCTETES.
Nothing evil has died, in this whole war.
The gods in their wisdom look after them;
450   It pleases them; they close the gates of Hades
To cheats and criminals, as if there was room
In the underworld only for honest men.
How can we understand? How can we praise
The gods, if we cannot praise the things they do?

NEOPTOLEMOS.
Philoctetes, my part in this is done.
From now on I'll watch the Trojan War
And the sons of Atreus from far away.
Now that honest men are dead and liars thrive,
Now that heroes are beaten and cowards rule,
I'll not stay to see it: I'll go back
460   To stony Scyros, and live content at home.
Now I must go to the ship. Philoctetes,
I leave you with the blessing of the gods.

May they answer your prayers, and cure your
  sickness.
Men, we must go. When the gods send fair wind,
We must be ready to set sail at once.

PHILOCTETES.
Neoptolemos! Will you go so soon?

NEOPTOLEMOS.
Yes. The wind's freshening. It's time.
We must go on board, and make ready at once.

PHILOCTETES.
Neoptolemos, I beg you, in the name
Of your father and mother, and all you hold dear
At home, I beg you, don't leave me here   470
Alone. You've seen how I suffer. You've heard
All the miseries I endure. Pity me.
Find a corner of your heart and pity me.

I know I'm not the cargo you would choose
To have on board – but bear me, put up with me!
You're a good man. Be kind, not cruel. Think
How your honour will suffer if you leave me here,
The glory and fame if you take me home.

I'll not trouble you long: less than one day.   480
Take me to the ship, and stow me where you like –
The stern, the hold, the prow, out of the way,
Wherever I will least offend the crew.

Say yes. I beg you in god's name, say yes.
Do as I ask. Look: I'm on my knees,
A sick man, a cripple. Don't leave me here,
Marooned alone in this desert. Pity me,
Take me to Scyros, home with you, or else
To the mainland, to Euboea, from where
It is just a little step home for me   490
To the hills of Trachis, the plain of Spercheius.
Home! To my dear father, if he's still alive.
I have sent him so many messages
By passing travellers: prayers to come himself

Or send a ship and crew to rescue me.
But no one came. He's dead, perhaps, or else
(And I think it more likely) my messengers
Cared nothing for me, and made their own way home.

500   Now you have come: messenger, rescuer, all
In one. I beg you, save me, pity me.
Remember, chance governs all human life.
When it's good, when we're up, we must look out
For trouble ahead, or we may come crashing down.

SAILORS.
Pity him, sir. He has told
Of unbearable suffering.
Pray god none of those we love
Ever has to suffer so.
If you hate them, sir,
510   The cruel sons of Atreus,
Turn the evil they have done
To this man to good.
Take him on board;
Take him swiftly home
Where he so longs to be.
Pity him, sir –
Help him, and be spared
The anger of the gods.

NEOPTOLEMOS.
It's easy now to stand by and pity him.
520   But once he's on board, when you're sick of the
        stench
Of his wound, will you be so generous then?

FIRST SAILOR.
Yes, sir. We understand, we accept him.
We'll not change. No one will blame us for that.

NEOPTOLEMOS.
When my men are so kind, so generous,
How can I refuse? If you agree, we sail.
Philoctetes, we'll take you on board.
Go to the ship, as quickly as you can.

O gods, grant us a safe journey – safe
Passage from here, a safe voyage home.

PHILOCTETES.
O blessed light of day. O dear boy ...   530
Dear friends ... how can I prove my gratitude?
Let us go, at once. Let us kiss goodbye
To this place, this dreadful place. I called it home.
Home! How did I bear it? Look for yourself –
The sight alone would frighten other men,
But I had to endure it; I had no choice;
Long suffering taught me patience in the end.

FIRST SAILOR.
Look, my lords: two men, coming from the ship.
One of the crew, sir, and another man,   540
A stranger. What is it? We must wait, and hear.

    Enter a SAILOR *and the* SERVANT *disguised as
    a* TRADER.

TRADER.
Son of Achilles, I found this man on guard,
With two others, beside your ship. I asked him
To tell me where you were, to bring me here.
It was a lucky accident that I found you.
That I happened to anchor here in this bay.

I am the captain of a small merchant-ship.
I am sailing from Troy to Peparethos
To pick up a cargo of wine. When this man said
That he and the others were sailors of yours,   550
I decided to come and tell you the news –
As much as I know – news you may thank me for.

Of course, I could have sailed on without a word.
But you know nothing of what is happening,
What the Greek generals are planning to do –
No, more than planning: what they are doing now.

NEOPTOLEMOS.
Thank you for your kindness, sir. I'll not
Be ungrateful. What is it? What is your news?   560

TRADER.
    They are sending warships to fetch you back.
    Phoinix is in command, and Theseus' sons.

NEOPTOLEMOS.
    To fetch me back? By persuasion, or force?

TRADER.
    My lord, I can't say. I've told you all I know.

NEOPTOLEMOS.
    Phoinix, and Theseus' sons. The orders came
    From the generals themselves, the sons of Atreus?

TRADER.
    My lord, they're on their way. They'll soon be here.

NEOPTOLEMOS.
    Where was Odysseus? Why was he so slow
    To volunteer? He can't have been afraid!

TRADER.
570   When I left port, he had already sailed
    With Diomedes, to fetch another man.

NEOPTOLEMOS.
    Oh yes? And who has Odysseus gone to fetch?

TRADER.
    His name was – no! Wait! Who is that man there?
    Lower your voice; whisper. Don't let him hear.

NEOPTOLEMOS.
    He is the famous Philoctetes, son of Poias.

TRADER.
    No more, then! Ask me no more! Get clear away
    From the island. Get clear while you still can!

PHILOCTETES.
    Neoptolemos, what is it? Who is this man?
    What are you bargaining behind my back?

NEOPTOLEMOS.
580   He has more to say. And whatever it is,
    He can say it openly, for us both to hear.

TRADER.
   No, Neoptolemos! I'm a poor man, sir;
   I make my living supplying the army;
   If you tell them ... if they get to hear of it ...

NEOPTOLEMOS.
   I am the sworn enemy of the sons of Atreus.
   He hates them too, and therefore is my friend.
   You came to do me a kindness. Do it, then:
   Don't hide what you know. Tell us everything.

TRADER.
   Take care, my lord.

NEOPTOLEMOS.
   I'm not afraid of them.

TRADER.
   It was your own choice.

NEOPTOLEMOS.
   It was my own choice. Speak.   590

TRADER.
   It's this. The two men I told you of,
   Lord Odysseus and Diomedes son of Tydeus –
   This is the man they have sailed to fetch.
   The whole Greek army heard Odysseus swear
   To bring him back, by persuasion or force.
   He made a solemn promise, before the gods:
   He's sure of himself, more than anyone alive.

NEOPTOLEMOS.
   What made them turn their minds to him,
   The generals, after all these years? How can
   He help them now? They marooned him, banished
      him –   600
   What do they want with him now? Have the gods
   Who punish wickedness stirred them at last?

TRADER.
   I'll tell you, everything as it happened.
   There was a noble prophet, Helenos,
   Son of King Priam of Troy. One dark night

The man no good is ever spoken of,
Odysseus, went out alone and captured him
By trickery. A glittering prize! He brought
Him back, and showed him to all the Greeks.

610   Then Helenos began to prophesy.
Of all the things he told them, this was the first:
The city of Troy, he said, would never be theirs
Unless they could persuade this man, Philoctetes,
To leave the island and go back to them.

When he heard that, Odysseus said at once
That he was the man to do it: he would fetch
Philoctetes back, and parade him there
For everyone to see. He thought the man
Would come back by choice; but if not, he said,
He would bring him by force. And if he failed
He would forfeit his own life, his own neck.

620   There, Neoptolemos, you've heard it all.
I advise you to get away now, at once –
You and anyone else you care about.

PHILOCTETES.
So he's sworn to persuade me back? To parade me
In front of them? Odysseus, the plague of Greece!
If I was dead, a corpse in the underworld,
He'd not persuade me back. He will not now.

TRADER.
Well, that's as may be. I must go back, now,
To my ship. May the gods send you all you need.

Exit TRADER.

PHILOCTETES.
Does he really think he can persuade me back?
Does he think he can gentle me with words
630   Into that ship, back to those Greeks? No!
Sooner than him, I'd listen to the snake
That destroyed me, that poisoned away my foot.
But he'll say anything, dare anything.
Neoptolemos, hurry. He'll soon be here.
A whole ocean must separate our ships.

Let us go, now: haste when the time is right
Eases the journey, brings peace and rest at last.

NEOPTOLEMOS.
No, we must wait for the wind. When it changes
We can sail. It's blowing against us now.   640

PHILOCTETES.
When you're running from danger, all winds help.

NEOPTOLEMOS.
No. It's against us. And against them too.

PHILOCTETES.
Against them? What wind has ever stopped
Pirates, criminals, from hunting their prey?

NEOPTOLEMOS.
If that's what you want, we'll sail at once.
Is there anything you need, inside the cave?

PHILOCTETES.
There isn't much – a few necessities.

NEOPTOLEMOS.
Necessities? The ship is well supplied.

PHILOCTETES.
One thing above all: a herb I have found
To poultice the wound and ease the pain.   650

NEOPTOLEMOS.
Go and fetch it, then. Is there anything else?

PHILOCTETES.
The arrows. I must count them, and check that none
Have been left for anyone else to find.

NEOPTOLEMOS.
Is that the famous bow, there in your hand?

PHILOCTETES.
There are no others. Yes, this is the bow.

NEOPTOLEMOS.
May I look at it closer? The bow of the gods!
May I handle it, and pay it my respects?

PHILOCTETES.
My dear boy, you know that it, and all I have,
Are at your service. You have only to ask.

NEOPTOLEMOS.
660   Only to ask ... If what I want is right
In the eyes of the gods, I'll ask for it.
But if it's wrong – well then, let it go.

PHILOCTETES.
You're right to respect the gods. What you ask
Is allowed. You have given me back my life;
You are taking me home to my native land,
To my dear father and the friends I love;
My enemies trampled me – you have raised me up.

Take the bow. Touch it, handle it. Now
Give it back. There. Now you can boast
That you and I are the only living men
To touch it. It is a reward for kindness:
670   My kindness to another, and now yours to me.

NEOPTOLEMOS.
My dear friend, thank you. A man who understands
How to reward kindness with kindness – that man
Is a friend beyond price. Now, go inside.

PHILOCTETES.
Come with me. Help me. Let me lean on your arm.

Exeunt PHILOCTETES *and* NEOPTOLEMOS.

SAILORS.
One other, one other only,
Has suffered so:
Ixion, bound to a wheel of fire.
He slept with Hera, Zeus' queen,
And he was punished.
680   But this man is innocent:
All his life he has lived
With justice among the just.
Why has he deserved such pain?

How has he endured such pain,
A life of tears, alone
By the breakers on the shore?
There was no one else: no one
To hear the cripple's groans
As the sickness gnawed him;   690
No one to gather soothing herbs
When scalding pus oozed
From his ulcers, his gangrened foot.
He crept, he crawled
Like a helpless child
Torn from its nurse's arms.

When the jaws of his pain
Parted a little, and set him free,
He crept out to look for food.
No seeds were his, no fruits   700
Of the bountiful earth,
Such as industrious farmers
Gather and store.
His was the meagre prey
His bow brought down
To feed his belly then.   710

First hunger, then thirst:
For ten long years
No taste of the wine
That brings us joy.
Instead, when he spied
A stagnant pool,
He stooped and drank.

Now he has met, at last,
A man of honour   720
Who will lift him up
To his old, high place.
In a fast ship
Butting the waves
He will take him home.

Home! Where nymphs play
By the river banks

Of Spercheius, and above
On the high hills
Heracles rules,
A man made god
In holy fire.

NEOPTOLEMOS *and* PHILOCTETES *re-enter*.

NEOPTOLEMOS.
730   Come on. Hurry. Why are you standing there dumb?
You're like a man thunderstruck. What's happened?

PHILOCTETES.
Oh!

NEOPTOLEMOS.
What is it?

PHILOCTETES.
It's all right. Go ahead, child.

NEOPTOLEMOS.
Is it the old agony, the old wound?

PHILOCTETES.
No, no. It's all right. It's better now.
O gods!

NEOPTOLEMOS.
Why are you groaning, and calling on the gods?

PHILOCTETES.
Oh gods, help me. Help me, heal me now.
Ah!

NEOPTOLEMOS.
740   What's the matter? Tell me. If you're in such pain
Tell me. What reason is there for hiding it?

PHILOCTETES.
You're right. There's no use hiding it.
I'm on the rack, Neoptolemos. The pain
Twists ... gouges ... tears me alive. O my child
Neoptolemos, I beg you, in the name of god,
Draw your sword, if you have it. Cut, here ...
Cut off this foot ... even if I die of it ...
750   Neoptolemos, please ...

NEOPTOLEMOS.
This agony, so suddenly – these groans and cries –
Is it some new attack? What has brought it on?

PHILOCTETES.
O my boy ...

NEOPTOLEMOS.
Yes?

PHILOCTETES.
My boy, my child ...

NEOPTOLEMOS.
What is it?

PHILOCTETES.
Can't you see? Can't you understand?

NEOPTOLEMOS.
I see how it tortures you.

PHILOCTETES.
Tortures me ... destroys me. Help me ... Oh help
    me.

NEOPTOLEMOS.
How?

PHILOCTETES.
Don't leave me. Don't leave me. Don't be afraid.
The pain ... this attack ... the Fury settles here
From time to time ... on me ... then someone
    else ...

NEOPTOLEMOS.
Philoctetes, I pity you.
I see your suffering, and pity you.   760
How shall I help? Shall I lift you up?

PHILOCTETES.
No. What you asked for before. Take my bow.
Take it. While the pain lasts. Keep it safe for me.
When the attack passes, I fall asleep.
The first sign that it's over. Leave me to sleep,
Don't wake me. If ... those other men come ...
Neoptolemos, I order you in the name of the gods,   770

Don't give them the bow, don't let them take it.
If you do, we both die. You murder us both,
Yourself and the man you have sworn to help.

NEOPTOLEMOS.
It's all right. I'll see to it. No one but you
Or I will touch it. Give it me. Pray for good luck.

PHILOCTETES.
There it is, child. Pray to the jealous gods
That they spare you pain such as they have given
  me,
Suffering like Heracles', who gave me the bow.

NEOPTOLEMOS.
God grant these prayers. And grant us, O god,
780   An easy voyage with a following wind,
Safe journey, wherever our fate is leading us.

PHILOCTETES.
No, child, no. Look! Prayers are useless ...
Wasted ... Look! There, inside ... fresh blood, fresh
  pus
Oozing ... Oh, it's here again ... Oh! Oh!
My foot ... my jailer, my executioner ...
It's here, it's here ...
Oh! Oh!

790   Don't leave me ...

If this were you,
Odysseus ... if it were only you
Transfixed by this agony ... Oh! Oh!
If only the generals ... Agamemnon, Menelaus ...
The sons of Atreus ... this should be their pain ...
Now, forever. Oh! Oh!

O death, I have called you so often –
Come down for me now. Why will you not come?
O my child, O Neoptolemos ... my boy ...
The fire, look! Be kind ... pick me up, and burn me
To ashes ... a funeral pyre. Then they will call me
800   The Lemnian. Please, Neoptolemos! Once I, too,
Did that kindness for Heracles, son of Zeus ...

A kindness, a favour ... he gave me the bow ...
He gave me the bow for it ... it's in your hands ...
O Neoptolemos, answer ...
Neoptolemos ... Neoptolemos ... what is it?

NEOPTOLEMOS.
I suffer for your suffering, in pain for your pain.

PHILOCTETES.
Be comforted. The Fury settles a little
And then flies on. It's not long. Don't leave me ...

NEOPTOLEMOS.
It's all right. I'll stay. There's no doubt of that.

PHILOCTETES.
In god's name, swear! No: I mustn't ask that.

NEOPTOLEMOS.
They won't let me go without you.   810

PHILOCTETES.
My son ... your hand ...

NEOPTOLEMOS.
There. I'll stay.

PHILOCTETES.
Lift me up ...

NEOPTOLEMOS.
Where?

PHILOCTETES.
Up there.

NEOPTOLEMOS.
It's empty sky. What are you looking at?

PHILOCTETES.
Let me go! Let me go!

NEOPTOLEMOS.
What is it?

PHILOCTETES.
Don't touch me! I'm dying. Don't touch me!

NEOPTOLEMOS.
Calm ... calm ... There.

PHILOCTETES.
O earth, mother earth, receive me. I'm dying.
I'll never stand up again. Twisted ... a
820   cripple ... sick ...

NEOPTOLEMOS.
His head is drooping. Soon, he will sleep.
He's covered in sweat; a dark trickle
Of clean blood is running from his foot.
Leave him now. Leave him to sleep in peace.

SAILORS.
Sleep that knows no pain,
No suffering, answer our prayers.
Breathe over us, blessed lord.
830   His eyes are closed:
Breathe over him rest and peace.
Come, sleep, and heal his pain.

FIRST SAILOR.
Now, sir, see where you stand.
What's to be done? What plan
Is best? The man's asleep:
What are we waiting for?
We know what to do –
We must do it, now.

NEOPTOLEMOS.
He can't hear us. The bow is a glittering prize –
840   But without him, if we sail without him, it's nothing.
His is the crown; the gods say he must be fetched;
How can we leave it half-done – and that half by lies?

FIRST SAILOR.
Sir, you must leave that to the gods.
And, sir, you must speak softly,
You must whisper what you say.
For a sick man's sleep
Is restless, easily disturbed –
Quick to hear, and start awake.

SECOND SAILOR.
  Now, sir, now it's time.
  You must do what must be done.
  Finish it! Win the game!   850
  Think, sir, and you'll see
  That the plan in your mind,
  The other plan, will fail.

THIRD SAILOR.
  The wind's behind us, sir.
  He can see nothing, do nothing –
  Stretched out, asleep in the sun.
  He doesn't move: hands, feet still.   860
  You might think he was dead.
  Sir, now it's time.
  No risk, no fear –
  Surely it's time.

NEOPTOLEMOS.
  Be quiet! Fool! Look: he's stirring.
  He's opening his eyes. He's awake.

PHILOCTETES.
  Bright sunlight ... I've been asleep. And you ...
  My friends ... you waited, against all hope.
  My son ... my dear boy ... I'd never have dared
    hope
  That you'd feel such pity, such friendly care ...
  That you'd wait, and help. The noble generals,   870
  The sons of Atreus, were not so long-suffering.

  You're a fine boy, the son of a noble father,
  And so you put up with it: the groaning,
  The smell, everything. You put up with it.

  And now the attack is over. The pain has gone,
  And the gods have given me a little rest.
  Lift me up, Neoptolemos, lift me up.
  When the dizziness clears and I can walk,   880
  We'll go to the ship, and set sail at once.

NEOPTOLEMOS.
So ill, and so soon recovered! My dear friend,
I'm glad. You were so tortured, at the height
Of the attack, I thought you were sure to die.
Let me help you up. Or else, if you prefer,
My men will carry you: they'll do as we say.

PHILOCTETES.
Neoptolemos, thank you. Help me up:
890   I'll walk. I'll not trouble them yet. The smell
Of my wound will be enough to bear on board.

NEOPTOLEMOS.
Just as you say. Stand up ... take hold of my arm.

PHILOCTETES.
I think I'll be able to stand again ... There.

NEOPTOLEMOS.
O Zeus! How can I bear it! What shall I do?

PHILOCTETES.
Neoptolemos, what is it? What do you mean?

NEOPTOLEMOS.
How can I tell you? How can I explain?

PHILOCTETES.
Explain what? I don't understand.

NEOPTOLEMOS.
There's no more choice. You must be told.

PHILOCTETES.
900   Must be told what? Is my sickness so foul,
So corrupt, that you're leaving me behind?

NEOPTOLEMOS.
The corruptness, the foulness, are here in me.
I chose to do wrong. I betrayed myself.

PHILOCTETES.
You helped a man who needed help. So like
Your father! How have you betrayed yourself?

NEOPTOLEMOS.
I chose to do wrong. Soon you'll understand.

PHILOCTETES.
All you've done is good. Your words make me afraid.

NEOPTOLEMOS.
Zeus, what can I do? To be a traitor, twice!
Shall I say nothing and hide it – or tell more lies?

PHILOCTETES.
Neoptolemos! Surely you don't intend 910
To leave me here, to leave me and sail away?

NEOPTOLEMOS.
If only I could! You have to come with me.
That's the truth, that's the torment I have to bear.

PHILOCTETES.
What do you mean, child? I still don't understand.

NEOPTOLEMOS.
Listen, then. It's this. You must sail back to Troy,
To the Greeks, to the army of the sons of Atreus ...

PHILOCTETES.
It's not true! It must be a lie!

NEOPTOLEMOS.
It's true. But listen ... let me explain ...

PHILOCTETES.
What else have you planned for me?

NEOPTOLEMOS.
My orders are these: to rescue you from here
And take you back to sack the land of Troy. 920

PHILOCTETES.
And what's why you came here?

NEOPTOLEMOS.
Philoctetes, I had no choice.

PHILOCTETES.
No choice? Murderer! Stranger! Give me the bow!

NEOPTOLEMOS.
I have my orders. I must obey.

PHILOCTETES.
No fire, no monster of hell, no foul scheme
Festering in the mind, is worse than you.
You tricked me, you cheated me. The man you
    helped,
930   The man who trusted you. Trusted you – for this!

You've stolen my bow, my life. I beg you,
On my knees I beg you, give it back.
By the gods you hold dear, give me back my life.

No. He'll not answer. He turns away.
He'll not give it back.

O rocks, hills, lairs of the mountain beasts,
Harbours and headlands, I cry aloud to you.
There's no one else. Hear me! Hear me!
940   Hear what Achilles' son has done to me.

He swore he'd take me home – he's taking me
To Troy. He held out his hand – and took my bow,
My sacred bow, the gift of Heracles son of Zeus.
He wants to brandish it in front of all
The Greeks, and boast how he won it, how he
    captured me
In all my strength. He has overpowered a ghost,
A shadow, an empty husk. And even so
He could only win by trickery. If I'd had
My former strength, he'd never have taken me.

You tricked me, destroyed me. What shall I do?
950   Give it back. I beg you, give it back ...
Be your own true self again. My boy, my child ...

Still he won't answer. Still he looks away.
Now I've nothing. O my cave, my double cave,
Your dear master's here, unarmed, alone.
I'll come inside; I'll wither and die.
No birds on the wing, no mountain beasts, will fall
To these arrows now. I'll die, alone,
A feast of flesh for the ones I feasted on,
The prey of my prey, my blood for their blood.

He seemed so honest, so innocent of guilt.   960
I trusted him, and he took my life away.

Will you change your mind? Will you pity me?
Then die in misery! Die a traitor's death!

FIRST SAILOR.
Sir, what shall we do? You must decide.
Shall we do as he begs us, or sail for Troy?

NEOPTOLEMOS.
I'm filled with a strange kind of pity.
Ever since I met him, I've pitied him.

PHILOCTETES.
Have mercy, my child. In god's name, pity me.
Who'll honour you for trickery and lies?

NEOPTOLEMOS.
What shall I do? What choice is left for me?
Why did I leave Scyros, and sail for Troy?   970

PHILOCTETES.
You're not wicked: you were trained in wickedness
By those others, those criminals. Leave it to them!
Give me my bow, and sail away from here.

NEOPTOLEMOS (*to the* FIRST SAILOR).
What do you think, friend? What's your advice?

    Enter ODYSSEUS.

ODYSSEUS.
Traitor! Coward! Give me the bow!

PHILOCTETES.
Odysseus! Is it Odysseus?

ODYSSEUS.
Odysseus, yes.   980

PHILOCTETES.
Then I'm betrayed, I'm dead. You plotted this:
This trickery of yours, to steal the bow.

ODYSSEUS.
Of course. The whole plan, every detail, was mine.

PHILOCTETES.
Boy! Quickly! The bow! Give me the bow!

ODYSSEUS.
He can't, whether he wants to or not. And where
The bow goes, you go. My men will see to that.

PHILOCTETES.
Your men? Have you sunk so low?
Have you brought soldiers here, to lay hands on *me*?

ODYSSEUS.
They're waiting. Will you come willingly, or not?

PHILOCTETES.
In the name of Lemnos, forged by the hand of god!
Am I a prisoner, to be dragged away by force?

ODYSSEUS.
Zeus is in command here, Zeus king of the gods.
990   I'm only his servant. This is his will.

PHILOCTETES.
Will you try to make Zeus your accomplice now?
Must he protect you? Must he lie for you?

ODYSSEUS.
Zeus does not lie. He commands. We must obey.

PHILOCTETES.
I won't go.

ODYSSEUS.
You must. There is no other choice.

PHILOCTETES.
O Zeus, was it for this that I was born?
Philoctetes son of Poias – to be a slave?

ODYSSEUS.
Not so. You're not a slave. You're brave, among
The brave: Philoctetes, Sacker of Troy.

PHILOCTETES.
I refuse! Do what you like to me.
1000   The cliff ... the headland, the precipice ... let me
go!

ODYSSEUS.
Go? Why?

PHILOCTETES.
Sooner than give way, I'll throw myself down,
And smash myself to pieces on the rocks.

ODYSSEUS.
Hold him, two of you. Don't let him escape.

PHILOCTETES.
Hunted, netted, trapped like an animal
For want of my dear bow ... and by Odysseus!
You can think no decent or honest thought;
You stole up on me, like a thief in the night;
You set a trap, and used this boy as bait.

What made you choose him? I didn't know him,   1010
He was a stranger. He's like me, not you –
He believes in justice and honesty. All he did
Was obey orders, and now he is suffering:
He betrayed me, and betrayed himself as well.
He was an innocent child: your serpent's tongue,
Sharp in the shadows, taught him his trade of lies.

And now you want *me*! You marooned me here
Alone; you deserted me; you left me to die –
And now you come back, to drag me away in chains.

Die! Die by the gods!
I have prayed that prayer so often. But the gods
Are deaf. You live and laugh. And I am in pain,   1020
A tortured wretch, lost in a sea of pain –
While you laugh, you and the sons of Atreus,
Your masters, the generals of all the Greeks.

You had to be tricked, *you* had to be forced
To accept the yoke, to sail with them to Troy.
I came willingly, *I* sailed with seven ships –
For this! To be robbed, to be thrown aside!
Was it your work or theirs? Each blames the other.
And now what will you do? Where will you take me?
   Why?
I am nothing. To you, I have long been dead.   1030

Have you forgotten my foot? The stench of it?
If I come with you to Troy, how will you pray,
How will you sacrifice? Have you forgotten?
That was your excuse for leaving me here before.

Die! Die in agony!
If the gods are just, die for your crimes to me!
Are they not just? Did they not spur you on
To launch your ship, and sail to fetch me home?

1040   O gods of my native land,
Punish them! Punish them! If you pity me,
If the time is right, rise up and punish them.
My life is torture — but if I see them dead,
If you punish them, I'll think my pain is cured.

FIRST SAILOR.
Stubborn words, Odysseus — stubborn words
From a stubborn man. He'll not give way.

ODYSSEUS.
I could answer him. There are many arguments.
But now is not the time. I'll say just this:
I make myself the man each occasion demands.
1050   When honesty and justice are required,
I am the justest, most honest man alive.
But in everything I do, I fight to win.
Except this once. This once, I give way to you.

Let him go. He's free.
He can stay on the island. We have the bow —
We don't need you. Prince Teucer is with us still,
A skilled bowman — and I am there myself,
As clever as you, I think, at archery.
1060   We don't need you. Stay here! Enjoy your island!

It's time to go. Perhaps this bow, this prize
Of his, will bring me the honour reserved for him.

PHILOCTETES.
You'll take my bow? You'll take it, and flaunt
Yourself with it, in front of all the Greeks?

ODYSSEUS.
There's nothing more to say. It's time to go.

PHILOCTETES.
    Son of Achilles, will you not answer me?
    Will you sail away, and leave me without a word?

ODYSSEUS.
    On, Neoptolemos! So decent, so honest –
    If you once look at him, we lose the game!

PHILOCTETES.
    My friends, pity me. Don't leave me here alone.   1070

FIRST SAILOR.
    We obey his orders. It's for him to say.

NEOPTOLEMOS.
    I know I'll be called soft-hearted, easy.
    But you can do as he asks. You can stay here
    While the ship's prepared, and sacrifice
    Is made for a fair wind. Perhaps he'll change
    His mind; perhaps he'll understand at last.

    Lord Odysseus and I will go on ahead.
    We'll signal when it's time. Come then, at once.   1080

      ODYSSEUS, NEOPTOLEMOS *and their sailors*
      go.

PHILOCTETES.
    Rock-tomb, rock-womb,
    Sun-warm, ice-cold,
    Home of my misery
    Forever, home
    Till the day I die.
    Weep for me, echo my grief.
    How must I live?
    Where must I turn   1090
    For food, for hope
    To nourish me?
    To the birds above?
    They fly free
    On the wind's wings:
    All my strength is gone.

FIRST SAILOR.
You chose this fate;
You burdened yourself.
It was not imposed
By a greater power.
You had a choice,
1100   And you chose this fate.

PHILOCTETES.
Distracted with grief
And torn with pain;
A hermit, stripped
Of all company
Till the day I die.
Stripped of my strength,
1110   The swift arrows
That brought me food.
Dark, twisted words
Choked my mind.
If only that man,
That cunning man,
Shared all my pain,
My endless pain.

FIRST SAILOR.
This is no trick,
Sir: this is fate.
We're not to blame.
1120   Turn your curses away,
Curse someone else.
We're your friends.

PHILOCTETES.
On the shore, by the grey sea,
He sits and laughs at me.
In his hands he waves my bow.
The bow of my life, the bow
That nourished me, the bow
No other man has held but me.

O my dear bow, stolen away
From the loving hands that held you,

If you could see, if you could feel,
How you would pity me: 1130
Heracles' friend, your old master,
Your master no more.

You have a new master now,
New hands to string, to bend, to fire.
Look at his face, and see deceit,
Injustice, treachery – my enemy,
And all the teeming agony
His cunning has made for me.

FIRST SAILOR.
 A person should speak only the truth: 1140
 No slander, no venom of the tongue.
 Odysseus was sent here, one man
 By many. He was obeying orders;
 What he did was a service,
 A service to help his friends.

PHILOCTETES.
 Birds of the air; wild beasts,
 Eyes gleaming in the hills
 Where I hunted you, now you are safe!
 Start up from your lairs and flee
 No more. My hands are empty,   1150
 My weapons, my arrows, gone.

There is no more terror now,
No more danger. The island
Is yours: walk freely
Where you will. Soon
It will be time to feast,
To glut yourselves on my rotting flesh,
My blood for yours.

My life will be over soon.
Soon I will die. For where,
And how, will I find my food?
Can a man eat empty air?   1160
Mother Earth, who feeds all men,
Gives me no nourishment.

FIRST SAILOR.
Come nearer: we are your friends.
What we say is good advice.
Remember: it's in your own power
To change your fate, to rid yourself
Of this burden of plague,
This suffering that eats your life.

PHILOCTETES.
1170   Must you torture me still?
Kindest of friends,
Must you open the wound
And torment me still?

FIRST SAILOR.
What have we done?

PHILOCTETES.
Why, why did you come?
Why did you ever hope
To take me back
To that detested Troy?

FIRST SAILOR.
We think it best.

PHILOCTETES.
Leave me! Leave me now!

FIRST SAILOR.
Very well. Your words
Are welcome. Let's go, men:
1180   The ship is waiting.

PHILOCTETES.
Don't go! In the name
Of the anger of Zeus, don't go!

FIRST SAILOR.
Be calm.

PHILOCTETES.
In god's name, wait.

FIRST SAILOR.
  For what?

PHILOCTETES.
  Pain ... pain ...
  Demon pain ...
  Twisting, torturing ...
  My foot ...
  How can I bear it?
  Why can't I die?
  O my friends, come back.   1190

FIRST SAILOR.
  Have you changed your mind?
  What must we do?

PHILOCTETES.
  Don't be angry.
  I was delirious.
  The jagged pain ...
  I said ... I didn't mean ...

FIRST SAILOR.
  Come with us. Do as we ask.

PHILOCTETES.
  No! Not if Zeus himself
  In a flash of white fire
  Scorches me, sears me to the bone.
  Topple, Troy, and crush them,   1200
  My enemies who took me
  A cripple, and left me here.
  O my friends, my dear friends, if only ...

FIRST SAILOR.
  What do you ask?

PHILOCTETES.
  Give me an axe, a sword, a spear ...

FIRST SAILOR.
  What new madness ... ?

PHILOCTETES.
>   Head ... arms ... hack them,
>   Butcher them ...
>   I must die now.

FIRST SAILOR.
>   Why?

PHILOCTETES.
1210   I must find him ... my father ...

FIRST SAILOR.
>   Where?

PHILOCTETES.
>   In Hades ... in the underworld,
>   Far from this light.
>   O my native land,
>   If only I could come home ...
>   Cursed, since the day
>   I left the holy river, and came
>   To the Greeks, my enemies,
>   To help them. No more ... no more ...

>   *Exit* PHILOCTETES.

FIRST SAILOR.
>   We should have gone to the ship long ago.
>   But here comes Neoptolemos – and Odysseus with
1220   him.

>   NEOPTOLEMOS *and* ODYSSEUS *re-enter.*

ODYSSEUS.
>   Where are you going? Why are you hurrying back?

NEOPTOLEMOS.
>   I did wrong before. Now I must set things right.

ODYSSEUS.
>   You're talking nonsense. What wrong did you do?

NEOPTOLEMOS.
>   I took orders from you and the other Greeks –

ODYSSEUS.
>   And you call that wrong? What was wrong in that?

NEOPTOLEMOS.
  I used trickery and lies to cheat a man.

ODYSSEUS.
  What do you mean now? What madness is this?

NEOPTOLEMOS.
  No madness. A debt. A debt I mean to pay.   1230

ODYSSEUS.
  What are you saying? You intend to give – ?

NEOPTOLEMOS.
  I intend to give back the bow I stole.

ODYSSEUS.
  You can't mean it! To give back the bow – !

NEOPTOLEMOS.
  I stole it, and now I intend to give it back.

ODYSSEUS.
  Is this a joke? In god's name, is this a joke?

NEOPTOLEMOS.
  It's no joke. I mean it. It's the truth.

ODYSSEUS.
  You'll really do it?

NEOPTOLEMOS.
  Are three times not enough?

ODYSSEUS.
  Once was enough.

NEOPTOLEMOS.
  Then there's no more to say.   1240

ODYSSEUS.
  You won't do it. You'll be stopped.

NEOPTOLEMOS.
  Stopped? Who by?

ODYSSEUS.
  The soldiers of Greece, and among them me.

NEOPTOLEMOS.
The wise Odysseus! You talk like a fool.

ODYSSEUS.
You're the fool, in all you do or say.

NEOPTOLEMOS.
Fool or not, what I intend is just.

ODYSSEUS.
Just? To give him back this prize – the prize
I helped you win?

NEOPTOLEMOS.
The prize you helped me steal.
I cheated; I lied. I must set things right.

ODYSSEUS.
1250   Aren't you afraid? The army of the Greeks –

NEOPTOLEMOS.
My army is justice. *You* should be afraid.

ODYSSEUS.
And if I use force?

NEOPTOLEMOS.
My mind's made up.

ODYSSEUS.
If I forget the Trojans, and fight with *you* . . . ?

NEOPTOLEMOS.
The choice is made.

ODYSSEUS.
Here is my sword.

NEOPTOLEMOS.
And mine. I'm ready. Will you stand, and fight?

ODYSSEUS.
No, I'll not kill you. I'll go back to them,
And give them my report. They'll deal with you.

NEOPTOLEMOS.
Wise Odysseus! Common sense at last!
1260   Remember this, and keep clear of trouble.

ODYSSEUS *goes*.

NEOPTOLEMOS.
Philoctetes, Philoctetes, son of Poias.

PHILOCTETES.
Who's there? Who's calling, outside the cave?

Enter PHILOCTETES.

Neoptolemos! What evil brings you again?
Have you brought new pain to top the old?

NEOPTOLEMOS.
Don't be afraid. Listen. Hear what I say.

PHILOCTETES.
I listened before. Honeyed words! I listened,
I trusted you – and you brought me to this!

NEOPTOLEMOS.
And if I say I've had a change of heart?   1270

PHILOCTETES.
A change of heart? You were like this before –
Until you stole my bow. You smiled – and lied.

NEOPTOLEMOS.
I'm not lying now. I want to ask you this:
Will you stay here, endure it to the end,
Or will you sail with us?

PHILOCTETES.
Enough! You waste words.
I'll not listen. I'll hear no more arguments.

NEOPTOLEMOS.
Your mind is fixed?

PHILOCTETES.
More firmly than you know.

NEOPTOLEMOS.
If I could have persuaded you, I would.
But if all my words are wasted –

PHILOCTETES.
Every one!   1280
You can say nothing that pleases me, nothing

I want to hear. You stole my life, my bow —
And now you bring me arguments instead!
That Prince Achilles should father such a son!
Die, all of you! The sons of Atreus first,
Odysseus next, and last Neoptolemos!

NEOPTOLEMOS.
You can save your curses. Here is your bow.

PHILOCTETES.
What did you say? Is this another lie?

NEOPTOLEMOS.
No lie. I swear by the honour of Zeus himself.

PHILOCTETES.
1290   Words of happiness ... if only they're true ...

NEOPTOLEMOS.
They're true. This is the proof. Take your bow.

ODYSSEUS' *voice is heard from offstage.*

ODYSSEUS.
No! I forbid it, in the name of god!
For the sake of the army, for the sake
Of the sons of Atreus, give me the bow!

PHILOCTETES.
Odysseus! That was Odysseus' voice.

ODYSSEUS (*entering*).
Odysseus, yes. And I am here: I have come
To take you by force to the plain of Troy,
Whether Achilles' son agrees, or not.

PHILOCTETES.
One arrow will stop these boasts.

NEOPTOLEMOS.
1300   Philoctetes, no!

PHILOCTETES.
Let me go, boy. In god's name, let me go.

NEOPTOLEMOS.
I can't.

        Exit ODYSSEUS.

PHILOCTETES.
Why did you stop me from killing him –
My enemy, the man I most hate in Greece?

NEOPTOLEMOS.
Enemy or friend, he's not for us to kill.

PHILOCTETES.
I tell you this: those leaders of the Greeks,
Those glib spokesmen, are brave enough with words,
But when it comes to fighting they cower, they
    cringe.

NEOPTOLEMOS.
He's gone. You have your bow. There's no more
    cause
For anger. I helped you: I'm no more to blame.

PHILOCTETES.
Neoptolemos, son of Achilles, you have shown   1310
The true spirit of your father, the finest of all
The heroes of Greece, alive or among the dead.

NEOPTOLEMOS.
Philoctetes, thank you. You give high praise
To my father and myself. Give one thing more:
A fair hearing for what I have to ask.
All mortals must bear whatever fate the gods
Allot them, good or bad – but when a man
Brings suffering on himself, and clings to it
As you do, no one forgives or pities him.   1320

You're like a savage; you take no advice;
When people offer you a friendly word
You spit with hate, as if they meant you harm.
Even so, I will speak. In your name, lord Zeus!
Hear what I say: imprint it on your mind.

The sickness you are suffering came from a god.
You strayed inside the sacred shrine of Chryse,
And disturbed the hidden snake, its guardian.
And now you are poisoned, you will find no cure
While the sun sets and rises, rises and sets,   1330
Until you come to Troy of your own free will.

We have doctors there, sons of Asclepius,
And they will cure your wound. Then, with this bow
And my help, you'll topple the towers of Troy.

I'll tell you how I know that this is true.
There's a prisoner in camp, a man of Troy,
The prophet Helenos. He has prophesied
Plainly that all this will happen – and more,
1340 That Troy will fall before this summer ends.
He'll give his life as forfeit if he lies.

You've heard it all. Give way. Do as I ask.
There are rich rewards: to be called a prince
Of princes, to find healing for your wound,
And this above all, to capture tearful Troy.

PHILOCTETES.
 Detested life, why do you keep me here
In the world above, and not send me down to Hades?
1350 What can I do? Must I reject his words,
The advice of a true friend – or give way to him?
A sick man, a cripple – if I go back,
How can I face them? What can I say to them?

It's not resentment for the past that stings,
But fear of the future. I understand these men.
Once the first wickedness is hatched, their minds
1360 Breed nothing but wickedness, nothing but crime.

And you, Neoptolemos: I don't understand.
You have every reason to stay away from Troy,
Not to persuade me back. They wronged you, too:
They plundered your father's arms – Achilles'
  arms! –
And gave them to Odysseus. Must you go back
And fight their battles? Must I fight too?

No, Neoptolemos! Take me home instead;
Go back to Scyros; leave those evil men
To die an evil death. If you help me now
1370 You will earn a double blessing, a double thanks –
Mine and your father's. But if he sees you
Helping those hated men, he'll hate you too.

NEOPTOLEMOS.
I hear what you say. Even so, I beg you:
Trust me, trust the gods. Sail back with me.

PHILOCTETES.
To Troy, to the accursed sons of Atreus?
A helpless cripple – and King Agamemnon?

NEOPTOLEMOS.
To skilful doctors who will heal your foot,
Dry up the ulcers and end your agony.

PHILOCTETES.
Cunning words! You're so full of good advice!   1380

NEOPTOLEMOS.
What I advise is best – for both of us.

PHILOCTETES.
The gods are listening! Are you not ashamed?

NEOPTOLEMOS.
Why should I be ashamed? The advice is good.

PHILOCTETES.
Good for the sons of Atreus, not for me.

NEOPTOLEMOS.
Yes, for you. I'm your friend. I'm helping you.

PHILOCTETES.
You're betraying me, helping my enemies.

NEOPTOLEMOS.
My poor friend, so stubborn, so determined to
suffer.

PHILOCTETES.
I hear my death in every word you say.

NEOPTOLEMOS.
You refuse to listen, refuse to understand.

PHILOCTETES.
This much I understand: they marooned me here.   1390

NEOPTOLEMOS.
They marooned you, and now they'll rescue you.

PHILOCTETES.
I'll never agree to go back to Troy.

NEOPTOLEMOS.
What can I do? You've rejected all
My arguments. Perhaps I should leave you here,
Without more words, to live the life you live
Here on the island, with no one to rescue you.

PHILOCTETES.
If it has to be endured, I'll endure it.
But remember your promise, Neoptolemos:
1400   Your promise to take me home. Oh, do it now!
Forget Troy. We've had pain and tears enough.

NEOPTOLEMOS.
I agree. Let's go.

PHILOCTETES.
Neoptolemos ... you agree?

NEOPTOLEMOS.
Walk with firm steps.

PHILOCTETES.
As firmly as I can.

NEOPTOLEMOS.
The Greeks will punish me.

PHILOCTETES.
Pay them no heed.

NEOPTOLEMOS.
If they attack my country ... ?

PHILOCTETES.
1410   I will be there.

NEOPTOLEMOS.
How will you help?

PHILOCTETES.
With the arrows of Heracles.

NEOPTOLEMOS.
You mean ... ?

PHILOCTETES.
I will drive them away.

NEOPTOLEMOS.
My true friend! My ally!
Kiss Lemnos farewell; come to the ship.

The god HERACLES *enters above.*

HERACLES.
Stop! Philoctetes, son of Poias,
Listen to my words.   1420
You hear, you see,
Heracles son of Zeus.
From the high place
Of Olympos I have come down
To tell you the will of Zeus
And prevent this journey.
Hear me. Hear me now.

Remember my story: my twelve labours,
And my reward, this immortality.
For you, too, there are labours to perform: 1430
For you, too, the rewards are glory and fame.

You will go back with this man to the towers of
    Troy;
You will find doctors there, to heal your wound;
You will be chosen champion of all the Greeks –
And with this bow, my gift, you will kill
Paris of Troy, who caused this suffering.
You will plunder his city, and carry home
Rich tribute, the prize of the battlefield:
Home to Poias, your father and your native land.   1440

Son of Achilles, my words are for your ears too.
Without his help, you will never topple Troy;
Without your help, he too must fall. For you
Are like lions, a pair of lions, joined in the hunt.

I will send doctors to Troy to heal his wound.
The city is doomed to fall, twice, to this bow.
And when you plunder Troy remember this,   1450
This above all: true reverence for the gods.

For nothing is greater in the sight of Zeus
Than reverence. It lives in all men's hearts.
They are mortal, they die; but reverence never dies.

PHILOCTETES.
O voice of god; dear friend
I longed to see again –
I hear, I will obey.

NEOPTOLEMOS.
I, too, hear and obey.

HERACLES.
Lose no more time.
1460 The hour and tide of fate
Are with you. The moment is now.

Exit HERACLES.

PHILOCTETES.
It is time to say a last farewell
To the cave that watched with me;
The spirits of brooks and fields
And the deep, full-throated roar
Where waves boom on the high cliffs;
My cave-shelter, wet with spray
Borne on the driving wind;
The Hill of Hermes, echoing
1470 My tears, my wintry grief.
It is time to leave the pools,
The bubbling streams; time to take
The unlooked-for gift of fate.
O Lemnos, my island, smile on me,
Send me safe sailing; I go
Where great Destiny leads, my friends'
Advice, and the all-powerful god
Who chose what has happened here.

SAILORS.
Gather now, and pray
1480 To the spirits of the sea
To lead us safely home.

Exeunt.

EURIPIDES

Trojan Women

translated by Marianne McDonald

Characters

POSEIDON, god of the sea
ATHENA, goddess of wisdom
HECUBA, queen of Troy
TALTHYBIUS, an army messenger
CASSANDRA, Hecuba's daughter
ANDROMACHE, wife of Hecuba's son Hector
MENELAUS, king of Sparta
HELEN, his wife
CHORUS OF TROJAN CAPTIVES
ASTYANAX, Andromache's son
GREEK SOLDIERS

Troy in ruins is smoking in the background. HECUBA *is lying on the ground.* POSEIDON *appears above her.*

POSEIDON.
 I, Poseidon, have come from the salty sea depths,
 where choruses of Nereids weave elaborate patterns
 in their beautiful dance. Apollo and I built this city's
 stone towers, measuring them carefully inch by inch,
 and never once did my heart falter in its love for this
 Phrygian city, smoking now, sacked, and destroyed
 by Argive spears. Phocian Epeius, the man from
 Parnassus, with Pallas Athena's help, built a horse   10
 pregnant with weapons, and sent it into the city with
 its deadly load. Men in times to come will call it the
 Trojan Horse, the horse that hid the spears of an
 ambush. Now the groves are deserted and the altars
 of the gods drip blood; Priam lies dead at the foot of
 the steps to the altar of Zeus, the defender of homes.
 Phrygian gold and treasures are loaded on the Greek
 ships, only waiting for a favourable wind; the Greeks
 who warred against this city for ten years are eager to
 see their wives and children. I'm defeated also by   20
 Argive Hera and Athena, who destroyed this
 Phrygian people, and I'm leaving this noble city and
 my altars. When cruel desolation seizes a city, belief
 in the gods grows weak and they are no longer
 honoured. Scamander's shore echoes with the
 weeping of the prisoners, allocated to their lords.
 Arcadians will own these, and Thessalians those; the
 leaders of Athens and the sons of Theseus win   30
 others. Those who have not been allotted are under
 these roofs, selected for the army's leaders, and with
 them is Spartan Helen, the daughter of Tyndareus,
 rightly counted one of the prisoners. But if one
 wants to look on misery, it's here to see: Hecuba lying
 in front of the doors, weeping tears for her many
 sorrows. She does not know that her child Polyxena   40
 died pitifully at Achilles' tomb; Priam and her
 children are gone; and Cassandra, whom lord Apollo

drove mad, Agamemnon, with no regard for what is
sacred, will drag to his bed for secret love.

Farewell my city, once prosperous with your
gleaming towers; if Pallas Athena, the daughter of
Zeus, had not destroyed you, you would still be
standing.

Enter ATHENA.

ATHENA.
May we set aside our quarrel, and may I address the
closest relative of my father, you who are great, and
50   honoured among the gods?

POSEIDON.
Yes, lady Athena. The ties between relatives are
tight; they do indeed bind my heart to yours.

ATHENA.
I'm glad you're not angry; I shall tell you something
that concerns us both, lord.

POSEIDON.
Are you bringing some new message from heaven,
perhaps from Zeus, or some other divinity?

ATHENA.
No. It's about Troy, here where we stand; I want us
to join forces and you to give me your help.

POSEIDON.
You've burned her to the ground; now has your
60   anger turned to pity?

ATHENA.
My question first. Will you be my ally and agree to
do what I want?

POSEIDON.
Of course, but I would like to know what you want;
whose side are you on, Greek or Trojan?

ATHENA.
I want to help the Trojans who were my enemies,
and make the Greek army's return home a bitter one.

POSEIDON.
  You're so fickle. Your mind leaps here and there:
  now you hate, and now you love, and both in excess.

ATHENA.
  Did you know that the Greeks violated my shrine?

POSEIDON.
  When Ajax assaulted Cassandra at your altar.   70

ATHENA.
  He was neither punished nor reprimanded by the
  Greeks.

POSEIDON.
  Yes, and they sacked Troy all because of your power.

ATHENA.
  Which I now want to join with yours to punish
  them.

POSEIDON.
  I'm ready to help; what will you do?

ATHENA.
  I want their homecoming to be miserable.

POSEIDON.
  While they are still on land, or out at sea?

ATHENA.
  When they have set sail for home from Ilium, Zeus
  has promised to send rain and thick hail and dark
  squalls from the heavens. He has given me his word
  that he will strike their ships with his thunderbolts
  and burn them to a crisp. You make the Aegean   80
  passage roar with huge waves and dizzying whirl-
  pools; fill the Euboean gulf with corpses, so that for
  the rest of time the Greeks may learn to honour my
  temples and give proper worship to all the gods.

POSEIDON.
  I'll do it. This favour needs no long speech. I shall
  make the Aegean seethe with storms; the shores of
  Myconos, and the Delian shoals, Skyros and
  Lemnos, and the Capherean headlands will be   90

littered with many corpses. Go to Olympus and get
the thunderbolts from your father's own hands, and
watch for the hour when the Greek army cast off
their ropes and set sail.

People are mad to sack cities, temples and tombs,
those holy places for the dead; those who send others
into darkness will soon enough end their own brief
day in night.

Exeunt gods.

HECUBA.
    Lift up your unhappy head,
    Raise your neck from the ground,
100   Troy is no more, no more do we rule.
    Accept the changes destiny brings,
    Sail with the stream, flow with fate,
    Don't oppose the waves of life,
    Just sail on the sea of chance.

    (*Keening, beating her breast with grief.*) *Aiai aiai.*
    What is left but my song of sorrow,
    Lost my country, children and husband?
    The sail is trimmed now,
    Those pretensions of noble ancestors,
    Now I see you were nothing.

110   Why should I be silent? Or not silent?
    Why should I weep?
    In pain I lie on this bed of doom,
    My back stretched on hard stone.
    My head hurts, my temples, my sides,
    I turn this way and that,
    Trying to ease my back, again and again,
    Keeping time with my ceaseless song of sorrow.
120   This is the muse for those in despair,
    That sings their destruction, a song without dance.

    From Greece's safe harbours,
    The prows of the ships,
    With swift beats of oars
    Keeping time to the hated songs of pipes and syrinx,

Sailed to holy Ilium
Over the deep purple sea,
Then docked secure with ropes of Egyptian weave.
You were pursuing the hated   130
Wife of Menelaus, reproach to the Eurotas,
And shame of Castor.
She killed Priam, the sower of fifty sons,
And drove me, Hecuba, into misery.

Such is my grief as I sit here waiting,
On the ground before the tents of Agamemnon.
I am dragged a slave out of my home,   140
An old grey woman, my head scarred with sorrow.
Come you miserable wives of Trojans
Who once bore spears of bronze,
And you daughters, brides of sorrow,
Let us sing our tears for Troy as it burns.
Like a mother of winged birds
I lead the shrill cry;
Not the song of yesterday,
When Priam leaned on his sceptre,   150
And my feet led the dance, tapping out the beat
To honour the Phrygian gods.

Enter SEMI-CHORUS A.

SEMI-CHORUS A.
Hecuba, why did you cry? Baying like a dog?
Have you heard any news? I heard your sad cry
Echo in the tents. Fear shot through our hearts,
We Trojan women waiting inside,
Weeping over our life of slavery.

HECUBA.
The hands of the Greeks are busy now
Readying the oars for the ships.   160

SEMI-CHORUS A.
Oh God, is this what they want? Will I
Sail away so soon from my father's land?

HECUBA.
I don't know, but I suspect the worst.

SEMI-CHORUS A (*keening*).
> *Io io.*
> Sorrow and suffering,
> For you Trojan women,
> Forced into hard labour,
> Driven from your homes;
> The Argives are ready to sail.

HECUBA (*keening*).
> *E e.*
> Do not send out my mad Cassandra,
170   A shameful sight before the Greeks,
> My maenad, who adds more pain to my pains.
> *Io io.*
> Troy, double-doomed Troy,
> You are no more,
> Your desolate people are leaving you,
> We who live, yes, but now as slaves.

> SEMI-CHORUS B *enters*.

SEMI-CHORUS B (*keening*).
> *Oimoi.*
> Terrified I left the tents
> Of Agamemnon when I heard you, Queen.
> Have the Greeks decided to kill us?
> Or are the sailors by the sterns of their ships
180   Ready to man their oars and set sail?

HECUBA.
> O daughters, my sleepless soul
> Is filled with terror.

SEMI-CHORUS B.
> Has some Greek messenger come?
> To whom am I assigned
> To serve as a miserable slave?

HECUBA.
> You won't have long to wait for decisions.

SEMI-CHORUS B.
> *Io io.*
> What Argive, or man from Phthia,

Or islander, will take me far from Troy
To a life of misery?

HECUBA.
Pheu Pheu.   190
Where will I, an old grey woman,
Go to be a slave?
A useless old drone,
Stand-in for a corpse,
Pale ghost of the dead?
Aiai aiai.
Will I be a doorkeeper,
Or nurse to some child,
I, who was honoured as Queen of Troy?

SEMI-CHORUS B.
Aiai, aiai.
What pitiful song
Can equal this outrage?
And I must leave my Trojan weaving,
Where I worked the shuttle back and forth.   200
For the last time
Shall I look on my dead children.
For the last time.
But there is worse to come,
Serving some Greek bed:
I curse that night, that fate.
Or shall I, a slave, draw water
From the sacred spring Pirene?
I'd like to go to Theseus' fair and famed land,
But not to the swirling Eurotas   210
That nurtured hated Helen,
To be a slave to Menelaus
The destroyer of Troy.

My second choice after
The god-haunted holy land of Theseus
Would be glorious Peneus,
Just before you reach Olympus.
I've heard of its rich harvests,
Flowers, and sweet fruits.

220   Perhaps the land of Hephaestus,
         That faces Phoenicia,
         And Etna, the mother of Sicily's mountains,
         Whose strong people win victory crowns.
         Or the land near the Ionian sea,
         Into which flows the stream Krathis,
         That makes hair golden, like a flame,
         And nourishes and enriches
         That land of brave men.

230   Look! A herald from the Greek army is hurrying this
         way with the latest news. What word does he bring?
         What will he say to us who are slaves of Greeks?

              Enter TALTHYBIUS, *soldiers with him.*

TALTHYBIUS.
    Hecuba, you know me, Talthybius. I've often come
    to you from the Greek camp, bringing messages to
    Troy. I have a new message for you now.

HECUBA.
    Here it is, women. The moment we dreaded.

TALTHYBIUS.
    Yes. You have been assigned masters by lot, if that is
240 what you dreaded.

HECUBA.
    Aiai.
    Is it a city of Thessaly, or Phthia? Tell me. Or
    Thebes, Cadmus' land?

TALTHYBIUS.
    Each woman has a different master.

HECUBA.
    Who gets whom? What woman of Troy will ever find
    happiness?

TALTHYBIUS.
    Ask about them one by one, not altogether.

HECUBA.
    Tell me. Who got my daughter, my poor Cassandra?

TALTHYBIUS.
She was lord Agamemnon's special choice.

HECUBA.
A slave to his Spartan wife Clytemnestra?
Io moi moi.   250

TALTHYBIUS.
To share his bed in secret.

HECUBA.
But she is a virgin dedicated to Apollo, the golden-
haired, who blessed her with a celibate life.

TALTHYBIUS.
That very sanctity made him desire her.

HECUBA.
Daughter, throw your holy keys away, and the
sacred wreaths you wear.

TALTHYBIUS.
Don't you realise how fortunate she is to share a
king's bed?

HECUBA.
And my other daughter – the one you took from me?   260
Where is she?

TALTHYBIUS.
You mean Polyxena. Is that your question?

HECUBA.
Yes. Who's her master?

TALTHYBIUS.
It was decided she would watch over Achilles' tomb.

HECUBA.
More woe for me. I gave birth to her so she could
watch over a tomb. Please tell me, is this some Greek
custom, or law?

TALTHYBIUS.
Consider your daughter fortunate. She's better off.

HECUBA.
What are you saying? She's alive, isn't she?

TALTHYBIUS.

270   It's all worked out for her, and she's free from care.

HECUBA.

And poor Andromache, the wife of Hector, our
leader in battle. Who drew her?

TALTHYBIUS.

Achilles' son took her as his prize.

HECUBA.

And this grey old lady, who leans on a walking-stick,
who am I to serve?

TALTHYBIUS.

Ithacan Odysseus won you to be his slave.

HECUBA.

E e.
280   Tear your hair, and rake your cheeks.
Io moi, moi.
Allotted to serve that filthy cheat,
Enemy of justice, law-breaking beast.
His double tongue turns an argument
This way and that
Until you don't know where you are,
Making foe a friend, and a friend foe.
290   Weep for me, women, my life is ended;
No worse luck could be imagined.

CHORUS.

At least you know what will happen to you.
What about us? What Greek will take us,
And where are we to go?

TALTHYBIUS (*addressing* SOLDIERS).

Go, men, bring Cassandra out to me quickly; I'm to
deliver her to our leader; after that I'll bring the
other prisoners to their masters. Hey! What's that
fire inside the tent? Are the Trojan women burning
300   it because they have to leave for Argos? Setting
themselves on fire, hoping to die? Those who are
born free suffer most freedom's loss. Open up! Open
up! The army won't tolerate it and I'll get the blame.

HECUBA.
 It's nothing. No fire. Only my child. My mad
 Cassandra is racing towards us.

 Enter CASSANDRA *with torches.*

CASSANDRA.
 Lift up the torches, here take them.
 I worship! I light the torch! See, here!
 I fill this temple with flame!   310
 Come Hymen, god of marriage,
 Bless the bridegroom, bless the bride
 Who serves a royal bed in Argos,
 Hymen, god of marriage.

 You, Mother, are drowned in mourning,
 In tears for my dead father
 And sweet land I called home.
 But I lift the torches high,
 Creating light, shining light,   320
 And its flashing splendour,
 A tribute to you, Hymen.
 And you, Hecate, bless us with your brilliant light,
 As is usual when a virgin becomes a wife.

 Dance, dance up to the sky!
 Shout 'yes', and celebrate
 The blessed fate of my father.
 You, Phoebus, lead the holy dance,
 There in your holy grove of laurels,
 Where I served you as my lord.   330
 Hymen, O marriage, Hymen.

 Dance, Mother, dance with me,
 Whirl your sweet foot with mine,
 Shout out a hymn to Hymen!
 Celebrate the bride
 With blessed songs and cries,
 Go maids of Phrygia, dressed in your best,
 Sing for my marriage and celebrate the husband   340
 For whose bed I'm destined.

CHORUS.
Queen, stop your mad daughter,
Before she dances straight into the Greek camp.

HECUBA.
Hephaestus, you light torches to celebrate marriage,
but this flame is a grim one for her. O sweet child,
what great hopes I had for you. How little I dreamed
that Argive spears would force you into marriage.
Give me your torches, dear, you can't hold them
350   straight in your wild dance. All your sufferings have
hardly made you wise; my child, you're still the same
. . . out of your head. Here, women, take the torches;
this marriage needs tears, not celebration.

CASSANDRA.
Mother, crown me with a victory wreath, and
celebrate my marriage to a king! Take me to him
and, if I hesitate, force me. For if Apollo told the
truth, my marriage to Agamemnon, leader of the
Greeks, will be more painful to him than Helen's. I
shall kill Agamemnon and destroy his home; he will
pay in blood for what he did to my brothers and
360   father. I won't talk about the rest: I won't sing about
the axe at my throat, or the murder of the others, or
the agony of matricide that my marriage will set in
motion, besides the overthrow of the house of
Atreus.

Now, Mother, I shall show you how we are more
fortunate than the Greeks. I've been rambling, but
I'll speak plainly now. They sent thousands to their
deaths for the sake of one woman, and one love
affair, when they chased after Helen. Look at this
370   clever general, who destroyed what he loved most,
for what was most hated; he gave up the pleasures of
his children at home for the sake of his brother's wife
who left home willingly: *she* was not raped. After
they reached the shore of Scamander the Greeks
died in droves, protecting neither their borders nor
high-towered city. Those who died did not see their

children, nor had they wives to bury them properly,
and they lie in a foreign land. Same misery back
home. Their wives die as widows, and the old men
have no sons to take care of them or, when they die,
to offer a sacrifice at their tombs. Should an army be   380
praised for this? Better is silence for such shame: this
suffering won't inspire my muse to song.

But the Trojans have the true glory, because they
died for their country. When they fell by the sword,
their loved ones took them home; they lie in their
native soil's embrace, and they were buried by the
hands of those who should have buried them. The   390
Trojans who were not killed in battle came home
each day to wife and children. No Greek had such
pleasures.

Look at Hector, whose death was so painful for you.
When he died, he was thought best of all the heroes.
All this, the coming of the Greeks achieved; if they
had stayed at home, no one would have seen his
glory.

Paris too married Zeus's daughter and, if he hadn't,
his marriage would not have been famous.

A wise man will avoid war, but if war comes, it's best   400
to die fighting for your city; not to do so would be
shameful.

So Mother don't weep for your country or my
marriage. This marriage of mine will destroy our
enemies.

CHORUS.
How lightly she laughs at her misery.
And sings of things that are still unseen.

TALTHYBIUS.
If you were not mad, I would punish you for sending
our leaders on their way with these curses.

(*Aside.*) These men in their high station, who are
reputed to be wise, are really not much better than   410
those like us of no account. This great lord of the

Greeks, the son of Atreus, lusts after this mad girl.
Poor as I am, I'd not have asked for a girl like her.

(*To* CASSANDRA.) You there, you're not right in
your mind, so the insults you gave to Greece, and all
your praise of the Trojans, I throw to the winds; I
didn't hear a word. Now follow me to the ship: a fine
420   bride for our leader.

(*To* HECUBA.) And you there, go with the son of
Laertes when he comes for you; people say that
Penelope, Odysseus' wife, whom you will serve, is a
good woman.

CASSANDRA.
Filthy slave. Why do we give him the honourable
name of herald, a man whom everyone hates, a
servant to tyrants and government. He says my
mother will go to Odysseus' halls, but Apollo told
me that she would die here. I won't insult her by
430   mentioning the rest.

Odysseus does not know the sufferings in store for
him. My sorrows along with Troy's are golden by
comparison. He will add ten years to the ten he spent
here until he finally reaches his land, all alone,
without his men. He will see the narrow straits
between rocks where fierce Charybdis lives, and the
Cyclops who eats raw meat and roams in the
mountains; Ligurian Circe who turns men into
swine; shipwrecks on the salty sea; his men enslaved
to the lotus; the sacred cattle of the sun, whose
slaughtered flesh will speak, a grim sound for
440   Odysseus; but to make a long story short, he will visit
Hades, the underworld, finally escape the sea, and
reach home, only to find a thousand more miseries.

Why do I fire these arrows
Of Odysseus' outrageous fortune?
Go! Take me quickly to my marriage in hell!
Oh you, leader of the Greeks,
Who prided yourself on your great achievements!
You, vile man, will be buried

Like a thief in the night, not in the day.
Close to my bridegroom's tomb,
My naked body will be thrown
Into a ravine washed by winter rains,
To feed wild animals, I, who served Apollo.   450
Farewell to the headbands, holy symbols of the god
Whom I loved most of all the gods.
No longer shall I go to holy feasts,
My former delight.
I tear these ornaments from my flesh,
Which is still holy,
And entrust them to the winds
To carry up to you,
My lord of prophecy.

Where is the general's ship?
Where shall I embark?
Stop looking for breezes to fill your sails.
In taking me from this land
You take a fury, one of the dreaded three.

Goodbye Mother,
Don't weep.
Goodbye to the land I love.
My brothers and father who bore me
Will soon welcome me in the underworld.
I shall come triumphant to the world of the dead,   460
Destroyer of the house of Atreus,
By whom we were destroyed.

Exit CASSANDRA *with* TALTHYBIUS.

CHORUS.
Attendants of aged Hecuba, don't you see how our
mistress has fallen to the ground without saying a
word? Won't you help her up? You are cruel to leave
her there, an old woman, who has fallen. Pick her up.

HECUBA.
Leave me alone and let me lie here. Help unwanted is
no help at all. This is right after all I suffer, have
suffered and shall suffer. You gods, you have proved
yourselves useless, but there's still something proper

470   in invoking the gods when things go wrong. First I
want to speak about my past life and how good it was,
to show you how great is the loss that now I face.

I was royal and I married royalty, and then I bore
the noblest of children, no ordinary ones, but leaders
of the Trojans. No Trojan, Greek, or barbarian wife
could ever boast of children such as mine. I saw
them slain by Greek spears, and I cut my hair as an
480   offering for their graves.

I did not hear about their father Priam's death: I saw
him with my own eyes slaughtered on our household
altar. And I saw our city sacked. Those daughters
that I raised for excellent marriages, I raised instead
for foreigners: they were ripped from my hands. I
have no hope of seeing them, or of ever being seen by
them again.

And last of all, to crown this sad tale, now I, an old
woman, will go as a slave to Greece. They will set me
490   tasks unsuitable for someone my age: to keep keys
and open doors, I who was the mother of Hector. Or
to bake bread, to lay my weak and wasted back on
the ground to sleep, after a royal bed. To wear rags
on my wasted body, torn clothes unsuitable for one
used to luxury. I suffered all this for one woman's
marriage, and there is more to come. O Cassandra,
my child, ardent worshipper of the gods, you will
lose your sanctity with so much suffering. And you
my poor Polyxena, where are you? Of all my sons
500   and daughters, there's no one left to help me in my
misery.

So why should I stand up? What hope is left? Bring
me, who was royally pampered, to my earthen bed
with a stone for a pillow: let me waste away in the
flow of my tears. Don't think any woman happy until
510   the day she dies.

CHORUS.
Muse, sing a song of sorrow for my Troy,
A song filled with tears, something new:

I shall chant its miserable death-dirge.
I was made prisoner by the spear,
Destroyed by the four-footed wooden beast,
When the Greeks left it at our gates,
That horse adorned with gold   520
And rattling its armour
So that even heaven could hear.
The Trojan people shouted
As they stood on the cliffs,
'Come, the war is over!
Bring in the holy wooden idol
To Ilian Athena, the maiden of Zeus.'
What young woman did not come,
Nor old man from their homes?
Celebrating in song,
They embraced their wily destruction.   530

All the Phrygian people
Raced to the gates
To bring the well-carved horse
Made out of mountain pine,
That trap from the Greeks
And death of Trojans,
As a gift for the goddess unwed,
Known for her immortal horses.
They dragged it with knotted ropes of linen;   540
Like the hull of a dark boat, it nosed its way
Into the shrine of Pallas Athena,
Onto its marble floors,
Soon to run with Trojan blood.
Over their toil and joy,
Night's darkness fell.
While the Libyan pipe played,
Phrygian songs were sung
And young girls danced away,
Singing a glad song.
In the houses a bright gleam of fire   550
Shed a dark sheen on those who slept.

I was singing and dancing
In honour of the mountain maiden,

Artemis, the daughter of Zeus,
When a bloody cry arose in the city,
And froze the heart of Troy.
Children clung to their mother's skirts
With frightened hands.
560   The god of war, Ares,
Lurched out of his hiding place,
That work of Pallas Athena.
Trojans were slaughtered at their altars,
And heads hacked off in bed.
The destitute women were prizes
To give birth to sons for the Greeks
And shame for our country.

> *Hector's wife* ANDROMACHE *is wheeled on stage
> with* ASTYANAX.

Hecuba, see here's Andromache,
570   Brought on an enemy wagon,
And dear Astyanax, the child of Hector,
Snuggling close to her beating heart.

HECUBA.
Where are they taking you, poor woman,
On this wagon loaded with spoils,
Hector's weapons and armour?
Now Neoptolemus will
Decorate his Phthian shrines
With his Trojan loot.

ANDROMACHE.
My Achaean masters are hauling me away.

HECUBA.
Oimoi.

ANDROMACHE.
Why do you sing my song of pain?

HECUBA.
Aiai.

ANDROMACHE.
My song of suffering.

HECUBA.
  O Zeus.   580

ANDROMACHE.
  And sorrow.

HECUBA.
  Children!

ANDROMACHE.
  Once, no more.

HECUBA.
  Gone my happiness, gone my Troy.

ANDROMACHE.
  You poor woman.

HECUBA.
  Gone are my noble children.

ANDROMACHE.
  Pheu pheu.

HECUBA.
  Pheu.
  That song for my ...

ANDROMACHE.
  Pain.

HECUBA.
  Pitiful luck.

ANDROMACHE.
  For the city.

HECUBA.
  All in smoke.

ANDROMACHE.
  Oh husband, husband, come to me!

HECUBA.
  Poor thing, you call for my son,
  But he's dead.   590

ANDROMACHE.
  Defend your wife!
  You who shamed the Greeks ...

HECUBA.
 You were the first child
 That I bore to Priam.

ANDROMACHE.
 Carry me off to Hades.
 I long so for death ...

HECUBA.
 Poor woman, this is the pain we suffer.

ANDROMACHE.
 Our city gone ...

HECUBA.
 Pain heaped on pain.

ANDROMACHE.
 The gods hate us,
 Because your other son
 Escaped death;
 He destroyed lofty Troy
 For the sake of his loathsome lust.
 Food for the vultures,
 Bloody corpses lie next to
 The goddess Athena,
600   And Troy now wears the yoke of slavery.

HECUBA.
 Oh my city, my city lost ...

ANDROMACHE.
 Abandoned, I weep for you.

HECUBA.
 Now you face a miserable end.

ANDROMACHE.
 The home where I bore my children.

HECUBA.
 Oh children! Your mother who has lost her city
 Is losing you too!
 What cries, what sorrow,
 What tears shed on tears,

For my home lost.
At least our dead are free from pain.

CHORUS.
Tears and songs of sorrow sung by the muse of
  suffering
Are sweet salves for those who suffer bitterness.

ANDROMACHE.
Oh mother of him whose spear brought destruction   610
on the Greeks, do you see what we suffer?

HECUBA.
I see the hand of the gods: those who are nothing
they raise to the heights, but those on top, they bring
down.

ANDROMACHE.
We are dragged off as booty, my child and I. For
those born noble slavery is a steep fall.

HECUBA.
Necessity drives us hard. Just now Cassandra was
taken from me, snatched from my arms.

ANDROMACHE (keening).
It seems another Ajax has appeared to rape her, but
there is more suffering for you.

HECUBA.
There's no limit to my suffering; each new horror   620
challenges the one before.

ANDROMACHE.
Your daughter Polyxena is dead; they slaughtered
her at the tomb of Achilles, a gift for his lifeless
corpse.

HECUBA.
Oh misery. That was Talthybius' riddle; unclear
then, but all too clear now.

ANDROMACHE.
When I saw her corpse, I left this cart to cover her
with a robe and beat my breast in mourning.

HECUBA.
Aiai. My child, for your unholy slaughter,
Aiai again, for this foul murder.

ANDROMACHE.
630   She's dead and gone; she's better off than I who live.

HECUBA.
Dying cannot be compared with living;
Death is nothing; in life there is hope.

ANDROMACHE.
Mother, oh Mother, listen as I try to word this well;
perhaps I can say something that will lift your
spirits. I think not to be born is the same as death,
and to live with suffering is worse than dying. If one
does not feel pain, then there is no pain; the sorrow
of a long fall from happiness into unhappiness drives
640   a soul mad. Polyxena is dead and it's as if she had
never seen the light; she is free from suffering.

I aimed high, at good repute, and I won it, but not
good luck. I brought to Hector's house all the virtues
of a good wife. First, if a wife does not stay indoors,
whether she is to blame or not, she gets a bad
650   reputation, so I tamed my desire and stayed at home.
I would not allow women's wheedling gossip inside
my house. My own good sense taught me, and I put
goodness into practice. My tongue was quiet, and
my eye modest; I knew when my judgement should
prevail and when I should give in to my husband.

My reputation reached the Greeks and this was my
ruin. When I was taken prisoner, the son of Achilles
660   wanted me for his bedmate; I shall be a slave in the
house of my husband's murderer. If I drive my dear
Hector out of my heart and open it to my present
lover, I will betray the dead; but if I show myself
unwilling, I shall be hated by my new master. They
say that a night in bed with a man wins a woman
over. That's disgusting and I despise the woman
who rejects her former husband for love in a new
bed. Not even a horse, if you take her mate from the

4

harness, will bear a new yoke easily. Yet animals lack   670
speech and are inferior in nature to man. You, my
beloved Hector, were the mate for me; you were
supreme in intelligence, birth, wealth, and bravery.
You took me pure from my father's house, and
tamed me, a virgin, in your bed. And now you are
dead. I shall sail to Greece, a prisoner of the spear, to
endure the yoke of slavery. As for the death of
Polyxena whom you mourn, don't you think she   680
suffers less than I do? I have no hope, that last
resource for the desperate; and I don't deceive
myself into thinking something good will happen,
sweet though that deception would be.

CHORUS.
You suffer as much as I do. Your weeping has taught
me the extent of my misery.

HECUBA.
I have never been on board a ship, but I know about
it from pictures, and what people tell me. If a storm
is manageable, the sailors are eager to save
themselves; this one steers, that one mans the sails,
and this one bales; but if a rough stormy sea   690
overwhelms them, they accept their fate and hand
themselves over to the racing waves. My troubles
rise up like these waves, but no voice, no speech rises
from my lips. This wave of misfortune from the gods
has silenced me.

But you, my dear child, you must forget Hector;
your tears cannot save him now. Honour your
present master and charm him with your sweet ways.   700
If you do this you will please us all, and so you might
raise the son of my son to be the saviour of Troy, and
your future children might one day rebuild it, and
Troy live once again. But here's a new worry. I see
that Greek lackey coming again. Are there new
decisions?

Enter TALTHYBIUS.

TALTHYBIUS.
Wife of Hector, bravest man of Troy, don't hate me
for the news I bring from the Greeks and their
710   leaders, the sons of Pelops. I wish I weren't the
messenger.

ANDROMACHE.
That's a bad beginning. What is it?

TALTHYBIUS.
They voted that your child ... How can I go on?

ANDROMACHE.
Is he to have a different master?

TALTHYBIUS.
None of the Greeks will be his master.

ANDROMACHE.
Are we to leave him here alone in Troy?

TALTHYBIUS.
There is no easy way to deliver bad news.

ANDROMACHE.
I admire your tact, but tact is not needed if the news
is good.

TALTHYBIUS.
They will execute your child; there you know the
worst.

ANDROMACHE (agonized scream).
Oimoi, I thought I had heard the worst, when I
720   heard whose bed I had to share.

TALTHYBIUS.
Odysseus won the Greeks over in assembly ...

ANDROMACHE.
Aiai again and again. Will my suffering ever end?

TALTHYBIUS.
He warned them against raising the son of noble
Hector.

ANDROMACHE.
May his sons also suffer the same.

TALTHYBIUS.

He must be thrown from the towers of Troy. Accept
it. You'll be the wiser for that. Don't stand in the
way, but bear your pain like the great lady you are
and don't imagine that you have any power to
change this: you don't. You are powerless; just look
around! Your city is destroyed and your husband is
dead; you are a slave; we can deal with a single   730
woman. So I do not want you to fight, or do anything
to incur anger, or call down any curses on the
Greeks. If you say anything that will anger the
Greek army, they will neither allow your child's
body to be buried nor mourned. So be still and
accept what you cannot change; that way your child
will be buried and you will find the Greeks kinder
towards you.

ANDROMACHE (*to her child*).

Oh darling boy, child that I prized too much, you   740
must leave your mother, and your enemies will kill
you. Your father's nobility has destroyed you, that
nobility that saved so many others, but was useless
for you. Oh doomed bed and marriage, for which I
came to Hector's halls! I did not bear a son for
Greeks to slay, but to be king over fertile Asia.

Oh my baby, you're crying. Do you know what
terrible things will happen to you? You cling to me
and hide in my clothes. You're like a little bird,   750
nestling under its mother's wings. Hector will not
rise out of the earth, seizing his famous spear to save
you, nor any of his relatives, nor any force from
Troy; but you will fall a horrible fall, smashed
piteously against the hard ground, your breath torn
away. Oh dearest child, nestling against your
mother, how sweet is your breath. It was for nothing
that this breast nursed you when you were a baby,   760
for nothing I suffered birth pains, and struggled to
raise you. Now for the last time kiss your mother;
put your arms around me and press your body close
to her who bore you, and kiss me, lips to lips.

O you Greeks you have found torture worse than any
barbarian's! Why do you kill this child who has
never done you any wrong? O Helen, daughter of
Tyndareus, you are not the child of Zeus. You are
the child of many fathers: an avenging Fury first,
then Envy, and Slaughter, and Death: as many
miseries as the earth has borne. I say you were never
770   Zeus's daughter, but rather evil incarnate, a curse on
both barbarians and Greeks. Your beautiful eyes
brought ugly destruction to the noble fields of
Phrygia.

(*To* TALTHYBIUS.) Here, take him away, carry
him off, throw him down, since that's your decision,
and feast on his flesh. I am destroyed by the gods,
and cannot save my child from death. Hide my
miserable body, throw me in the ship. I go to a fine
marriage after losing my child.

CHORUS.
Poor Troy, you have lost thousands for the sake of
780   one hateful woman and her marriage.

TALTHYBIUS.
Come child, let your poor mother go,
Leave her embrace,
Go to the top of your ancestral towers,
The crown of the city.
Where they voted
You will breathe your last.

(*To the* GUARDS.) Take him.

(*Aside.*) A man to deliver messages like these
Should be pitiless and shameless,
Not think and feel the way that I do.

    Exeunt GUARDS, BOY *and* TALTHYBIUS.

HECUBA.
790   Child, son of my poor son,
Your life is ripped away from us,
From your mother and me.
This is a crime.

What will my life be now?
What can I do to help you,
My poor little one?
All that we can do is strike our heads,
Beat our breasts!
I'll begin the mourning
For the city and
Laments for you.
What has not happened to us?
What keeps us now from
Hurtling to the bottom of hell?

CHORUS.
King Telamon, who made his home
On the bee-humming island of Salamis,
Washed by its many waves,   800
Lying opposite the holy hills
Where Athena first revealed
The branch of grey olive,
That heavenly crown,
A wreath to adorn shining Athens,
Telamon, you came from Greece,
One hero with another hero,
The bow-bearing son of Alcmena,
To sack the city of Troy,
Troy, our city,
That first time long ago.

He led the flower of Greece,
Angered by the fraud of the promised steeds.
He shipped the sea-stroking oars
By the shores of fair-flowing Simois,   810
And fastened the ropes from the sterns.
He took his bow in his hand from the ship
To deal death to Laomedon.
He destroyed the well-measured walls of Phoebus,
With a blast of red fire;
He destroyed the land of Troy.
Two times were the walls of Troy spattered with
    blood,
Two times did the bloody spear shatter the city.

820   In vain do you walk with graceful step
To fill the golden goblets,
Ganymede, child of Laomedon,
Cup-bearer of mighty Zeus,
In fairest servitude.
She who bore you
Flames with fire,
And the sea shores moan
With the cry of a bird
830   Who has lost its young.
Here women weep for their husbands,
These weep for their children,
And those for their grey-haired mothers.
Gone are the cool pools where you bathed,
Gone are the fields where you used to run.
You stand gracefully with smile serene
Next to the gleaming throne of Zeus
While Greece's spear
Razes the city of Priam.

840   Love, you came to the halls of Troy,
Love, you seduce even the gods!
You raised up Troy to greatness
Blessing her with divine relations.
I shall not blame Zeus.
But the light of white-winged Dawn,
So dear to man, shed an evil glow
850   And gazed on the death of Troy.
The goddess Dawn had a husband from this land,
And bore him children;
The golden chariot with four horses from the stars
Took him up to heaven,
Fine hope for his native land,
But gone is the love of gods for Troy.

Enter MENELAUS, *with some* GUARDS.

MENELAUS.
860   Oh far bright light of the sun on this day, when I lay
my hands on my wife Helen again. I, Menelaus who
fought with the Greek army for all these years, did

not come to Troy as most people think for the sake of
my wife. No. I came for him who betrayed his host
and stole my wife from out of my house. He paid the
price with the god's help, he and his land which fell
to Greek spears. I'll take away the wretched creature
whom I hesitate to call by the name of wife as I once
did. She is one of the defeated slaves, along with the   870
other Trojan women. My men, who conquered
Troy, handed her over to me to kill, or not kill, or
take her back home if I want. I think it's best not to
kill her at Troy, but take her home on my ship and
then execute her in Greece as payment for all my
men who died in Troy.

Go to the tents and bring her to me; drag her here by   880
her bloodstained hair. When the wind starts to blow,
we'll take her to Greece.

HECUBA.
O god, who guides and rules the earth,
Whoever you are, dark riddle of the universe,
Whether law of nature, or mind of man,
I pray to you who silently but surely
Leads mankind in the ways of justice.

MENELAUS.
What's that? Some new prayer you have made up?

HECUBA.
Please Menelaus: kill your wife. But be careful; if
you look at her you will come under her spell. Her   890
eyes enslave men, destroy cities, and set homes on
fire; such is the power of their enchantment. I, and
all those who have suffered because of her, know her
all too well.

    Enter HELEN, *dragged by* SOLDIERS.

HELEN.
Menelaus, this beginning could well make a woman
afraid. I am dragged by force from my tent by your
servants. I imagine you must hate me, but I want to

know what you and the other Greeks have decided to
900   do with me: am I to live or die?

MENELAUS.
Nothing ambiguous about that vote; the whole army
agreed to hand you over to me, whom you've
wronged, to kill.

HELEN.
May I at least answer the charges, and show that if I
die, it is unjust?

MENELAUS.
I have not come to debate with you, but to kill you.

HECUBA.
Oh listen to her Menelaus, don't let her die without a
hearing, and then let me answer her. You do not
know the terrible things she did at Troy; after you
hear the whole story you will kill her, and she won't
910   have a chance to escape.

MENELAUS.
I suppose I can spare the time. Let her speak if she
wants to. But I want her to know that it is because
you ask; I do not grant her this for her sake.

HELEN.
I see you are against me, so whether I speak well or
not does not matter; you will not talk to me because
you regard me as the enemy. I shall guess what you
would say and answer your charges, point by point.
920   First, she, by giving birth to Paris, was the cause of
all these evils. Second, the old king, in not slaying
the child, Paris, that grim firebrand, destroyed me
and Troy. Listen to what followed. He became the
judge in a contest between three goddesses. Athena
promised him that he could head an army of
Phrygians and conquer Greece. Hera promised that
he would rule Asia and Europe's borders, if he
would declare her the winner. Aphrodite, boasting of
930   my beauty, promised me to him if she would be
chosen fairest. Look what happened then: Aphrodite

won, and my marriage helped Greece: it is not
conquered by barbarians, nor subjected to war, nor
ruled by a tyrant. All these benefits came to Greece,
but I was ruined, sold for my beauty; and I am now
blamed rather than crowned with a victory wreath,
as I should have been. You will say this is off the
point because I have not said why I left your house
in secret; he came, that nemesis, Paris, with a great   940
goddess at his side; and you, you fool, you left him
alone with me when you sailed from Sparta to Crete.
There you are.

Now I shall question myself, because you may well
ask what inspired me to leave your house and follow
this stranger, betraying my country and my home.
Punish the goddess, and be stronger than Zeus who
rules all the gods and yet is her slave. So you see, I
deserve forgiveness. You might well ask, when Paris
died, and my heaven-sent marriage was over, why   950
did I not leave his house and go to the Greek ships?
But that's exactly what I tried to do. And I have
witnesses, those who guarded the tower gates and
the walls: how many times did they find me dangling
from strong ropes, stealthily trying to lower my body
from the ramparts down to the ground. My new   960
husband, Deiphobus, seized me by force, and made
me his wife, even though the Phrygians disapproved.
So why is it just that I die, my husband, since he
took me forcibly, and my domestic life here was as a
slave not an honoured prize? Go on, fight the gods!
If you want to be stronger than the almighty, you are
mad!

CHORUS.
Queen, defend your children and your country;
destroy her case. Her clever words cover foul crimes,
and that is terrible.

HECUBA.
First I shall defend the goddesses and show that
what she says can't be right. I hardly think that Hera

970   or the virgin Athena would ever descend to such
       foolishness, to come to Ida and compete in a beauty
       contest. For a beauty contest would Hera sell out her
       Argos to barbarians, and Athena enslave Athens to
       Phrygians? Is the goddess Hera concerned about her
       beauty so that she could win a husband mightier
       than Zeus? Or Athena, who begged her father that
       she could keep her virginity, does she now seek
980   marriage with one of the gods? Don't turn the
       goddesses into idiots to cover up your own crime;
       you won't convince any sensible person. And you say
       Aphrodite came with my son to Menelaus' halls?
       That's a big laugh! Even if she stayed at home in
       heaven, couldn't she have brought you and Amyclae
       too to Troy?

       My son was the handsomest of men, and when you
       saw him, your own desire became Aphrodite's. Men
990   call their foolishness 'Aphrodite', and it's no
       accident that love and lunacy share the first letter.
       You saw him wearing his foreign robes which shone
       with golden splendour and you went mad for him.
       Argos simply wasn't up to your taste, so you
       exchanged your Sparta for a Phrygian city flowing
       with gold and you hoped to spend it all. Menelaus'
       halls were not good enough to satisfy your desire for
       wanton luxury. So you say that my son forced you to
       leave? Hardly. What Spartan heard you call out?
       What cry for help did you raise? Your brothers,
1000   young Castor and his twin, were still alive, not yet
       stars in the sky; why didn't they hear you?

       You came to Troy, with the Argives hot on your
       track: they battled with deadly spears. If news came
       that your husband was winning you would praise
       him and shame my child who had this great rival for
       his love; but if the Trojans were winning, Menelaus
       was worthless. You always looked to the winning
       side; intrinsic merit meant nothing to you. You say
       you were kept here against your will, and you
1010   secretly tried to let your body down from the towers

using ropes to escape? Did anyone find you trying to commit suicide by fitting a noose to your neck or sharpening a sword, as any woman who missed her former husband would have done?

How many times I pleaded with you, saying, 'Daughter, please go. My son can find a new bride. I'll secretly escort you to the Argive ships. Put an end to this war between the Greeks and us.' But that was not what you wanted to do. You ran riot in the   1020
halls of Paris and wanted barbarian obeisance. This was what was important to you. And look at you now, dressed to the hilt, looking shamelessly on the same sky your husband does, you despicable woman. You should have come without airs, dressed in rags and trembling with fear, your head shaven for shame, and shown more modesty than audacity before the husband you wronged.

Menelaus, in brief, crown Greece with her death,   1030
and do what you know is right. Show women that if they betray their husbands, they will die.

CHORUS.
   Menelaus, show yourself worthy of your ancestors and punish your wife. Be a brave foe to your enemies and by her death eradicate this blot on womankind.

MENELAUS (*to* HECUBA).
   I agree with you: she went of her own accord from my home into a foreign bed. That's just empty boasting when she talks about Aphrodite.

   (*To* HELEN.) Go and let my people stone you; compensate for the long suffering of the Greeks with the brief moment of your death, and learn what it   1040
means to shame me.

HELEN.
   No! Clutching your knees, I beseech you; do not blame me for heaven's madness. Forgive me!

HECUBA.
Do not betray your dead allies; I beg you on their behalf and for the sake of your children.

MENELAUS.
Stop, Hecuba. She means nothing to me. I'll give my orders to my servants now: take her to where the ships lie, and she will sail with us.

HECUBA.
Don't take her on the same ship with you.

MENELAUS.
1050   Why not? Put on weight, has she?

HECUBA.
Once a lover, always a lover.

MENELAUS.
No. It depends on what that beloved has done. But I'll do what you say. She won't go on the same ship with me. You give good advice. When we get to Greece she will die a terrible death for the terrible things she did, and be a lesson for all women to control their lust. This is not easy for me. But her destruction will terrify them in their sexual misdeeds, were they even more shameless than she.

Exit MENELAUS *with* HELEN.

CHORUS.
1060   Zeus, you betrayed your own shrine to the Achaeans,
Even while its altar was smoking with incense and
    flame of sacrifice,
And holy Pergamon whose smoky myrrh floats to
    heaven;
The vales of Ida covered with ivy
And washed by streaming snow,
Ida, the limit of the world,
First to be struck by the sun's rays,
1070   That shining holy haunt of the gods.

No more sacrifices,
No sacred chants and dances in the dark,
In all-night worship of the gods.

Gone the sacred wooden images covered with gold,
And the twelve holy rites for Phrygia's full moons.
This is now my worry, Zeus:
Do you care at all for these rites, you who are
Seated high above on your heavenly throne?
Any care for me and my city in ruins
Or the raging storm of fire that brought it down?   1080

Oh, you my dear husband,
You are now a ghost,
Wandering unburied,
Unwashed by hands that loved you.
A ship will take me over the sea,
Swiftly sailing on wings of pine
To horse-blest Argos
With its stony Cyclopean walls
That rend the sky.
Our children crowd the gates
And shout as they weep.
A little girl cries out,   1090
'Mother, the Greeks are taking me away,
All alone, far from your eyes,
To a dark-blue ship with sea-faring oars
Off to holy Salamis,
Or the Isthmian heights that split two seas,
Where Pelops rules behind lion gates.'

How I wish the double-pronged lightning,   1100
The thunder-bearing fire of the Aegean,
Would strike the ship of Menelaus
As it sails on the high sea,
When he takes me from Troy to Greece,
A slave weeping many a tear,
While Helen the daughter of Zeus
Holds her golden mirrors,
Those delights for young girls.
May he never reach his Spartan home,   1110
Nor enter his ancestral hearth,
Nor walk in the streets of Pitana,
Nor enter the brazen-gated temple of the goddess,
Since he took her back, and by his rotten marriage

Brought shame on great Greece
And untold misery to the streams of the Simois.
Io io.
New miseries pile up on the old for our land.
1120   Unhappy Trojan wives, see our dead Astyanax,
Whom the Greeks threw pitilessly from the city's
     towers;
Now his murderers bring him to us.

   Enter TALTHYBIUS, *carrying the body of*
   ASTYANAX.

TALTHYBIUS.
   Hecuba, one last ship, with its oars manned, is ready
   to take back to the shores of Phthia the booty left
   behind for Achilles' son. Neoptolemus himself set
   sail because he heard of his father Peleus' new
   troubles: Acastus the son of Pelias has exiled him.
   Neoptolemus did not delay, but left quickly and took
   Andromache with him. As she wept for her country
1130   and sobbed over the grave of her husband, Hector,
   she made me weep. She begged Neoptolemus that
   her child, who breathed his last when he fell from
   the walls, that child of your Hector, be granted a
   funeral.

   She asked too that, instead of in cedar or stone, he be
   buried in Hector's bronze shield, the same one his
   father wrapped around his own body for protection
   and that struck terror in the Greeks. Andromache
1140   begged that it not be hung on the wall of her new
   room, where she would be bedded, as a grim
   reminder of her past. She asked that I lay this child's
   dead body in your arms, so that you might cover him
   with some clothing and wreaths, from whatever is
   left to you, since her master's hasty departure
   prevented her from burying him herself. When you
   have prepared the body, I shall heap a mound over
   him and stick a spear in the earth to mark it. Do what
   you have to do as quickly as possible.

One trouble I spared you: when I crossed   1150
Scamander, I washed his body in the stream and
cleaned his wounds. I'll go and dig him a grave, so
between us both we'll shorten the work and hasten
our return home.

HECUBA.

Lay Hector's rimmed shield on the ground, now a
joyless sight and bitter for me to see. O you Greeks
who have more strength in the spear than the brain,
why did you fear a child so much that you
committed this barbaric murder? Did you think he
would raise again our fallen Troy? Did you consider
yourselves so weak? When Hector was winning, with   1160
all his allies at his side, we still died in droves. Now
that Troy is taken, and Phrygia no more, do you fear
this little child? I hate the fear that comes when
reason flies away.

O my best beloved, how unlucky you were in your
death. If you had grown up and died fighting for
your city, had wed, and ruled like a god, you would
have been happy, if happiness can be found in such   1170
things. You saw all this and knew what it was in your
young mind, but you had no chance to experience it
yourself and never enjoyed it in your own house.
Poor sweet child, how cruelly your father's walls,
built high by Loxias, have shorn from your head the
curls your mother used to caress and kiss. The
broken bones grin between bloody gashes; why
should I conceal the horror of it? Your hands, sweet
miniatures of your father's, now lie limp.

O sweet mouth that made such grand promises, you   1180
are now silent. You lied when you clung to my dress,
snuggling close, and said, 'Grandmother, when you
die I'll come with lots of friends to visit your grave,
and cut off some of my curls and leave them as an
offering and tell you how much I loved you.' You
did not bury me, but I, an old woman, now without a
city or child, must bury your poor young corpse. Oh
terrible, those kisses, and all my care of you,

watching over you as you slept, all for nothing. What
will some poet inscribe on your tomb? 'This is the
innocent child that the Greeks feared and
1190   murdered!' An inscription to bring shame on
Greece.

You who had no share in your father's heritage, at
least will have his brazen shield in your grave. O
shield that protected the mighty arm of Hector, you
have lost your noble master. How sweet to see the
marks my son left on your handle, and the sweat that
stained the smooth rim, that sweat that dripped
down the face of Hector as he held you close to his
beard in the heat of battle.

1200   Bring me some covering, any scraps you have for this
poor body. We've not much left for adornment.
What I have, he will have.

A man is a fool who, when things go well, thinks that
his happiness will endure; fate is like a madman,
lurching here and there. No one's happiness ever
lasts.

CHORUS.
Here is what is left from the ruins of Troy;
We give it into your hands to cover his corpse.

HECUBA.
Your father's mother adorns you from the treasures
which once were yours, not to celebrate a victory
1210   with horses or in archery, two sports the Phrygians
honour, but not in excess. Now Helen the god-
cursed has deprived you of all this: she slew you and
destroyed all our city.

CHORUS.
E e.
You touch my heart,
Touch it with sorrow.
You were once a great prince in the city.

HECUBA.
Here I cover your skin with fine Phrygian robes, that

you should have worn for your wedding with the
most powerful princess of Asia.   1220

You, dear shield, mighty mother of Hector's
countless victories, receive your crown: you who are
deathless will die with this corpse, you, so much
more deserving of honour than the armour won by
that crafty criminal Odysseus.

CHORUS.
  Aiai aiai,
  Bitter sorrow,
  The earth will receive you, child.
  Mother, weep ...

HECUBA.
  Aiai.

CHORUS.
  Keen for the dead.   1230

HECUBA.
  Oimoi moi.

CHORUS.
  Oimoi.
  Deathless memory of sorrow.

HECUBA.
  I bandage your wounds, but I can heal nothing, all I
  can do is try, a useless effort. Your father will take
  care of you among the dead.

CHORUS.
  Strike your head
  And strike again,
  Keep the beat with your hands,
  Io moi moi.

HECUBA.
  Dearest women ...

CHORUS (*seeing her struggle to speak*).
  Hecuba, say what is in your heart.

HECUBA.
  All the gods have given us was suffering, to me and 1240

Troy, hated above all cities; in vain we sacrificed to
them. But if god had not overthrown us, and buried
us, no one would have had any fame. But now we are
celebrated in hymns, and shall provide songs for
future generations.

Go, bury the corpse in his sorry grave. It now has
the offerings that are due the dead. I think to be
buried with pomp and luxury means little to the
1250   dead; it is just vain show for the living.

CHORUS.
Io io.
Your poor mother who had such great hopes for you.
You had so much wealth and luxury, and came from
noble ancestors.
Ea ea.
What is this I see?
People brandishing flaming torches
On the heights of Ilium?
New evils on top of the old
Assail Troy.

TALTHYBIUS.
1260   Now, captains who are ordered to set Troy on fire,
don't hold back any longer, but do your work
quickly. After the city is razed to the ground, then
we'll sail happily home from Troy.

You women, I have two messages for you. When the
army leaders sound the trumpet, go to the Greek
ships to sail away from this land.

(*Pointing to some* SOLDIERS.) And you, old
woman, unhappiest of all, follow them. They have
1270   come from Odysseus; the lot gave you to him as a
slave and takes you away from this land.

HECUBA.
Oh miserable. This is the last and worst of all the
sorrows I've suffered. I leave my country and my
city burns. Old feet, make an effort, carry me to the
embrace of the flame so that I may die along with my

city. O Troy, great among all the barbarian cities,
soon your famous name will be forgotten. They have
set you on fire, and me they take away from this land
as a slave. O gods! But why do I call on the gods?   1280
They never listened to my prayers before. Come,
let's run into the fire, so that I may die gloriously in
my city's flames.

TALTHYBIUS (*to his* SOLDIERS).
Seize her, and don't let her go. You have to hand her
over to Odysseus; she is his war prize.

(*To* HECUBA.) Poor creature, your suffering has
driven you mad.

HECUBA.
Otototototoi!
O son of Cronus, lord of Phrygia, Father,
And begetter of our race,
Do you see what indignities we suffer?
We, the offspring of Dardanus?   1290

CHORUS.
He has seen.
But Troy, the greatest of cities,
Is a city no longer.
Troy is no more.

HECUBA.
Otototototoi!
Troy is burning bright,
The buildings of Troy blaze with fire,
The heart of the city,
With its high walls.

CHORUS.
Our land, fallen to the spear,
Is utterly destroyed,
And floats heavenward
On a wing of smoke.
O halls raging, running with flames,   1300
Defeated by fire and the foeman's spear.

HECUBA.
Children hear me!
Heed your mother's voice!

CHORUS.
You call the dead with your cries.

HECUBA (*throwing herself to the ground*).
An old woman, I lie on the ground,
And beat the earth with my two hands.

CHORUS.
We follow you and kneel on the ground,
Calling on our poor dead husbands.

HECUBA.
1310   We are carried off, dragged away ...

CHORUS.
Pain, pain you cry.

HECUBA.
Leaving my country for a house of slavery.
Io io.
Priam, Priam,
You are dead, without a tomb,
No loved one close,
No knowledge of my suffering.

CHORUS.
Dark death covered his eyes,
A holy man in unholy slaughter.

HECUBA.
O shrines of the gods,
Beloved city.

CHORUS.
E e.

HECUBA.
Bloody flame and spear shafts rule.

CHORUS.
Now nameless you are rubble on our beloved earth.

HECUBA.
  On smoke's wing,   1320
  As it flies to the sky,
  Ash covers my home,
  I see it no more.

CHORUS.
  The name of this land, unknown.
  One person vanished here, another there.
  Troy, poor Troy, is no more.

HECUBA.
  Did you see?
  Did you hear?

CHORUS.
  The fall of Troy.

HECUBA.
  An earthquake,
  A violent shaking, collapsed the city.
  Io io.
  Trembling frail legs, trembling body,
  Carry me on.
  Go to the first day of this life of slavery.   1330

CHORUS.
  O suffering city ...
  But we must leave now,
  And go to the ships of the Greeks.

    Exeunt.

EURIPIDES

Bacchae

translated by J. Michael Walton

Characters

DIONYSUS, son of Zeus and Semele
TEIRESIAS, a prophet
CADMUS, founder and former King of Thebes
PENTHEUS, his grandson, now King
SERVANT
FIRST MESSENGER
SECOND MESSENGER
AGAVE, mother of Pentheus
ATTENDANTS
CHORUS OF ASIAN BACCHAE

Before the palace of Thebes. Enter DIONYSUS.

DIONYSUS.
    Here am I, Dionysus.
    Son of Zeus and Cadmus' daughter, Semele.
    I have returned to this land of Thebes
    Where I was born from the lightning bolt.
    Now I stand by the springs of Dirce and the waters
        of Ismenus,
    A god ... disguised as a man.
    By the palace I see my mother's memorial,
    Smouldering with the deathless fire of Zeus,
    My mother who proved only too mortal
    Faced by Hera's unrelenting spite.
    Cadmus is my grandfather. I admire him.   10
    He had his tomb erected on hallowed ground.
    I had it wreathed with vine-leaves in profusion.
    I have left behind the gold-rich lands of Lydia and
        Phrygia,
    Deserted the sun-parched shore of Persia,
    The Bactrian fortress and the cruel land of the Mede.
    Through Arabia I came, prosperous Arabia,
    And through all of Asia where Greeks and foreigners
    Mix in the lofty cities by the shore.
    Now I have come to Greece, this city first.   20
    The dances and ceremonies invented across the sea
    To celebrate my godhead, I now bring here.
    Here, in Thebes, I have first excited women's cries –
    These women of Thebes, the first to dress in
        fawnskin –
    Placed in their hands my thyrsus, the ivy-covered
        shaft.
    Why these? Because these sisters of my mother,
    These aunts of mine, denied that I was born of Zeus.
    The last who should have done so, they defamed my
        mother,
    Semele, proclaiming my god-like birth a trick
    Devised by Cadmus to save a harlot-daughter's face.   30
    That was why, they said, Zeus incinerated my
        mother,

For her presumption. I have driven them mad.
Homes abandoned, they roam the mountains,
Out of their senses, deranged: every last woman in
Thebes,
Up there amongst the rocks and the trees,
Witless and homeless, Cadmus' daughters too.
40 Thebes will have to learn to appreciate me
And my rituals. My mother will receive her
recognition
When all acknowledge my divinity.
Cadmus has grown old and abdicated his throne
To his grandson Pentheus. This Pentheus wages
holy war
On me, offers no libations, ignores me in his prayers.
I am going to have to show this Pentheus, show all of
Thebes,
50 What kind of god I am. And when I have succeeded,
I shall move on. But if Thebes takes it in mind to
resist
And tries to drive my Bacchants from the mountains,
Then I must lead my women as their general.
Which is why you see me now in human form.

Come now my women, come now my dears.
This is not Tmolus, you're no longer in Lydia.
Come now my acolytes, my fawnskin fawners,
Drawn from far places, eager to serve me.
Rattle your castanets, clatter your drums,
Cymbals and tambours of Rhea, the great Mother.
60 Clash them and strike them. Batter the palace,
Din down on Pentheus. The city must witness.
While I to the mountains depart by myself,
There to accompany the mad Maenad dances.

Exit DIONYSUS. *Enter* CHORUS.

CHORUS.
Far from Asia, land of Asia,
I have come and I cry,
I have come and I praise,
I laud the name of Bromius,

Dionysus.
I praise his name, I laud his name,
Toil but a sweet toil,
The burden sweet as we praise his holy name.
Bacchus. Dionysus.
Where? What? Who can resist us?
Who on the road? Who in the doorway?
Beware. Let them beware.   70
Let them stand aside, say nothing, stay dumb.
One name we cry. Let none say another.
Dionysus.

Happy. Happy is the one. Blessed is the one
Who comes to know the mysteries,
The mysteries of the gods,
Who hallows life, who yields.
Who yields, lets the soul dance.
Pure is our dance in the mountains,
Purified the dancer in the name of Dionysus.
Sacred are the rites, secret rites for Cybele, the
    Mother.
Break through, yield. Break through, yield.   80
Break through with thyrsus aloft.
Serve him, serve Dionysus.
Come, Bacchants, come.
Dionysus is your god, god son of god.
Escort him home, home from Phrygia,
Home to Greece, the broad streets of Greece.
Bring him home, your Dionysus.

Dionysus god. Mother labours.
Lightning flashes. Zeus destroys, but Zeus
    preserves.   90
Mother dies, but Zeus preserves.
Preserved from the fire, concealed in his thigh,
Fastened there with golden pin,
All too quick for jealous Hera's eye.
In due time, as Fate decrees,
He is born, but what a child,   100
What a child from Zeus' thigh.
A savage child with horns and serpents in his hair.

His Maenads wear them still,
The child, Dionysus.

Thebes, city of Semele, Semele's nurse,
Crown her with ivy, crown her with fir,
Crown her with evergreen, berry and flower.
110   Brandish the thyrsus, twine wool through the fawn.
Then free her to dance
In the name of our god.
Free from the shuttle,
Free from the loom,
She waits for her leader,
Possessed by the god,
Dionysus.

120   And Crete with its deep holy birthplace of Zeus,
Crete where the Corybants first beat the drum,
Drummed and mixed drumming with Phrygian
    flute,
The sweet thunder from which they offered to Rhea,
A gift which she used as the true Bacchic note.
130   A gift which was raped by the satyrs' mad band,
Who created a dance for the god they adore,
Dionysus.

Sweet, sweet it is to run through the hills.
Sweet to wear the fawnskin.
Sweet to fall enraptured.
Sweet is the hunt, sweet the goat,
140   Sweet the taste, sweet the raw blood.
To run through the hills, through Phrygia, sweet,
To follow through Lydia the lead of our god,
Dionysus.
The earth flows with milk, the earth flows with wine,
With honey it flows.
The smoke like incense from brandished brand.

Run, shout, scream and cry.
150   Dance and fly,
Hair streaming behind.
On Bacchae, on Bacchae.
Far from Tmolus,

Golden Tmolus,
Praise him, praise him,
Praise his godhead.
Sacred song   160
And sacred dance,
Mountain high and mountain wide,
Deepest drum and shrillest pipe,
Celebrate his furious flight.
Dionysus.

Enter TEIRESIAS.

TEIRESIAS.
Gatekeeper. Are you there?   170
Call Cadmus, son of Agenor
Who left Sidonia to fortify this place.
What's keeping you?
Tell him Teiresias wants him.
He knows why I'm here. We made a bargain,
One old man to his elder,
To dress up in fawnskins, thyrsus in hand
And wreaths about our brows.

Enter CADMUS.

CADMUS.
I thought it must be you, old friend.   180
I heard your voice indoors. Sound words from a
    sound man.
Here I am, fit and ready, all dressed up
As the god requires. After all, he is my daughter's
    boy,
Dionysus, revealed to man as a god,
And we must do our best by him.
Where should we go and dance, do you think,
Shaking a leg, an aged head if it comes to that?
You'd better lead, Teiresias. We are neither of us
As young as we were, but you're the clever one.
I feel I could dance day and night, non-stop,
Beating the ground with my thyrsus;
And never a thought to age.

TEIRESIAS.

190   I share your enthusiasm. I feel young and I shall
         dance.

CADMUS.

Excellent. Let's order my chariot to take us to the
mountains.

TEIRESIAS.

No chariot. We would dishonour the god.

CADMUS.

No chariot. I'll help you, then, one old man with
another.

TEIRESIAS.

We'll never weary. The god will be leading us.

CADMUS.

Will we be the only men dancing for Bacchus?

TEIRESIAS.

We alone are in our right minds. No one else.

CADMUS.

We may as well get moving, then. Take my hand.

TEIRESIAS.

Where are you? Ah, there. Now, don't let go.

CADMUS.

I'm only a man, not one to scorn a god.

TEIRESIAS.

200   It is not for us to reason about the gods.
         We hold what our fathers held,
         And their fathers before them, from time
             immemorial.
         They didn't waste time rationalising
         And philosophising. Suppose someone says
         I look a fool at my age going off to dance
         With ivy in my hair, it is no shame to me.
         The god has decreed that we should dance,
         Young and old, and dance I shall.
         No half measures for this god. No one is exempt.

CADMUS.
    Being blind you will not have seen, Teiresias,   210
    So I'd better warn you. Here's Pentheus in a hurry,
    My grandson to whom I abdicated.
    He looks rather cross. Bad news, perhaps.

    Enter PENTHEUS, *attended.*

PENTHEUS.
    I only have to leave town,
    Go away for a few days and what happens?
    What's this I hear about strange goings-on,
    Women leaving home to roam around the
      mountains,
    Prancing through the trees in honour of this
      fashionable god,
    Dionysus, whoever he may be?   220
    And, of course, in the midst of all this revelry,
    Drink. Then off they creep to bed down
    With some man in a quiet corner. Dionysus?
    It's the goddess of lust they're celebrating.
    I've caught some of them, chained them up.
    There they stay in the public prison.
    As for the rest, Ino is among them,
    Actaeon's mother Autonoë, and even Agave
    Who bore me to my father Echion.   230
    I will hunt them down,
    And when I have them safe under lock and key,
    I'll put a stop to this Bacchic nonsense.
    I hear too that some foreigner has turned up,
    Some juggling charmer from Lydia,
    All golden hair and perfume,
    Flushed with drink and oh so beautiful.
    It's he debauches them night and day.
    When I get my hands on him,
    I'll stop him swinging his twig.   240
    I'll part his head from his neck.
    He's the one who claims Dionysus is a god,
    Who was sewn in Zeus' thigh,
    When we know perfectly well the mother
    Was blasted together with the child

For claiming Zeus as her lover.
The nerve of him. I don't care who he is.
Hanging's too good for him.

Oh, here's another marvel.
250   Teiresias the prophet, all dolled-up in a fawnskin.
And my grandfather too.
How ridiculous he looks with that stick.
Dear old man, I hate to see you so witless.
Take off the ivy. Please. Give me the thyrsus.
Grandfather, please. This is your fault, Teiresias.
It suits you to introduce some new god,
So you can pocket a commission.
If your senility did not protect you,
I would lock you up with the women for introducing
260   These foul practices. It's always the same.
The moment you allow drink at a women's festival,
Things turn unhealthy.

CHORUS.
Profanity. Profanity.
Strange man, have you no respect?
Respect for Cadmus, sower of the earth-born,
   dragon-spawn?
As Echion's son, do you scorn your own house?

TEIRESIAS.
A wise man with a good cause finds eloquence easy.
You talk well enough but there's no sense in your
   words.
270   Bold you may be, and capable too,
But, without sense, a man like you is a public
   liability.
He is new, perhaps, this god whom you mock ...
But I cannot begin to tell you how great his influence
Will one day be throughout Greece.
You are a young man. Listen to what I say.
There are two main principles in human experience,
Just two. The first is Demeter,
Mother Earth, whatever you care to call her.
She nurtures us humans by the gift of solid food.

Then there's Semele's son who discovered wine,
A liquid to match her mortal gift with his,
A gift to soothe the troubled mind
And bring us restful sleep, the best of all remedies.   280
We pour libations so that he, a god,
May benefit from mankind.
Oh, you make fun, do you, of that stuff
About Zeus' thigh, and the baby sewn up in it?
Let me tell you the truth about that.
It's just a story, a beautiful story.
When Zeus rescued Dionysus from the ashes,
After the lightning-bolt, he carried the baby away to
    Olympus.
Hera wanted to throw the god-like child out of
    heaven.
Zeus, with all a god's cunning, concocted this plan.   290
Out of the ethereal layer which surrounds the earth,
He constructed a surrogate, a phantom child
Which he gave to Hera, thus protecting
The real Dionysus from his wife's anger.
But in time men confused 'ethereal layer'
With 'laid in the thigh', a simple error of
    transmission.
So myths are made.

Another thing you should consider
Is that Dionysus is a god of prophecy.
Bacchants, like madmen, have method. When the god
Invades a man, that man can see the future.
Or you could find Dionysus in the field of Ares,   300
God of war. Have you never heard of soldiers
Drawn up under arms, stricken with panic
Before they can lift a spear?
That is the 'madness' of Dionysus.
It's Dionysus you can see
Hurtling over the rocks at Delphi,
Hair streaming, wand shaking,
His powers already formidable in Greece.

Pentheus, listen.   310
Do not be so proud as to think that brute force

Is all that makes a man strong.
Only a diseased mind sees power as physical
    strength.
Accept this god in your kingdom, reverence him,
Crown him, worship him, in his particular way.

As for the women, Dionysus does not require
    chastity,
But a temperate mind controls any circumstance.
Take note of that. The Bacchic rites alone
Never lead to corruption.
You know yourself what a joy it is to stand at your
    gates
Before a cheering multitude. No harm in that.
Allow him, then, his due, the respect which pleases
320   him.
Cadmus and I, decked out in our finery,
We will dance for him. An aged pair but,
Mock if you must, we will dance.
Nothing you can say will make us oppose a god.
It is you, alas, who have lost your sanity,
Sick beyond any drugs to cure.

CHORUS.
Wise words, old man. Apollo could not grudge
Your reverence for Dionysus, a mighty god.

CADMUS.
330 My boy, I tell you, Teiresias offers good advice.
Become one of us. Do as we do.
Your head's in the clouds. Think again.
There is this too. Even if this god is not really a god,
As you believe, you could at least say that he is.
It's just a little white lie. Semele gives birth to a god,
And our family gets the credit.
You saw what happened to your cousin Actaeon,
Torn to pieces by the man-eating hounds he'd
    reared.
And you know why he suffered.
All for claiming he was better than Artemis at
340   hunting.

May you never suffer like that.
Come, let me crown you with ivy.
Join us in honouring the god.

PENTHEUS.
Leave me alone. Go on. Dance about, if you must.
I want none of this foolishness.
But the man who taught you this folly,
He shall get what he deserves.
Go immediately to his seat of prophecy,
And uproot it. Use crowbars if you have to.
Leave nothing standing.   350
Throw all his trumpery to the winds.
Perhaps then he'll take me seriously.
The rest of you, search the city.
I want him found, this freak who infects our women,
Corrupting our beds. And when you catch him,
Tie him up and bring him here.
We'll see how he dances when it's raining stones.

> *Exit* PENTHEUS.

TEIRESIAS.
Oh, you fool, you do not realise what you are saying.
Witless before, you're now stark mad.
Cadmus, we must go, do what we can for the man,   360
However brutish his behaviour:
Do what we can for our city, god preserve it.
Pick up your staff and follow me. Help prop me up,
And I'll support you. It would be shaming
For a pair of old men to fall over. Still we must go.
Son of Zeus, Dionysus must be served.
Pentheus' name means grief. That is no prophecy,
Cadmus. It is a fact. A foolish man. Foolish words.
May he never bring grief upon your house.

> *Exeunt* TEIRESIAS *and* CADMUS.

CHORUS.
Reverence, queen of gods,   370
Flying, gold-winged, over man.
Reverence, do you realise,
Did you hear what Pentheus said?

Do you hear how he slights,
How he sneers at the name of Dionysus?
Dionysus is Semele's son, blessed and crowned,
380   Lord of the dance and lord of laughter,
Redeemer from care at the feast of the vine,
And when the wine's drunk and the festival over
He delivers the ivy-clad Bacchants to sleep.

What is the result of an unbridled tongue,
What is the end of lawless misjudgement?
The outcome disaster, only disaster.
A life lived in quiet, a life tranquil and sane,
390   Preserves the house and keeps it from harm.
The gods, far off, still gaze upon mortals.
Overstepping the mark is simply fool's wisdom,
Gaining him nothing who chases too far.
400   This way lies madness, attempting the summit,
Ill-judged and ill-starred, crashing to earth.

Let me come, let me come, to Aphrodite's isle,
To fairest Cyprus where love's charms are fashioned.
Three hundred-tongued the rivers give richness
To land untouched by rain.
Or let me come to Pieria,
410   Lovely Pieria where the Muses live,
To the slopes of Olympus, the holy.
Bromius, Dionysus, lead me there, dancing god.
There to the home of Desire and the Graces.
Lead me where dancing to Bromius is welcome.

Our lord, son of Zeus, delights in the feast.
One goddess I name who pleases him more.
Giver of comfort, giver of joy,
Allowing young men to relish their youth.
420   The goddess he loves is the goddess of Peace.
To rich and to poor he brings gifts of enchantment,
Gifts he bestows through the virtue of wine.
But the man who declines, by day or by night,
To live life as pleasure, he loathes.
430   Wisdom is keeping apart from the rational.
Grant me instead what the simple believe.

Enter SERVANT *and* DIONYSUS.

SERVANT.
  Pentheus. Lord Pentheus.

  Enter PENTHEUS.

  We've caught the prey you sent us after.
  Here he is, tame enough.
  He made no attempt to escape,
  Never turned a hair. He didn't turn pale,
  But stood there with a smile on his face
  And told us to bring him here. He held out his
      hands.
  It made my job easier, but I felt a bit ashamed.   440
  So I told him so. 'It's not up to me, friend,' I said,
  'Pentheus sent me.' And then there are those
      Bacchants
  You had locked up in the public gaol.
  They've gone. They got free,
  And now they're leaping about in the fields
  Calling upon their Bromius. The chains fell off
      them.
  The doors unbolted themselves without a hand laid
      on them.
  This man, well, I tell you. There's some funny things
  Going on in Thebes, and he's the cause,
  Though it's up to you to decide what to do about it.   450

PENTHEUS.
  You're losing your wits, the whole pack of you.
  Now I've got my hands on him, he'll not get away in
      a hurry.
  So, my friend. You're not so bad-looking, I see,
  Not as far as women are concerned,
  Which is why you came to Thebes, no doubt.
  Such long hair. Not a wrestler, I think. All down
      your cheeks.
  Very luscious. How pale you are. Not much in the
      sun,
  Are you? Under cover mostly, hunting Aphrodite?
  Right then. We'll start with where you come from?

DIONYSUS.
460   That's easy enough though nothing to boast of.
    Have you ever heard of Tmolus of the flowers?

PENTHEUS.
I've heard of it, the area round Sardis.

DIONYSUS.
That is where I come from. I'm a Lydian.

PENTHEUS.
And these rites you bring to Greece, where do they
    come from?

DIONYSUS.
Dionysus, the son of Zeus, initiated me.

PENTHEUS.
You have your own Zeus, do you, who spawns new
    gods?

DIONYSUS.
There is only one Zeus, Semele's husband.

PENTHEUS.
And were you awake when this Dionysus
Forced himself upon you, or was it a dream?

DIONYSUS.
I confronted him face to face. He looked at me
470   And gave me his mysteries.

PENTHEUS.
Ah yes, mysteries. What sort of mysteries would
    they be?

DIONYSUS.
They are secret except to initiates.

PENTHEUS.
Then what are the benefits for his devotees?

DIONYSUS.
Considerable, but you may not be told them.

PENTHEUS.
You're trying to intrigue me.

DIONYSUS.
These mysteries are not for the unbeliever.

PENTHEUS.
You say you've had a good look at this god. What's he like?

DIONYSUS.
Whatever he wishes. I cannot tell him how to appear.

PENTHEUS.
That's no kind of answer.

DIONYSUS.
Any fool finds wisdom foolish. 480

PENTHEUS.
Is this the first place you have introduced this god?

DIONYSUS.
His rites are danced everywhere abroad.

PENTHEUS.
Where they have less control of their senses than us Greeks.

DIONYSUS.
Perhaps more. Practices differ.

PENTHEUS.
These practices. Do you practise by day or at night?

DIONYSUS.
Mainly at night. Devotion needs the dark.

PENTHEUS.
So does corrupting women.

DIONYSUS.
That can be done in daylight.

PENTHEUS.
You'll pay for this disgusting sophistry.

DIONYSUS.
And you for your mindless irreverence. 490

PENTHEUS.
Really. Very brave, this Bacchant, quite a juggler
with words.

DIONYSUS.
Tell me my fate. What terrible punishment lies in
store for me?

PENTHEUS.
I shall start by cutting off your curls.

DIONYSUS.
My hair is sacred, dressed for the god.

PENTHEUS.
Then there's your thyrsus. Hand it over.

DIONYSUS.
It belongs to Dionysus. You take it.

PENTHEUS.
You, we'll chain up inside.

DIONYSUS.
The god will free me whenever he wants.

PENTHEUS.
Very fine with your Bacchants all around you.

DIONYSUS.
500   Take care. He came with me and sees what I suffer.

PENTHEUS.
Where exactly would he be, may I ask?
He is not immediately apparent to my eyes.

DIONYSUS.
With me. To a blasphemer invisible.

PENTHEUS.
He mocks me. He mocks Thebes. Tie him up.

DIONYSUS.
I give you fair warning. It would be unwise to bind
me.

PENTHEUS.
We shall soon see who has the power here.

DIONYSUS.
   You see nothing. Not what you do, what you are,
      who you are.

PENTHEUS.
   That I can tell you, Pentheus, son of Agave and
      Echion.

DIONYSUS.
   Pentheus, an ill-omened name. It suits you.

PENTHEUS.
   Take him down. Put him in the stables.   510
   He can dance in the dark in there.
   As for this pack of followers he brought with him,
   I'll sell them or set them to work sewing
   Instead of making all this din.

DIONYSUS.
   As you wish. I cannot suffer what I may not.
   He will repay you for your behaviour, Dionysus,
   Whose existence you deny.
   When you place a restriction on me
   It is Dionysus you affront.

      Exeunt DIONYSUS, SERVANT *and*
      PENTHEUS.

CHORUS.
   Dirce, maiden, mistress.
   Acheloüs' daughter,
   Once you kept Zeus' son   520
   Safe in your spring water.
   In his thigh Zeus placed him,
   Snatched him from the pyre.
   'Enter my male womb,
   Safe from deathless fire.'
   Bacchus, Dionysus.
   Dirce, blessed mistress,   530
   Why reject me now?
   Why disown my worship,
   The garlands on my brow?
   Why do you oppress me?

This I swear, one day
You'll accept the worship
Which you now deny.
Bromius. Dionysus.

540 Dragon-seed Pentheus betrays his birth,
True son of Echion, sprung from the earth.
Hardly a human, so savage a creature,
God-fighting giant, bloody in feature.
There where our leader lies in the gloom,
Bromius' servant he seeks to entomb.

550 Do you see from Olympus our witnesses' plight?
Come and protect us from tyranny's might.

Where Dionysus? Carrying the thyrsus?
On beast-haunted Nysa, in shade of Olympus?
On crest of Corycia? Where Dionysus?

560 There he lingers, there he lingers,
There where, charming beast in tree-lined glade,
Charming forest, Orpheus played.
You Bromius reveres, blessed Pieria:
Dancing he comes, here he comes prancing,
570 Never grows weary.

From the land of fine horses
Across Axius and Lydia,
From the land of fine waters
He hastens, he hastens
Our Maenad leader.

DIONYSUS (*within*).
Ahhh, Bacchae. Hear me, Bacchae. Hear my voice.

CHORUS.
Who? Where? A shout. A cry.
His, Whose? Calling. Who?

DIONYSUS (*within*).
580 Hear me, Bacchae. I call again.
It is I, Bacchae, son of Semele, son of Zeus.

CHORUS.
Dionysus. Master. Dionysus. Join us.
Lead us, Dionysus.
Welcome, Bromius, Dionysus.

DIONYSUS (*within*).
  Come, earthquake, come.
  Shake the world to its roots.

CHORUS.
  Help us. Look. Look there. There.
  The palace of Pentheus. See how it shakes.
  Shaking to pieces. It falls. The palace is falling.
  Dionysus within. Worship him. Worship.   590
  We revere. We revere.
  Look at the stones, the pillars, the beams.
  Bromius cries and the whole house replies.

DIONYSUS (*within*).
  Lightning bolt! Flashing fire!
  Engulf and consume all Pentheus' domain.

CHORUS.
  See how it blazes. Blazing fire
  Licking over the holy tomb. Over Semele's tomb,
  Semele, blasted by thunderbolt, thunderbolt of
    Zeus.
  Fling yourself earthwards. Fling yourself fearfully.   600
  Cast down your bodies. Fall down, you Maenads.
  All-overturning, Zeus' child breaks the house down.

    Enter DIONYSUS.

DIONYSUS.
  Women. Outsiders. Were you so terror-stricken
  You fell to the ground? I do believe you may have
    noticed
  How Dionysus wobbled the palace of Pentheus.
  Up you get. Calm yourselves.
  There, that's better.

CHORUS.
  Light of our light, lord of our Bacchic rites,
  We're overjoyed to see you.
  So desolate have we been.

DIONYSUS.
  You lost heart, did you, believing   610
  I had fallen into one of Pentheus' dark traps?

CHORUS.
How could we help it? What protection was left us?
But how are you free from that vile man's authority?

DIONYSUS.
Saving myself was really no problem.

CHORUS.
Your hands were tied, bound with chains.

DIONYSUS.
I made a fool of him. He thought he had tied me up,
But he never touched me. Delusion.
By the stable, when he thought he was securing me,
He trussed up a bull, shin and hoof.
620   It was he who snorted all the while,
And gnawed his lips, sweat pouring off him,
As I stood quietly by, surveying the scene.
Then came Dionysus to burn up house and tomb.
When the king saw that, he ran about
Shouting at servants to fetch water.
They were all too busy, slaving away ... naturally,
To no avail. Deciding that I had escaped,
He changed tack, grabbed a sword and rushed
    indoors.
Dionysus, or so I suppose – this is only what I
    assume happened –
630   Fashioned a phantom inside the house.
Pentheus made straight for it, this ethereal, shining
    thing,
Thinking to kill me. Dionysus mocked him even
    more,
Razing the house to the ground. He turned it upside
    down.
That will teach him to tie me up.
Pentheus dropped his sword when he saw that.
A man daring to take on a god. Imagine!
As for me, I simply slipped out here to you.
Pentheus is nothing. I think I hear him coming.
What will he have to say, I wonder?

Not that his bluster upsets me greatly.
Controlling one's temper is a sign of a wise man. 640

    Enter PENTHEUS.

PENTHEUS.
  This is humiliating. That foreigner
  Chained as he was a minute ago, he's got away.
  So, the fellow's here, is he? What is all this?
  How did you get out? What do you think you're
    doing
  Standing here in front of my house?

DIONYSUS.
  Don't take it too hard. And don't come any closer.

PENTHEUS.
  How did you get out?

DIONYSUS.
  Did I not tell you that someone would free me?
  Perhaps you were not listening.

PENTHEUS.
  What someone? Give a straight answer, can't you? 650

DIONYSUS.
  The god who grew the clustering vine for mortals.

PENTHEUS.
  That, I suppose, is a Dionysian benefit.

DIONYSUS.
  You can bear witness to his presence here.

PENTHEUS.
  I'll have every gate in the walls bolted.

DIONYSUS.
  To what end? Cannot a god jump over a wall?

PENTHEUS.
  So clever, aren't you? But maybe not that clever.

DIONYSUS.
  That clever, certainly. Born wise.

Enter FIRST MESSENGER.

Perhaps you should pay attention to this messenger
And what he has to say. Don't worry. I'll not run off.

MESSENGER.

660   Pentheus, Lord of Thebes. I come from Cithaeron
Where the snow can fall so thick and white ...

PENTHEUS.

Do you have any news or don't you?

MESSENGER.

Bacchants. That is what I've seen,
Rushing about like mad things.
Barefoot. All over the place.
I tell you, my lord, they're amazing,
These things they get up to.
Do you want everything or the edited version?

670   To tell the truth, my lord,
I'm a bit worried how you'll take it.

PENTHEUS.

Tell me it all. You'll come to no harm from me.
I have no need to take out my temper
On decent people. The worse the tale you have to tell
About these Bacchants, the more severe
My punishment for their corruption will be.

MESSENGER.

It was soon after daybreak, the sun just getting
    warm.
My cattle were heading for the tops when I saw
    them,

680   Three groups of these dancing women.
Autonoë was the leader of one group,
Your mother, Agave, the second, Ino, the third.
They were all fast asleep, stretched out,
Some reclining on pine branches,
Others amongst the oak leaves.
They were lying anywhere, but decently,
No sign of the drink and music you had led us to
    expect.

No debauchery in the bushes.
Then your mother, when she heard my cattle
    lowing,
Gave a great shout and jumped up   690
In the middle of the others crying
'Rouse your bodies from sleep.'
And they all threw off their sleepiness
And stood upright, old and young,
Married and unmarried, a marvellous sight.
They let down their hair, tied up their fawnskins
Where they had become disarranged,
And hung on their dappled fur snakes
Which licked their cheeks. Some young ones,
With milk at the breast, their newborn babes
    deserted,   700
Nursed gazelles or fed young cubs instead.
Then they dressed their hair with ivy,
Oak or flowering briony.
One struck her thyrsus on a rock
And a stream of water flowed out.
Another planted hers in the ground.
That one sprayed out god-given wine.   710
Those who required milk had only to scratch at the
    earth
And milk poured out. Their ivy wands dripped
    honey.
I tell you, if you'd been there,
If you'd seen all this, you would be praying
To the god you now pour scorn upon.

We got together, herdsmen and shepherds,
Arguing about all these wonderful things.
Some clever fellow, no countryman,
Made an announcement.
'How about it, men of the hills?   720
Shall we hunt down Agave, the king's mother,
Out of these revels, and do our lord a favour?'
It seemed like a good idea,
So we laid an ambush in the brush and waited.
In no time at all, they all started shaking their wands,

Shouting to Iacchus, calling on Bromius, son of
    Zeus.
And the whole mountain went wild for Dionysus,
Animals too. They began to run. Everything ran.
Agave came leaping past where I was hiding.
730   I tried to grab her but she let out a scream.
'Hounds, my swift hounds.
They are hunting us. Men.
Arm with your thyrsi. Arm. Follow me.'
And we fled.
They'd have torn us to pieces, these Bacchants.

They turned instead on our herds where they were
    feeding.
With her bare hands your own mother
Wrenched and tore at a bellowing cow.
740   Others ripped at calves, stripping them.
Hooves torn off. Ribs, wherever you looked.
Pieces of flesh hanging bloody from the trees,
Dripping.
Even bulls, with pride of horn,
Were dragged down,
Set upon by dozens of girlish hands,
Which grabbed at them, defleshing them,
As quickly as you could wink, my lord.
Then off they sprinted, swift as birds,
750   Down to the fertile Theban plain,
To Hysia and Erythrae beneath Cithaeron.
Like enemies they invaded, scattering everything.
Snatched children out of houses,
Slung them over their shoulders where they stuck
    fast,
As did anything they carried,
Even iron and steel, nothing falling to earth.
They bore fire in their hair.
It didn't even scorch them.
The villagers, meanwhile, furious at the raid,
760   Fell to arms. But there's another mystery, my lord.
The steel javelins of the villagers
Didn't so much as draw blood,

But the thyrsi cast by the Bacchants
Wounded them and put them to flight.
Men, routed by women, but not without the help of
  a god.
Then they went back where they'd come from,
To the fountains the god had raised up for them.
They washed off the blood,
While snakes licked clean their cheeks.
This god, my lord, whoever he is,   770
Accept him in the city.
His power is phenomenal, greater even than I have
  told you.
He is the one, as they say, who gives us wine
To ease our ills. And without wine, there's no love
  either,
And precious little else for a man to enjoy.

CHORUS.
  I hesitated to speak of freedom before such a tyrant,
  But speak I must. Second to no god is our god,
  Dionysus.

PENTHEUS.
  It is upon us already, spreading like wildfire,
  This Bacchanalian frenzy. The whole of Greece   780
  Will be jeering at us. We must act.
  You, go to the Electran gate. I want the shield-
    carriers,
  The cavalry and bowmen. Fast riders, the best
    shots.
  We march against the Bacchae. It's past all enduring
  To put up with these women's conduct.

DIONYSUS.
  Pentheus, you take no notice of what I say.
  I have suffered at your hands,
  But I am giving you fair warning.
  Do not bear arms against a god.
  Calm down. Dionysus will never allow you   790
  To drive his followers from the mountains.

PENTHEUS.
Don't give me orders. You're free. Isn't that
   enough?
Or are you looking for further punishment?

DIONYSUS.
It seems to me you would do better to offer him a
   sacrifice
Rather than get so excited. You cannot fight
Against the inevitable, mortal against immortal.

PENTHEUS.
I'll offer a sacrifice all right ... all those women.
In the woods of Cithaeron they'll get the sacrifice
   they deserve.

DIONYSUS.
You will simply run away, even with metal shields
Against wooden thyrsi. And you will all look rather
   foolish.

PENTHEUS.
I've had enough of this foreigner.
Nothing I do or say will stop his mouth.

DIONYSUS.
My friend, listen to me.
This still could be turned to your advantage.

PENTHEUS.
What can I do? I cannot let my subjects
Overrule me, women at that.

DIONYSUS.
I'll bring the women back, unharmed.

PENTHEUS.
You're plotting something.

DIONYSUS.
Why should I be plotting anything
Beyond using my skill to assist you?

PENTHEUS.
You're in this together, plotting
To install this religion here.

DIONYSUS.
  Why yes, I am. I am in this together with a god.

PENTHEUS.
  That's enough from you. Fetch me my armour.

DIONYSUS.
  One thing more. You would like to watch them
  Up there in the mountains, wouldn't you?   810

PENTHEUS.
  Watch them? Why, yes. I'd pay
  Good money to see what they are up to.

DIONYSUS.
  Why this great desire to see them?

PENTHEUS.
  There's no great pleasure in watching women drunk.

DIONYSUS.
  But you would like to take a look, pleasant sight or
    not.

PENTHEUS.
  Yes, I would. As long as I was sitting quietly
  Out of the way among the trees.

DIONYSUS.
  They'd sniff you out if you tried to watch them
    furtively.

PENTHEUS.
  That's very true. Out in the open then.

DIONYSUS.
  Do you want me to show you a way? Is that what you
    want?

PENTHEUS.
  Yes. You show me the way. Now, I want to go now.   820

DIONYSUS.
  You'll have to put on a dress. Linen, something like
    that.

PENTHEUS.
  Dress? What do you mean? Dress like a woman?

DIONYSUS.
They'd murder a man if they saw him, now wouldn't they?

PENTHEUS.
Yes, of course. You're right. You've thought it all out.

DIONYSUS.
Call it inspiration. From Dionysus.

PENTHEUS.
A clever idea. Now what?

DIONYSUS.
Come indoors. I'll help you get dressed.

PENTHEUS.
I don't think I've the nerve. Not dressed like a woman.

DIONYSUS.
Do you want a peep at the Maenads, or do you not?

PENTHEUS.
830   A dress, you say? What sort of a dress?

DIONYSUS.
A full-length dress. And a wig, a long one.

PENTHEUS.
Any other kind of decoration?

DIONYSUS.
You ought to have a headband.

PENTHEUS.
Is that everything?

DIONYSUS.
Yes, except for a thyrsus and fawnskin.

PENTHEUS.
Dress up as a woman? I couldn't do it.

DIONYSUS.
The alternative is bloodshed and a battle against the Bacchae.

PENTHEUS.
    All right. I'll do it. I have to see them before
      anything else.

DIONYSUS.
    Far more sensible than countering one evil with
      another.

PENTHEUS.
    How will I cross the city without being recognised?   840

DIONYSUS.
    We'll use quiet roads. I'll take you.

PENTHEUS.
    Rather than have those Bacchants
    Laugh at me. I'll go inside. I want to think about it.

DIONYSUS.
    As you wish. I'm ready, whatever you decide.

PENTHEUS.
    I'll go then. I'll go and prepare my weapons.
    Either that, or do what you suggest.

    Exit PENTHEUS.

DIONYSUS.
    Straight into the trap. Where he will find,
    Oh my women, his Bacchants and a death sentence.
    Dionysus, close at hand, now it is up to you.
    We will pay him out, but first befuddle his wits,
    Make him mad. Never in his right mind
    Would he put on a dress. Possessed, he will.   850
    After all those dire threats of his,
    I want Thebes helpless with laughter
    As he prinks,
    Ladylike, through the streets.
    I will go and help him
    Into the shroud he must wear
    When his mother tears him apart.
    He will discover, at first hand,
    Dionysus, son of Zeus,   860
    Most fearful of gods by nature, though the mildest
      too.

Exit DIONYSUS.

CHORUS.

> I long to dance through the night without sleeping,
> Barefoot,
> Neck stretched up to the dew-dropping air,
> Like a fawn as she plays in the field,
> Fear flown,
> Flight-free,
> Escaped from the hunter's snare,
870   Where she strained as she strove as she ran,
> Past meadow,
> Past stream,
> Till she found forest peace, far from man.
>
> Where is the beginning of wisdom?
> What gift of the gods could be finer for man
> Than to raise up his hand o'er the head of his foe,
880   Triumphant?
> Nothing finer,
> Delightful.
>
> The power of the gods proceeds slowly but surely,
> Chastening
> The insensitive,
> Those whose mad arrogance trusts only itself.
> Hidden away lie the traps for the godless.
> Time passes,
> Slowfoot.
890   The gods have good time to await the unwary.
> We must know and must care for the custom of ages,
> What's right and what's natural.
> These the ideals that religion gives sanction to.
>
> Where is the beginning of wisdom?
> What gift of the gods could be finer for man
> Than to raise up his hand o'er the head of his foe,
900   Triumphant?
> Nothing finer.
> Delightful.
>
> Happy the man who escapes the sea's tempest.
> Peace,

A haven he finds,
Delivered from hardship.
One achieves one thing, another another,
Fortune and happiness,
Hope upon hope.
So to thousands of men may be myriad ambitions.
Some may achieve while others fall backward.
Happy the man who can daily progress.   910

Enter DIONYSUS.

DIONYSUS.
Pentheus, so keen to see what you ought not to see,
Come out, Pentheus, out from your palace.
Let's have a look at you, tricked out like a Bacchant
To go and spy on your mother and her troupe.

Enter PENTHEUS, *dressed as a woman.*

There now, every inch a daughter of Cadmus.

PENTHEUS.
I can see two suns, I think,
And the seven-gated city of Thebes, double.
A bull. I think you look like a bull,   920
Horns on your head? A wild animal.
Did you used to be an animal? You've become a bull.

DIONYSUS.
The god is with us.
He was ill-disposed before, but now he has joined us.
You are seeing what you ought to see.

PENTHEUS.
Who do I look like? Ino, surely,
Though perhaps more like my mother, Agave?

DIONYSUS.
Their living image. You could be either one.
Wait. A lock of hair is out of place.
Tuck it back in the hood where I set it.

PENTHEUS.

930   I must have loosened it
When I was shaking my head about, Bacchant-
    fashion.

DIONYSUS.

Let me be your dresser. Keep your head still. There.

PENTHEUS.

Set me to rights. I am in your hands now.

DIONYSUS.

The girdle could be tighter, and your dress
Doesn't hang quite right at the ankle.

PENTHEUS.

I see. On the right. The left's all right, though, isn't
    it?

DIONYSUS.

How you will thank me when you finally see the
940   Bacchants
And find out that you are wrong about them.

PENTHEUS.

What's the right way to hold a thyrsus? This hand, is
    it?
I want to be like a real Bacchant.

DIONYSUS.

Right hand, and you raise your right foot in time.
Good, that's it. I do commend this change of heart.

PENTHEUS.

I wonder if I could lift up Cithaeron
On my shoulders, and all the Bacchae with it.

DIONYSUS.

Anything you like. Your wits were distracted before.
Now they are sound again.

PENTHEUS.

What about taking a crowbar? Or shall I just
Put a shoulder against the cliffs
950   And heave them over, with brute force?

DIONYSUS.
  You do not want to do any harm
  To the holy places of the nymphs, now do you,
  Or the haunts of Pan which echo with his pipes?

PENTHEUS.
  No, of course. And it would never be right to use
    force
  Against a woman. I'll hide in the trees.

DIONYSUS.
  You will find the right hiding-place
  For someone who wants to peer at the Bacchae.

PENTHEUS.
  I can see them already in the bushes,
  At it, like sparrows.

DIONYSUS.
  That is why you are going – as a watchdog.   960
  Perhaps you will catch them. Unless they catch you
    first.

PENTHEUS.
  Take me through the centre of Thebes
  As I am the only man with the nerve to go.

DIONYSUS.
  You bear responsibility for Thebes, all by yourself.
  You alone. Your trial awaits. Follow me.
  I will deliver you safely. Someone else will return
    you.

PENTHEUS.
  My mother.

DIONYSUS.
  For everyone to see.

PENTHEUS.
  That is why I am going.

DIONYSUS.
  You will be carried back ...

PENTHEUS.
  In triumph.

DIONYSUS.
In your mother's arms.

PENTHEUS.
You will ruin me.

DIONYSUS.
You could say that.

PENTHEUS.
970   Not that I don't deserve it.

Exit PENTHEUS.

DIONYSUS.
What a remarkable man you are,
But you face an ordeal so remarkable
It will bring you fame in heaven.
Such an ordeal and so young a man.
But I will win. You will see. Bromius and I will win.

Exit DIONYSUS.

CHORUS.
Go. Swift. Hounds. Madness.
Sting. Madness. Sting.
Cadmus' daughters,
980   Madness, sting.
Maenad decked out as female.

Mother spies. Spy from rock or spy from tree.
'Spy, Bacchae, racing Bacchae.'
Spy's mother. 'No, women.
990   Lion-cub. Gorgon-spawn.'

Sword of Justice, sword through throat
Of the godless, lawless, worthless man.

Echion's son, stung with madness,
Fighting your mysteries, Dionysus.
1000   And his mother's. Fights from weakness,
Crazed with daring, fighting mysteries.

Carefree life? Behave like mortals.
Cleverness for the clever. I choose better.
Reverence, honour, respect for the gods,
These man should practise by day and by night.

Sword of Justice, sword through throat 1010
Of the godless, lawless, worthless man.
Come, Dionysus, appear as a bull,
As a many-mouthed dragon,
As a fire-breathing lion.

Come, Bacchus. Come, Bacchus. 1020
Hunt, mock, trap, Bacchus.
Pursue him, sneer at him, snare him,
The man who would chase your Maenads.
Collapsed at their feet
He will find what he looked for.

Enter SECOND MESSENGER.

MESSENGER.
Nothing but grief. I'm only a slave
But I grieve for my masters, as a good slave must.
This family, till now so prosperous throughout
  Greece,
Family of Cadmus, the dragon-seed sower ...
  grief ...

CHORUS.
Tell us. What news of the Bacchae?

MESSENGER.
The son of Echion, Pentheus. Dead. 1030

CHORUS.
Dionysus, lord, you show your true face.
Great is the god Dionysus.

MESSENGER.
What? What are you saying, women?
You rejoice at this family's disaster?

CHORUS.
No family of mine. I am free to sing my foreign
  songs,
Safe from the fear of restraint.

MESSENGER.
Thebes has men enough ...

CHORUS.
Dionysus is my master, not Thebes, Dionysus.

MESSENGER.
Maybe so, but even you should not rejoice
1040   At such terrible things. It can't be right.

CHORUS.
Tell me. The whole story. How did he die,
This evil worker of evil deeds?

MESSENGER.
We left the last cottages of Thebes behind,
And crossed the Asopus, heading for Cithaeron.
Just Pentheus, me following my master,
And that foreigner to show us the way.
As soon as we got there we crouched down
In a grassy hollow to watch, silent and unseen.
1050   There's a rift between tall cliffs,
Waterfalls running down them,
All shaded by pine-trees.
That's where we saw the Maenads, hard at work, but
    content.
Some were decorating thyrsi with sprigs of new ivy.
Others sang Bacchic songs to one another,
Frisking, free as colts.
Pentheus couldn't see the whole company
And he said, poor man,
'I cannot get a proper look from here
1060   At these self-styled Maenads.
If I could climb up higher,
In one of those pines perhaps,
I could get a decent look at this debauchery of theirs.'
Then I saw the foreigner do a remarkable thing.
He took hold of a soaring branch of one of the pines,
And he pulled it, pulled it right down to the dark
    earth.
He bent it over like a bow or the curved felloe on a
    wheel.
Just so did this strange man take that tree
In his two hands, and bend it to the ground.

No ordinary man could have done it.
His strength was superhuman. 1070
He sat Pentheus astride the branches,
And let the tree slowly straighten,
Taking care not to unseat him.
Up it went, up towards the sky, my master on its
    back,
For all the Maenads to see, plainer than he saw
    them.
No sooner was Pentheus up there in full view
Than the foreigner disappeared and a voice
Came out of the air, as it were the voice of Dionysus.
'Ladies,' he cried, 'here is the man
Who would make mock of us and our mysteries. 1080
I offer him to you for punishment.'
He spoke and a blinding flash of fire
Struck earth from heaven.
Everything went quite still, air, trees, animals even,
Quite still.
The Maenads got to their feet,
Some having missed his words,
And stared about them. He called again.
This time Cadmus' daughters realised what he
    required.
And they ran. 1090
They ran, swift as birds,
Agave, her sisters, all of them,
Over river and rock, mad,
For the god had breathed on them.
Then they saw my master perched on his tree.
They hurled stones at first and sticks,
Climbing the cliff opposite.
Some threw thyrsi at their wretched target. 1100
He was too high even for their frenzy,
But could only sit there appalled.
They snatched off branches from the oaks
To lever up his pine, but their efforts bore no fruit.
Then Agave spoke.
'Circle the trunk, Maenads, grasp it.
We need to catch this clamberer

Before he reveals god's dances.'
Dozens of hands hauled at the tree,
1110   Then heaved it out of the earth.
Down fell Pentheus,
Down to the ground with an awful cry.
He knew now what was happening.
His mother started it, the ritual slaughter.
Desperate Agave. As she fell upon him,
He tore off the headdress so she would recognise him
And grabbed her cheek.
'Mother, it's me. It's Pentheus, your son.
Pity me. I've done no wrong.
1120   Don't kill me.' But her eyes were rolling.
She was frothing, imagining god knows what
In her Dionysiac frenzy.
She ignored his words, and took his left hand in hers,
Planted a foot in his ribs
And ripped off his arm at the shoulder.
Her strength was supernatural.
Ino set to work on the other side,
Tearing out handfuls of flesh,
1130   And Autonoë and the whole mob of Bacchants.
A single, terrible scream,
Pentheus' agony, their exultation.
One ran off with an arm, another a foot still in its
      shoe.
His ribs were stripped to the bone.
Bright red hands toyed with lumps of flesh.
The remains were strewn about,
By the rocks, in the undergrowth, anywhere.
We'll never find them.
But the head, the poor head,
1140   His mother chanced to snatch it up,
And stuck it on her thyrsus.
She left her sisters dancing away
And set off through Cithaeron,
Brandishing the head as though it were a mountain
      lion's.
She arrived in the city glorying in her frightful
      trophy,

Shrieking about her splendid Dionysus,
Fellow-huntsman, victorious. A victory of tears.
I can't stay to see this sight,
Not Agave's homecoming.
Balance. Reason. That's all we can aim for.   1150
Honour the gods and stick to that.

Exit MESSENGER.

CHORUS.
Dionysus, we dance for you,
Call on your name, Dionysus.
Dionysus, we praise you.
Defeat for the dragon-born,
Dragon-spawn Pentheus,
Dressed like a woman,
Sporting his thyrsus,
Flaunting his death-warrant,
Led by the bull-god, Dionysus.

You've achieved a famous victory,   1160
Bacchants of Cadmus,
A victory for suffering,
A victory for tears.
Fine victory for a mother,
Paddling in her own child's blood.
And here I see her, the mother of Pentheus,
Wild-eyed Agave. Welcome to our revelling
    company.

Enter AGAVE.

AGAVE.
Bacchae from Asia.

CHORUS.
You call? Ahhh.

AGAVE.
See what I've brought home from the mountains.   1170
The garlands are quite fresh. Happy hunting.

CHORUS.
Fellow-reveller, I see you and welcome you.

AGAVE.
Look. My lion-cub, caught without a trap.

CHORUS.
Where did you find it?

AGAVE.
On Cithaeron.

CHORUS.
Cithaeron?

AGAVE.
Cithaeron killed him.

CHORUS.
Who was the first to ...

AGAVE.
I was. Fortunate Agave. That's what they're calling
1180   me.

CHORUS.
Any others?

AGAVE.
Cadmus' daughters.

CHORUS.
Cadmus'?

AGAVE.
They fingered the prey. But after me. After me.
Good luck in the hunt. Will you share the feast with
me?

CHORUS.
Share, poor woman, share?

AGAVE.
Just a cub. Soft mane and downy whiskers.

CHORUS.
Mane, yes, and whiskers.

AGAVE.
Dionysus himself, clever hunter, set us onto our
1190   prey.

CHORUS.
Our lord, the hunter.

AGAVE.
Have I done well?

CHORUS.
Of course. Very well.

AGAVE.
Soon all the men of Thebes ...

CHORUS.
And Pentheus, your son, Pentheus.

AGAVE.
He'll be pleased with his mother for capturing such a
lion-cub.

CHORUS.
A rare prize.

AGAVE.
Rare is right.

CHORUS.
Are you pleased?

AGAVE.
Ecstatic.
Anyone can see what a fine creature I have bagged.

CHORUS.
Show it then. Show everyone this trophy,   1200
Poor woman, this trophy you bring.

AGAVE.
Citizens of our dear Thebes, draw near
And examine the spoil. We, Cadmus' daughters,
Have captured it without spear or net.
With just our white fingers.
So much for the boasting of men and their weaponry.
This creature we dismembered with our bare hands.
Where's my old father? Send for him.   1210
And Pentheus. Where's my son, Pentheus?
He should climb up with this lion's head
And nail it over the door.

Enter CADMUS, *attended*.

CADMUS.
>Follow me in. Bring him here,
>Here in front of his own house –
>What's left of him. Poor Pentheus.
>I found his body spread over Cithaeron,
>All torn, in pieces.

1220
>I found something in the wood ...
>I was on my way back from revelling
>With old Teiresias when they told me
>What my daughters had done.
>I went back to the mountain and found the boy.
>The Bacchae had ... killed him.
>Actaeon's mother, Autonoë was there.
>Ino too, in among the oak groves, still raving.
>But someone told me that Agave
>Had wandered back here in her mania.

1230
>How right they were. I cannot look.

AGAVE.
>Father. Now you can be proud of us.
>What daughters you have sired,
>The best in the world.
>And especially me.
>I've given up weaving for hunting,
>And with my bare hands.
>Look here. No, what I'm holding in my arms,
>A trophy to mount on the palace walls.
>Here, take hold of it, father,

1240
>And let's call our friends to a celebration.
>They'll think well of you for this.

CADMUS.
>No man could measure the horror of what I see.
>Murder, vile murder, at those frightful hands.
>This is the victim you want Thebes to celebrate.
>My grief is for you. For me too.
>A just revenge? No, too cruel.
>Dionysus is one of our family,

1250
>But he has destroyed our house.

AGAVE.
How grumpy an old man can get,
Looking at me like that.
I want my son to take after his mother,
Race to the hunt with the young men of Thebes.
All he does is fight gods.
You should put him right, father. It's your place.
Call him here, someone,
So he can see how well I have done.

CADMUS.
Oh my dear. When you realise what you've done,
Your pain will be unbearable. Madness   1260
Is the best that you can hope for.

AGAVE.
What's wrong? Why so solemn?

CADMUS.
Look up. Look at the sky.

AGAVE.
What am I meant to be looking at?

CADMUS.
Is it the same as before, or do you see a change?

AGAVE.
It's brighter, perhaps, a little clearer.

CADMUS.
And the confusion in your mind. Is that still with
    you?

AGAVE.
I don't understand. I was confused.
But that seems to be passing.   1270

CADMUS.
Can you hear what I'm saying? Tell me if you can.

AGAVE.
What were we talking about, father? I can't
    remember.

CADMUS.
What family was it you married into?

AGAVE.
You gave me to Echion, the one they call the dragon-
spawn.

CADMUS.
Yes, and the son you bore your husband?

AGAVE.
Pentheus. Our son is Pentheus.

CADMUS.
And whose . . . whose head is that you're cradling in
your arms?

AGAVE.
A lion's. That's what the hunters told me.

CADMUS.
Look at it. No, fully. Look.

AGAVE.
1280   What is it? What am I holding?

CADMUS.
Look again. Carefully. Now do you realise?

AGAVE.
What I see is unbearable. God help me.

CADMUS.
Is it anything like a lion?

AGAVE.
God help me. The head is Pentheus.

CADMUS.
We wept. We knew. You never realised.

AGAVE.
Who killed him? Why am I carrying this?

CADMUS.
The truth is terrible. Best not to know.

AGAVE.
Tell me. My heart is pounding. I have to know.

CADMUS.
You killed him. You and your sisters. You killed
him.

AGAVE.
Where? At home? Somewhere else? 1290

CADMUS.
There, where his own hounds ripped Actaeon to
pieces.

AGAVE.
Whatever was the poor boy doing on Cithaeron?

CADMUS.
He went to make fun of your Dionysus and his rites.

AGAVE.
Our Dionysus? What were we doing there?

CADMUS.
You didn't know what you were doing. The whole
city was deranged.

AGAVE.
Now I see it. Dionysus has destroyed us.

CADMUS.
He was slighted. You slighted him, denying his
divinity.

AGAVE.
Where is my son's body, father?

CADMUS.
There are the remains. It wasn't easy ...

AGAVE.
The body is ... all there? 1300

CADMUS.
Don't look. The head you have. That is what I could
find.

AGAVE.
How did Pentheus get involved in this madness of
mine?

CADMUS.
Like you, he disdained the god.
We were all involved in this disaster,
You, the son you see here dead, and me as well.
No male heirs. The family is destroyed.
This house looked up to you, my boy.
My grandson, my support.
1310 They went in awe of you in Thebes.
No one could insult the old man with you around.
Or else you made him pay.
Dishonoured I must leave my home,
Cadmus, the great, founder of Thebes,
Sower and reaper of the finest of races.
I loved you most. In death I love you still.
Never again to hug you,
To feel your touch on my cheek, or hear your voice:
'Is something the matter, grandfather?
1320 Is someone upsetting you?
Tell me. I'll soon put a stop to it.'
Now I am desolate, and so are you.
Mother, daughters, pitiful.
If any here cast doubt on supernatural power,
Let him consider this boy's death, and take heed.

CHORUS.
Cadmus, you have my pity. Your daughter's child,
He got what he deserved, but the pain is yours.

AGAVE.
Father, you see the change in me . . .

[*The manuscript breaks off here. Translator's conjectural reconstruction:*]

Sane now, I see what I could not see.
My own child, Pentheus.
How did I not know him? My sisters too?
My son's blood is upon their hands,
Loving hands which tore away his life.
And I am left to mourn the son
Who should have mourned for me.
Whose fate is worse?

Here, place the head and cover it. Cover it quickly.
Dionysus was the cause and now I know his power.
What mortal man could stand and face his fury?

Enter DIONYSUS, above.

DIONYSUS.
 What mortal man, indeed?
 I am Dionysus, son of Zeus and your sister Semele.
 I came to Thebes to seek my earthly home.
 But how was I received?
 The city rejected me. My family cast me out,
 Me, a god, they banished from their mortal company.
 My mother Semele's sisters I drove mad.
 Up into the mountains,
 And they have done what I had them do.
 So all of you as exiles must seek your own redemption,
 An expiation which only time can bring.
 Pentheus, my cousin, who dared to sneer at my rites,
 I mocked in my turn, and sent him
 Bacchus-mad to where his mother was waiting.

[*Manuscript resumes:*]

For Cadmus, my grandfather, and Harmonia his
 wife,   1330
A different fate is in store. You shall turn into
 snakes –
Zeus' oracle has forecast this – and lead great armies.
Strange deeds and in strange places,
With no peace at the last.
Leading barbarian hordes, you will sack cities,
And even Apollo's oracle, though that will bring a
 grim return.
But Ares, Harmonia's father, will preserve you
And take you eventually to the land of the Blessed.
That is my immortal decree, and I am the son of
 Zeus,
Dionysus, a good friend to the wise.   1340
A pity you did not realise it sooner.

CADMUS.
Dionysus, we implore you. We admit that we were
wrong.

DIONYSUS.
Too late. You acknowledge me far too late.

CADMUS.
We know that, but you are too severe.

DIONYSUS.
You offended me, me a god.

CADMUS.
A god should not show passion like a man.

DIONYSUS.
Zeus agreed to all this long ago.

AGAVE.
1350   Come now, father, exile is our fate.

DIONYSUS.
Go then. Why put off the inevitable?

CADMUS.
We have come to a terrible pass, my child,
Every one of us, your sisters too.
I must go and live in foreign lands, an old man
Fated, with Harmonia, my wife, daughter of Ares,
To lead an alien army against Greece:
Changed to a snake, but warlord
Against the altars and tombs of my country.
No piece for me until I cross Acheron's stream.

AGAVE.
1360   I must go too, father, and I must part from you.

CADMUS.
Why cling to me, poor child,
Like a young white swan still clinging to an old?

AGAVE.
Where can I turn, cast out from my country?

CADMUS.
I don't know, my dear. Your father can't help you
now.

AGAVE.
Farewell. Home, city, country. An exile.

CADMUS.
Go to Aristaeus. He will protect you.   1370

AGAVE.
Father, I feel pity for you.

CADMUS.
And I for you. Your sisters too.

AGAVE.
This punishment Dionysus has visited on our
family. It is terrible.

DIONYSUS.
What you made me suffer was terrible,
My name made light of in Thebes.

AGAVE.
Father. Farewell.

CADMUS.
Farewell, my child. Though what can fare well mean? 1380

AGAVE.
Take me to my sisters, my fellow-exiles.
I want to go where cursed Cithaeron
Shall never see me more, nor I set eyes on Cithaeron.
Some place where I can forget the thyrsus.
All that I leave to others.

Exeunt AGAVE *and* CADMUS.

CHORUS.
Olympian Zeus ordains.
The gods accomplish, strangely.
Things rarely end as you expect.
The unexpected is God's way,   1390
The lesson of this story.

Exeunt DIONYSUS *and* CHORUS.

A Note on the Translators

MARIANNE McDONALD is a professor of Theatre and Classics at the University of California, San Diego, and a member of the Royal Irish Academy. She was one of the earliest writers on modern versions of the classics and has over one hundred and fifty publications. They include *Terms for Happiness in Euripides*; *Euripides in Cinema: The Heart Made Visible*; *Ancient Sun, Modern Light: Greek Drama on the Modern Stage*; *Sing Sorrow: Classics, History and Heroines in Opera*; *Amid Our Troubles: Irish Versions of Greek Tragedy* (ed. with J. Michael Walton); various books on mythology, and translations. She established a computerised database for early Greek (Thesaurus Linguae Graecae) and Irish literature (Thesaurus Linguarum Hiberniae). Her translation of *Antigone* was performed in Ireland, Greece and Austria and her adaptation of *Trojan Women* at the Old Globe in San Diego. She is the recipient of many awards, including the Order of the Phoenix from Greece and the Golden Aeschylus Award from Italy; and honorary degrees from, among others, University College and Trinity College, Dublin, the University of Thessaloniki and the University of Athens.

KENNETH McLEISH's translations, of plays by all the Greek and Roman dramatists, Ibsen, Feydeau, Molière, Strindberg and others, have been performed throughout the world on stage, film, TV and radio. His original plays include *I Will If You Will*, *Just Do It*, *The Arabian Nights*, *Omma* and *Orpheus*. His books include *The Theatre of Aristophanes*, *Guide to Shakespeare's Plays* (with Stephen Unwin), *The Good Reading Guide* and *Guide to Greek Theatre and Drama*. He was editor of the Drama Classics series for Nick Hern Books and a Fellow of the Royal Society of Literature. He died in 1997.

FREDERIC RAPHAEL is the author of five volumes of short stories and nineteen novels, including *The Limits of Love*, *April, June and November*, *Heaven and Earth* and

A Double Life. He has written biographies of Somerset Maugham and Lord Byron. His latest book is *Personal Terms*, a writer's notebook 1950–1969. He is co-editor of a philosophical series for Orion, to which he is contributing a study of Karl Popper. His screenplays include the Oscar-winning *Darling*, and his work for television includes *The Glittering Prizes*, *Oxbridge Blues* and *After the War*. His translations with Kenneth McLeish include plays by Aeschylus and Euripides and the complete poems of Catullus. He has recently completed a new translation of Petronius' *Satyricon*. He is a fellow of the Royal Society of Literature.

J. MICHAEL WALTON worked in the professional theatre as an actor and director before joining the University of Hull, where he is Professor of Drama. He has published four books on Greek theatre, *Greek Theatre Practice*; *The Greek Sense of Theatre: Tragedy Reviewed*; *Living Greek Theatre: A Handbook of Classical Performance and Modern Production*; and *Menander and the Making of Comedy* (with the late Peter Arnott). He edited *Craig on Theatre* for Methuen and *Amid Our Troubles: Irish Versions of Greek Tragedy* (with Marianne McDonald). He is Series Editor of the thirteen volumes of Methuen Classical Greek Dramatists. He has translated plays by Sophocles, Euripides, Menander and Terence. He is founder/director of the Performance Translation Centre in the Drama Department at the University of Hull and was a Getty Scholar in 2002.

Methuen Classical Greek Dramatists

Aeschylus Plays: One
(Persians, Seven Against Thebes, Suppliants,
Prometheus Bound)

Aeschylus Plays: Two
(Oresteia: Agamemnon, Libation-Bearers, Eumenides)

Aristophanes Plays: One
(Acharnians, Knights, Peace, Lysistrata)

Aristophanes Plays: Two
(Wasps, Clouds, Birds, Festival Time, Frogs)

Aristophanes & Menander: New Comedy
(Women in Power, Wealth, The Malcontent,
The Woman from Samos)

Euripides Plays: One
(Medea, The Phoenician Women, Bacchae)

Euripides Plays: Two
(Hecuba, The Women of Troy, Iphigeneia at Aulis,
Cyclops)

Euripides Plays: Three
(Alkestis, Helen, Ion)

Euripides Plays: Four
(Elektra, Orestes, Iphigeneia in Tauris)

Euripides Plays: Five
(Andromache, Herakles' Children, Herakles)

Euripides Plays: Six
(Hippolytos, Suppliants, Rhesos)

Sophocles Plays: One
(Oedipus the King, Oedipus at Colonus, Antigone)

Sophocles Plays: Two
Ajax, Women of Trachis, Electra, Philoctetes)

Methuen Student Editions

Jean Anouilh	*Antigone*
John Arden	*Serjeant Musgrave's Dance*
Alan Ayckbourn	*Confusions*
Aphra Behn	*The Rover*
Edward Bond	*Lear*
Bertolt Brecht	*The Caucasian Chalk Circle*
	Life of Galileo
	Mother Courage and her Children
	The Resistible Rise of Arturo Ui
Anton Chekhov	*The Cherry Orchard*
	The Seagull
Caryl Churchill	*Serious Money*
	Top Girls
Shelagh Delaney	*A Taste of Honey*
Euripides	*Medea*
John Galsworthy	*Strife*
Robert Holman	*Across Oka*
Henrik Ibsen	*A Doll's House*
	Hedda Gabler
Charlotte Keatley	*My Mother Said I Never Should*
Bernard Kops	*Dreams of Anne Frank*
Federico García Lorca	*Blood Wedding*
	The House of Bernarda Alba
	(bilingual edition)
John Marston	*The Malcontent*
Willy Russell	*Blood Brothers*
Wole Soyinka	*Death and the King's Horseman*
August Strindberg	*The Father*
J. M. Synge	*The Playboy of the Western World*
Oscar Wilde	*The Importance of Being Earnest*
Tennessee Williams	*A Streetcar Named Desire*
	The Glass Menagerie
Timberlake Wertenbaker	*Our Country's Good*

Methuen World Classics
include

Jean Anouilh (two volumes)
Brendan Behan
Aphra Behn
Bertolt Brecht (seven volumes)
Büchner
Bulgakov
Calderón
Čapek
Anton Chekhov
Noël Coward (eight volumes)
Feydeau (two volumes)
Eduardo De Filippo
Max Frisch
John Galsworthy
Gogol
Gorky
Harley Granville Barker
  (two volumes)
Henrik Ibsen (six volumes)
Alfred Jarry
Lorca (three volumes)

Marivaux
Mustapha Matura
David Mercer (two volumes)
Arthur Miller (five volumes)
Molière
Musset
Peter Nichols (two volumes)
Clifford Odets
Joe Orton
A. W. Pinero
Luigi Pirandello
Terence Rattigan
  (two volumes)
W. Somerset Maugham
  (two volumes)
August Strindberg
  (three volumes)
J. M. Synge
Ramón del Valle-Inclán
Frank Wedekind
Oscar Wilde

Methuen Contemporary Dramatists
include

John Arden (two volumes)
Arden & D'Arcy
Peter Barnes (three volumes)
Sebastian Barry
Dermot Bolger
Edward Bond (six volumes)
Howard Brenton
 (two volumes)
Richard Cameron
Jim Cartwright
Caryl Churchill (two volumes)
Sarah Daniels (two volumes)
Nick Darke
David Edgar (three volumes)
Ben Elton
Dario Fo (two volumes)
Michael Frayn (three volumes)
David Greig
John Godber (two volumes)
Paul Godfrey
John Guare
Lee Hall
Peter Handke
Jonathan Harvey (two volumes)
Declan Hughes
Terry Johnson (two volumes)
Sarah Kane
Barrie Keeffe
Bernard-Marie Koltès
David Lan
Bryony Lavery
Deborah Levy
Doug Lucie
David Mamet (four volumes)

Martin McDonagh
Duncan McLean
Anthony Minghella
 (two volumes)
Tom Murphy (four volumes)
Phyllis Nagy
Anthony Nielsen
Philip Osment
Louise Page
Stewart Parker (two volumes)
Joe Penhall
Stephen Poliakoff
 (three volumes)
David Rabe
Mark Ravenhill
Christina Reid
Philip Ridley
Willy Russell
Eric-Emmanuel Schmitt
Ntozake Shange
Sam Shepard (two volumes)
Shelagh Stephenson
Wole Soyinka (two volumes)
David Storey (three volumes)
Sue Townsend
Judy Upton
Michel Vinaver (two volumes)
Arnold Wesker (two volumes)
Michael Wilcox
Roy Williams
Snoo Wilson (two volumes)
David Wood (two volumes)
Victoria Wood

Methuen Modern Plays
include work by

Jean Anouilh
John Arden
Margaretta D'Arcy
Peter Barnes
Sebastian Barry
Brendan Behan
Dermot Bolger
Edward Bond
Bertolt Brecht
Howard Brenton
Anthony Burgess
Simon Burke
Jim Cartwright
Caryl Churchill
Noël Coward
Lucinda Coxon
Sarah Daniels
Nick Darke
Nick Dear
Shelagh Delaney
David Edgar
David Eldridge
Dario Fo
Michael Frayn
John Godber
Paul Godfrey
David Greig
John Guare
Peter Handke
David Harrower
Jonathan Harvey
Iain Heggie
Declan Hughes
Terry Johnson
Sarah Kane
Charlotte Keatley
Barrie Keeffe
Howard Korder

Robert Lepage
Stephen Lowe
Doug Lucie
Martin McDonagh
John McGrath
Terence McNally
David Mamet
Patrick Marber
Arthur Miller
Mtwa, Ngema & Simon
Tom Murphy
Phyllis Nagy
Peter Nichols
Joseph O'Connor
Joe Orton
Louise Page
Joe Penhall
Luigi Pirandello
Stephen Poliakoff
Franca Rame
Mark Ravenhill
Philip Ridley
Reginald Rose
David Rudkin
Willy Russell
Jean-Paul Sartre
Sam Shepard
Wole Soyinka
Shelagh Stephenson
C. P. Taylor
Theatre de Complicite
Theatre Workshop
Sue Townsend
Judy Upton
Timberlake Wertenbaker
Roy Williams
Victoria Wood

For a complete catalogue of Methuen Drama titles
write to:

Methuen Drama
215 Vauxhall Bridge Road
London SW1V 1EJ

or you can visit our website at:

www.methuen.co.uk